ID0899866

Shoreline

Shoreline

SEASONS AT THE LAKE

Elizabeth A. Schultz

Michigan State University Press · East Lansing

♾ The paper used in this publication meets the minimum requirements
of ANSI/NISO Z39.48–1992 (R 1997) (Permanence of Paper).

Michigan State University Press
East Lansing, Michigan 48823-5202

Printed and bound in the United States of America.

07 06 05 04 03 02 01   1 2 3 4 5 6 7 8 9 10

Library of Congress Cataloging-in-Publication Data
Schultz, Elizabeth A.
Shoreline : seasons at the lake / Elizabeth A. Schultz.
p. cm.
ISBN 0-87013-593-7 (cloth : alk. paper)
1. Schultz, Elizabeth A.–Homes and haunts–Michigan–Pinewoods Camp.
2. Pinewoods Camp (Mich.)–Social life and customs. 3. Pinewoods Camp
(Mich.)–Biography. 4. Higgins Lake (Mich.)–Social life and customs.
5. Natural history–Michigan. I. Title.
CT275.S3464 A3 2001
977 .4'76–dc21
2001003709

Book and cover design by Sharp Des!gns, Inc., Lansing, MI
Cover was edited from a photo by Jane Kohring that can be found in the second photo essay.

———————————

Visit Michigan State University Press on the World Wide Web at:
www.msupress.msu.edu

To

Lucy Helen Shaw Schultz,

my mother

CONTENTS

MY GRATITUDE goes to Don Worster, Marilyn Schirmer, and Marion Foster, who read *Shoreline* sensitively and wisely in its early stages, and to Martha Bates, who guided it in its later stages at the Michigan State University Press. The story would not have been told without the contributions and concern of my father and of my brother and his family; my thanks to them all are boundless. Of Jane Kohring and Prue Thompson, for their trust and for their profound sense of beauty, I am also deeply appreciative.

Shoreline

Beginnings

ANTECEDENTS

ecently, I've been feeling haunted. I have lived in Kansas since the fall of 1967, longer than I've lived anywhere else, long enough to bear witness to the attitude Gertrude Stein called, "the aggressive way of the casual stranger."[1] This is the attitude of those who fly by on I-70 toward Colorado and who believe Dorothy is the state's most famous inhabitant and tornadoes its most important feature. I've also been in Kansas long enough to appreciate a certain luminescence in the evening sky as a more constant characteristic. But the longer I stay on, the more I remember the lake and the community in Michigan where I have spent a part of almost all of my summers, the more I realize the ways in which that place and those people have shaped my vision.

That first fall in Kansas I was conscious that the trees were not showing off with the same degree of flamboyance that Michigan trees habitually displayed before the winter, and I cautioned myself, saying, "comparisons are odious." I know now that Kansas trees have their own version of the last fling (in shades of red and russet, tangerine and ocher) and that the place to watch for the seasons' subtle changes is in the grasses. I have also learned that comparisons, at least those that derive from a struggle to appreciate differences, significantly extend one's vision. And so I have continued to live in Kansas with the companionable ghost of Michigan. My Michigan ghost, however, is not generalized. It comes to me repeatedly as memories of Pinewoods Camp, a summer community on Higgins Lake in Roscommon County.

Another very particular ghost—H. D. Thoreau—haunts both my memories and my writing. His integration of savagery and high morality, practical economies and transcendental connections, keeps me from sleeping. His perceptions steer me, for he is the secret sharer, the paddler in the stern. I wonder, as I think about Higgins and its surroundings—its shore, trees, plants, birds, animals, people—if I know them only because Thoreau put them into words. Can they exist for me apart from his perceptions? I quarrel with his occasional smugness, with his ignorance of women's lives and the lives of poor people, and with his refusal to take responsibility in his friendships. But he heard the tree falling in the woods and was the first to tell me how it sounds. In telling me that wherever "I sat, there I might live, and the landscape radiated from me accordingly,"[2] Thoreau gave me the deed to my lake.

Long before there was Thoreau, however, my mother was constructing Pinewoods and Higgins for me. More than Thoreau's meditation on Walden, her vision of the summer community and the surrounding lake and woods has been the shore which shaped the waters of my shifting thoughts and feelings about them. She saw the lake when the only lights rimming it at night were constellations, when its stillness was disrupted by echoing whippoorwills, when loons clowned with canoes, when the fringed gentians on its shores were not an endangered species. My mother's lakescape is not mine, yet hers intersects with mine in interminable ways as waves ripple across the expanding circles set in motion by a water strider settling on the lake's calm. I struggled with her authority; I honor her wisdom. Her memories of Pinewoods cradled me, even as my memories of her rock this writing. Her presence in my essays—as mother and mentor, as bearer of legends, and at over ninety now a legend herself—revises Thoreau's solitariness.

On Independence Day in 1845, Thoreau declared himself and moved to Walden Pond. He moved, he said in words now well known, intending "to live deliberately, to front only the essential facts of life, and see if I could not learn what it had to teach, and not, when I came to die, discover that I had not lived."[3] Perceiving his living at Walden as an experiment, he stayed two years and two months. When he left Walden, however, he wasn't finished with that place of "liquid joy and happiness,"[4] for in remembering it and writing and rewriting about it for seven more years, he went on living there. So the task that Pinewoods set for me as a child has pursued me in Kansas: to try to live fully and well and to grow in relationship to all living beings, natural and human. Thoreau and my mother continue as my guides. They hover close by, nurturing, instructing. If I tussle with them, they sustain me, sending me back on my own. In Pinewoods's pulsating weave of life, the lessons of lake, woods, and community are never complete, and so in summer after summer and in memory after memory I resume my task, as conscious as the monarch butterflies in their annual move from Mexico through Kansas up to Michigan.

Although I have kept no journal of my years at Pinewoods, I have a century of reminiscences from people who, like my family, summer(ed) at Higgins—some of these are written, others are recorded from oral story in my memory. Geological and human history appear to structure my essays initially; observations of natural phenomena alternate with human events, personal experience with accounts of the gregarious summer community. Yet the final form of the essays seems even now to be evolving, for I test the waters as I write, paddling vigorously for a while and then drifting to watch the bottom of the lake or the cloud shadows on its surface. As it seems possible to take the canoe out on the lake an infinite number of times without wearying of the process, I feel I'm only beginning to see Pinewoods and its inhabitants. Yet the most important things—like love—seem always evolving and ever the most elusive.

TRUTH-TELLING

Mother does not entirely approve of my writing about Pinewoods. She knows about my writing because on occasion I've had to call her to verify a fact—natural or historical—and she has commented on some of the short, early sections. Her primary concern is that my revelations will precipitate pain among Pinewoods people, and her distress has led to proclamations.

In the summer of 1994, I spent several days sitting in the alcove off the living room of our cottage reading years of minutes from the Pinewoods annual meetings. One afternoon Mother came down from a nap and, without prologue, pronounced, "I have learned one thing in this life: I don't want to do anything unkind." Prior to this announcement, I had been sharing notes with her from my reading that related to the family or to some aspect of the early days of Pinewoods, which I thought she would enjoy. Her proclamation, however, made me realize that she was more concerned about the present than the past. My investigations were preventing her from sleeping. I could only issue a proclamation in return, stating that I had to tell my story, that I had to tell my truth. That fall she sent me a letter in Kansas, indicating she was continuing to mull over her concerns: "If you are considering publishing your P'woods musings, would you please delete any sensitive material which would be unbearably hurtful to our friends, no matter how much you wish to be honest to yourself."[5]

I spoke with friends at Pinewoods and with friends in Kansas, all caring people. All recognized the ways in which mothers, even into their nineties, may try to regulate their daughters' lives, and the ways in which daughters will react against such regulation. They also recognized the witches' brew of guilt, pressure, and pain in my mother's special concerns. I queried my friends and myself further. Can any one version of the truth be clear of personal desires and obsessions? Can any one truth be separated from the truths of others? Can any one truth be more valuable than another?

The fond convictions of Mary Hale Bruske (known as Grandma Bruske), writing in 1928, that at Pinewoods "we are bound together in our joys and our friendships by ties that are sweet and enduring," suggest a vision I cherish.[6] I yearn for it. But I cannot say that I am always part of this "we," this "our." Certain Pinewoods traditions, for example, are not mine. The sporting events which delighted young and old in my childhood were Ping-Pong and sailing, whereas now it's the annual Rat Race on the tennis court, water volleyball in front of one cottage and racquetball at another—running and jumping exercises which embarrass me, which bore me. In an attempt to complement these exercises, I once placed a notice in *Pinewords,* the camp's out-of-season newsletter, regarding the possibility of organizing an all-camp reading of *A Midsummer Night's Dream;* it received only one interested response.

Some Pinewoods families I feel I hardly know. I did not play in their cottages as a child; their stories did not intersect with mine when I was growing up. Some Pinewoods families divided and merged, grew and grew up when I was away—in Japan, in graduate school. Now those babies have babies, and I know them not, nor do they know me. In the salad line at the dining hall a few years ago, a young woman asked me if I was my mother's sister. Tangled in the spaghetti, which is how my niece Lucy describes the Pinewoods social scene, are new fiancées, fourth cousins, step-grandchildren, mothers of in-laws. During the long summers of my childhood, we kept track of each person who came and went through the dining hall by name and costume. In recent summers I do not reach the lake until early August, and I miss the Pinewoods people who come in July. In recent Pinewoods directories there are many names without faces, and faces and costumes come and go in the dining hall without names. I cannot tell their truths.

I cannot tell the truth of two brothers who grew up in Switzerland but return every other summer for two-week intervals to the cottage where their father spent his boyhood summers. To them, Pinewoods may seem exotic, elitist, anachronistic, mythic, or merely smug in its comfort and ease. Nor can I tell the truth of a young Pinewoods friend. She called me in Kansas some nights ago to spin out a series of Pinewoods memories, full of anger, full of grief, full of yearning. Out of this matrix of desperation, she expressed her desire for her daughter to have that perfect Pinewoods vacation with a gang of friends.

Neither can I tell my niece Lucy's truth. When I visited her in her Chicago apartment some years ago, she spoke about Pinewoods as she never had in Michigan. Perhaps it was because we were on neutral ground. She, too, is heavy with memories—of going with her gang out to deep water on a float boat and being told she'd have no trouble swimming because she was so fat, of playing hospital with her sister and other kids and having the day change color when the boys showed their penises. Lucy told me on a visit to Kansas that Pinewoods is her salvation and sanctuary; in its stasis, she said she feels as secure as if she were wrapped in a warm blanket. Sometimes, however, it's as if she's still in the backseat of her parents' car.

Her memories of Pinewoods occasionally give her bad dreams. She dreams of a large cocktail party in our pavilion, with everyone turned toward the lake where she is swimming alone; they stand scrutinizing her, and she realizes she must teach herself to fly to escape their gaze. She succeeds and rises up out of the lake, but then can only bounce from one cottage roof to another. Her experiences at Pinewoods mystify her. At the lake one summer, Lucy joined her parents in their early-morning ritual to see the sunrise at the island. Upon reaching the island's cove, her dad cuts the motor. The boat drifts in the stillness; they watch the birds lifting off the island's point and listen to their greetings; they wait for glory. But to Lucy, "it was terrifying. Out there, there was nothing. Why was I there? Why were we there? There was nothing, but I've never felt so smothered in my life." When Lucy and I are in camp at the same time (which is not often, lately), we go out to the end of our dock after dinner, when the sun has gone down and left the lake smeared with shades of peony and primrose, and we share stories. If we miss each other at the lake, we have our dock conversations by letter and phone, and so I've come to know that, like each of us at Pinewoods, her Pinewoods story is in process, and that her Pinewoods truth is her own.

I often wonder if, after all, I can tell my own truth. So much is lost—vanished into thin air, buried beneath the sand, lost in deepest black water, taken into the black hole of time, the black lake of Lethe. I can't recover the stories of individual Chippewa at the lake. I can barely recover my lady grandmother's story. A few artifacts, a few photographs, a few sentences stand in for the whole. And the translation of each is so suspect. I struggle to retrieve a shadow of my own story. Its details disappear daily due to ignorance, indolence, layers of illusions, fear of hurt, simple loss of memory. Do I know the best questions? Could I ask them if I knew them? Why do I omit telling about spying on my brother and his friend when they were playing dirty or telling about playing dirty myself? Why do I find it necessary to scapegoat motorboat owners? I know only that by trying to tell my own truth, I reach a shoreline of continuing revelations. By trying to tell my story, I am constantly surprised by the shape emerging from the waters.

Anticipating charges of subjectivity from the first pages of *Walden*, Thoreau candidly reminds his readers that in any book, "it is, after all, always the first person that is speaking."[7] Certain of himself, he thus can assign eternal values to a particular pond in Massachusetts with joyous equanimity. Here, then, are the particular pines, paths, pavilion, shore, island, and people of Pinewoods as I cherish them; here I seek to discover their shaping properties as I have known them and to share them as best I can that others may find their own places and stories to cherish.

The Place

GEOGRAPHY

You really have to see it—Higgins, the lake. Via the twisting stream, always known as The Cut, in the middle of the northern part of Michigan's Lower Peninsula, it is connected to Houghton Lake, the two lakes appearing like moth holes unraveling in the tip of Michigan's mitten. Maps of Higgins are tacked on the living room wall in our cottage: the topographical one from the Michigan Department of Natural Resources in shades of green and yellow; the other, a 1919 Christmas card, on blue graph paper with a grid of white lines, and this message printed by hand around the edges—"It's a Little Bit of Heaven, and We Love It More and More." Formed from two bays wedded together at Huckleberry Point in the west and Stony Point in the east, Higgins looks like a pair of old-fashioned water wings on the map. My image of the lake as a child was that of a big peanut, with one lobe smaller than the other. Pinewoods Camp, together with two other associations of summer cottages—Lakeside Camp and Cottage Grove—and the stretch of forest between them, occupies about two miles of shoreline along the northern edge of Higgins's large bay. In order to sail from our shore across the big bay, between Huckleberry and Stony Points, all the way over to The Cut in the little bay and arrive back home in time for dinner, you need a good wind from the southwest.

Glaciers moving out during the last age of the Pleistocene epoch created Higgins, forming moraine deposits on the north and southwest shores and filling the basin between with melting ice.

With little bottom vegetation "due to sandy shoals and excessive wave action," Higgins, in a report by the Michigan Institute for Fisheries, is defined as "a cold-hard-water lake."[8] Springs still fill the lake with water that can feel like melting ice; swimming even in the shallowest water, you suddenly tingle with the chill when you pass over one of these "cold spots." At Cold Springs, an artesian well, in a low-lying cedar thicket near the northwest shore, pools and pours through several fingers out into the lake; wading into these rivulets is to experience such a freezing numbness in your feet that they feel detached from your body. From the springs of Higgins, water flows through The Cut to Houghton and down the Muskegon River 225 miles, dropping 561 feet to Lake Michigan.

Early European-American visitors to the lake commented on the lake's purity. The 1852 field notes of William Burt, U.S. deputy surveyor, stated that, "Higgins Lake is a beautiful sheet of water . . . remarkable for its clearness and purity."[9] A. Button, seeking lands for Civil War veterans in 1873, reported, "The water is so pure and wonderfully transparent that its pebbly bottom can be seen at a depth of twenty-five or thirty feet."[10] Writing about Higgins in 1949, Bertha Carpenter claimed that "The water is so clear that a dime can be seen at a depth of forty feet and has a peculiarity of always showing at least four different colors on its surface."[11] When the cottages were first built in our camp in the late nineteenth century, water for drinking, cooking, bathing, and laundry all came from the lake. In its early days Lakeside Camp used a windmill to pump water up to its central dining hall. The little shed down by our dock, a collect-all now for sailing, swimming, and boating equipment, is still called the pumphouse, for when Mother was growing up a kerosene motor inside worked night and day to transfer water from the lake up the steep bank to the kitchen and bathrooms and bedrooms of the cottage.

If you look out across the lake from the pavilion in front of the cottage at sunset, from a canoe in the middle of black water in the early morning when the mist is just rising, from the end of the dock on a clear moonlit night, Higgins remains "a beautiful sheet of water." With human beings increasingly inscribing their summer lives upon this sheet, however, its clarity and purity are being transformed. Fuels from power boats, fertilizers from lawns, and sewage from septic tanks set close to the shore are seeping into the water, spawning a strange new grammar. Black gunk rims boats and buoys at water level; cladophora, indicative of accumulated phosphates, attaches itself in short green beards to stones along the shore; an unknown, hard, dark fungus has joined assorted squishy fish eggs on the lake bottom. Roger Rasmussen, the caretaker of Pinewoods, has a word for the process of transforming pure water into marl and muck—utrification. He points out that Higgins now has fewer fish and more ducks. Still, limnologists from the Environmental Protection Agency in the summer of 1993 declared Higgins to be one of the cleanest recreational lakes in the country.

FIRST SETTLERS

The Chippewa first called the lake "Majinabeesch," which means "something sparkling." In time, however, they changed its name to a phrase that was translated as "The Devil's Hole" and, according to Chief David Shoppenagons, the last of the Chippewa to visit Pinewoods, they came to shun the lake as "a dark and dangerous body of water."[12] On the one hand, Higgins was known to have swallowed up whole war parties, and on the other, it had mysteriously resurrected, through an underwater passageway, a certain chieftain who had supposedly drowned far to the north in Lake Superior, as well as his personalized burial canoe. Offshore about seventy-five feet, a "boiling spring" is noted on the original survey map of 1838, and on a calm day in 1919 a party of men, fishing offshore about twenty feet, reported that the water beneath them began to churn and swirl as if the bottom of the lake had opened up.

Chippewa legends, however, were not the stuff of which my mother's stories were made. In the memoirs and histories of Higgins and its campers that I have read, only one mentions that the Chippewa might have resented an encroachment upon their lands. The *History of the Ottawa and Chippewa Indians of Michigan,* written by Chief Mack-e-te-be-nessy (A. J. Blackbird) in 1887, as well as other histories authorized by Michigan's indigenous peoples, reveal several causes for Chippewa resentment. Treaty after treaty took their lands and their livelihood. Although they were given annuity payments for land, these payments, according to one account, were "often timed for political advantage." The payments typically "drew a crowd of white merchants and whiskey sellers, so these monies soon returned to white hands. The same was true of land allotments. Corrupt Indian agents and local officials joined forces with land speculators and powerful lumber interests to defraud Indians." In addition, "While the Michigan constitution of 1850 granted suffrage to Indians, the right to vote was contingent upon renouncing tribal affiliation."[13] Although the Chippewa may have been erased from the memoirs of Pinewoods, they have not vanished from Michigan. Nor have they renounced their tribal affiliations despite disease, discrimination, economic deprivation, and relocation on reservations. While many moved to Michigan's urban centers, others continue to live close to their ancient lands, "using the skills of their ancestors daily and preserving a part of their inheritance from the past."[14]

Shoppenagons lives. As a man who, according to several accounts, "knew every foot of the ground from Saginaw Bay to the Straits of Mackinac,"[15] Shoppenagons declined to stay on the Chippewa reservation near Mt. Pleasant in Isabella County and considerably south of Higgins. He returned often to the lake from the 1880s into the early years of the new century, first as a hunting guide for the founders of Lakeside Camp, later as a merchant of his handcrafted canoe paddles, baskets, and snowshoes, and in his last years as a campfire entertainer. His Chippewa name was Shop-nee-gaunse, meaning "sewing needle," but the syllables of his name were rearranged by white folks over the years and finally reduced to "Shop." Although he lived with his family on the Au Sable River close to the nearby town of Grayling, accounts about Shoppenagons indicate that he always returned to Higgins alone. He continued to hunt and fish until the end, but his cronies by that time were all white men. They introduced him to their children as a "live Indian chief," and some of these children, on whom he bestowed Indian names, came to love him.

Shoppenagons allowed his own name and picture to be used in advertising brochures and on freight car sidings for a Grayling lumber and flooring company, and on its behalf, he was taken all over the country to lumber conventions where he posed in full Chippewa regalia and handed out cards identifying himself as "David Shoppenagons, Chief of the Chippewas and Guardian of the 'Swim High Like Cork' pine forests ceded to Salling-Hanson and Company at the last council of the Chippewa braves." The *Grayling Centennial* essay on Shoppenagons claims that, although he gave the town its most stunning "local color," he was "a real person, who served a real purpose and is definitely a part of our local heritage. . . . 'The Chief' was a natural promotional object." The essay continues to subvert its praise of Shoppenagons by casting him as the Grayling version of a wooden cigar-store Indian: "The old guide and trapper became a symbol of Grayling and the fine products produced by its mills."[16]

Leading the parade for Saginaw's semicentennial celebrations on 4 July 1907 as its proud guest of honor, Shoppenagons wept when the parade wound past his birthplace and his parents' burial ground. Upon his own death in 1911, the *Crawford County Avalanche* wrote that "Shoppenagon had a history which he might have told, but his familiar acquaintances of Grayling knew nothing of it. He chose to keep his counsel."[17] He willed his prized crescent-shaped silver breastplates, prominent in all of his photographs and portraits, to one of the Lakeside founders, and a subdivision on the southern shore of the lake and a hotel in Grayling carry his name. He has a corner in the Crawford County Historical Museum, formerly the Grayling train depot, and the docent there will tell you that when asked to give a speech at conventions or parades, Shoppenagons recapitulated the history of Native Americans succinctly and enigmatically: "Two hundred years ago—more two hundred years ago—injun all skin—all skin—no blanket. When now injun—all blanket—all blanket—no skin."[18]

One afternoon when I was a kid and messing around behind the Bruske cottage at the lake, I spotted an arrowhead in the sandy soil. It had a talismanic shape, which raised more questions than it answered—How long had it lain there? Whose was it? What was its trajectory? The arrowhead kept its counsel, and I gave it to my grandmother who, unable to answer its questions, placed it snugly in her curio cabinet at home. It rested there behind glass with tokens from other cultures—carved in crystal, lava, or ivory—for us to muse over, teasing us with their connections every time we visited the old Bay City house.

ECONOMICS

Establishing headquarters for his American Fur Company on Mackinac Island in 1817, John Jacob Astor sent out tentacles into the rivers and streams of northern Michigan. At the trading post on the confluence of the Au Sable and the Muskegon Rivers, trappers exchanged their furs for the guns, blankets, and whiskey brought in by Astor's agents, who had transported them by enormous cargo canoes. A busy spot, this post became the site of Roscommon Village. Such settlements and commercial activities prepared the way for the Saginaw Treaty of 1819 between the U.S. government and native peoples, which was followed by federal surveys in 1838, 1849, and 1852. Surveyors measured the lake, remarked upon the usefulness of its minerals and its flora and fauna, and named it for Sylvester W. Higgins, assistant to the first Michigan state geologist and topographer. It is uncertain whether Higgins ever saw the lake named for him, but other surveyors went on to enclose it in a grid of townships and plats defining Roscommon County in 1875.

Lumber barons rushed in to stake land claims in the surveyors' wake. They clear-cut the pine throughout the county, built boom towns around their sawmills, and developed transportation systems to move their logs and lumber out. Initially, most logging occurred during winter when many men were freed from farming chores. Brought by sled or big wheels to frozen lake and river banks, the logs awaited the spring thaw when they would be sent downriver. The connecting waterways provided by Higgins and Houghton Lakes, the Cut, and the Muskegon River took them down to the mills of the city of Muskegon on Lake Michigan. What Bruce Catton calls "the backwoods production line" was off and running.[19]

Terry E. Jones, in a document prepared for the Higgins Lake Foundation, notes that "in Michigan . . . the 'green gold rush' out-valued the 'yellow gold rush' in California by more than a billion dollars over a sixty-year period. . . . Of the 55 billion board feet of lumber processed in Muskegon, the central area of Michigan, which includes the Roscommon area, accounted for 22 billion board feet. . . . In its heyday, the Muskegon mills were turning out over 500 million board feet of lumber yearly. The Higgins area provided as much as 20 percent of this amount."[20] A November 1885 headline in the *Roscommon News* announced, "Roscommon Lumbermen Plan to Harvest 146 Million Feet of Logs."[21]

In 1877 a narrow-gauge railway line—the first in the country whose sole purpose was transporting logs from remote cutting areas to the rivers—was completed to speed up the process of transforming Higgins's living forests into deadwood and to do it cheaply and easily. Roscommon County's first township, just east of Pinewoods, is named Gerrish after the developer of that early railway. Thus, waterways were quickly supplemented by the development of railway lines, including the powerful Jackson, Lansing, and Saginaw Railroad (J. L. & S.) linking established urban centers in the south of the state with the new boom towns of the north. Lumbering turned spectator sport when newspapers encouraged people to ride the rails north to watch the forest disappear before their very eyes.

Paul Bunyan, "The Logger Lover," and the Lumberman's Monument of Alpena testify to the aggrandizement of the men who logged with their big axes, their big wheels, and their big hunger. Only a few of the great pines remain, standing as sentinels to the past, and some of these rim the north shore of Higgins, preserved by those lumber barons and their friends who had staked out this shore for their personal camps. In "The Lamentation of the Overflowing Heart of the Red Man of the Forest," which concludes his 1887 history, Chief Mack-e-te-be-nessy grieves for the loss of a "beautiful old basswood tree":

> That tree was planted there by the Great Spirit for me to sport under, when I could scarcely bend my little bow. Ah, I watched that tree from childhood to manhood, and it was the dearest spot to me in this wide world. . . . But alas, alas, the white man's ax has been there! The tree that my good spirit had planted for me, where once the pretty brown thrush daily sat with her musical voice, is cut down by the ruthless hands of the white man. 'Tis gone; gone forever and mingled with the dust. . . . Ah, could we but once more return to our forest glade and tread as formerly upon the soil with proud and happy heart! On the hills with bended bow, while nature's flowers bloomed all around the habitation of nature's child, our brothers once abounded, free as the mountain air, and their glad shouts resounded from vale to vale, as they chased o'er the hills the mountain roe and followed in the otter's track. Oh return, return! Ah, never again shall this time return. It is gone, and gone forever like a spirit passed.[22]

"A Legend of Higgins," written by a family staying in Pinewoods in 1924, summarizes these sweeping transitions. Composed in the metrical language of Henry Wadsworth Longfellow's *Hiawatha*, which was still recited in the 1920s, the "legend" records the losses of indigenous peoples and the campers' oblivion:

> Later came the White man seeking,
> Seeking lumber for his dwellings,
> Saw the stately pine trees towering
> On the shores of Majinabeesch;
> Loved these woods and shining waters

Breathed the cold clear air and loved it;
Wanted it for his young children.
So the campers settled 'round here
Knew no more of Indian warriors
Knew no names or stories ancient
Later names and later memories
Cover now the ancient story.
Still the lake and pines continue
Heritage of "Majinabeesch."[23]

Other campfire songs paid romantic homage to the first human settlers at Higgins. As with team mascots and decorators' motifs of wigwams and small birch bark canoes in cottage decor, however, they subscribe to the myth of the Vanishing Indian and are oblivious to the changing, complex cultures of native peoples.

Arthur Rosenau writes in his history of Lakeside Camp: "Many lumbermen had predicted that the cutting could go on indefinitely such was the limitless extent of Michigan's pine. But each mill wanted endless supplies of logs to keep its operation profitable while competition grew keener each year among the large and small mill towns along the rivers and the railroads. Suddenly the big timber was gone! The mills moved—to the Upper Peninsula, to Minnesota, to the far West."[24] Although the mills moved, the railroad remained. Having sent logs and lumber south to build houses in Chicago and Kansas City, in the last decades of the nineteenth century, it began bringing land speculators, farmers, immigrants, and "pleasure-seekers" north. Bereft of its timber, the land was being advertised to farmers as "a rich, dark sandy loam, with a clay sub-soil that produces the finest variety of vegetables and fruits." Other promoters proclaimed that "the fruits and vegetables grow to an enormous size and are very solid and firm," that "several enterprising farmers . . . are growing sugar beets and tobacco. At the prices we are selling these lands one good crop will pay for the land."[25] Huckleberries were also known to flourish under the pines, with 4,000 bushels a week picked in Roscommon County in 1885; in prime seasons, wages for pickers were higher than those for loggers.

To promote real estate sales on Higgins itself, the Michigan Central Railroad Company, successor to the J. L. & S., identified it as "the most beautiful summer resort on earth" and provided excursion rates, ran special trains up to the lake, and offered to give away one free lot for every one purchased. "No Taxes, No Assessments for Sidewalks, Sewerage, or Street Improvements," one broadside asserted. Another boasted, "We expect 2,000 HOUSES AND COTTAGES built around the lake this coming season. There are already 68 built. All good class, a great many of them belonging to millionaires of Saginaw and Detroit and other Michigan cities."[26] These late-nineteenth-century "pleasure-seekers," defined by Rosenau as "an omnibus term that included hunters, fishermen, boaters, swimmers, and out-of-doors lovers generally,"[27] could believe the boosters because, unlike the struggling farmers, they had the leisure to see "HIGGINS LAKE . . . a beautiful crystal sheet of water."[28]

Roscommon County's sandy soil finally broke the hearts of the Civil War veterans and the Swedes who followed them in the early twentieth century as they dragged out the stumps remaining from the logging boom in desperate attempts to create fields for corn and potatoes. Some of the Swedes supplemented their farming with poultry and dairy cows while others provided carpentry and domestic services for the growing number of summer resorts on Higgins Lake. Still others abandoned their farmsteads, in the same way that the lumberjacks and timber barons left their towns before them, leaving haunted houses and ghost towns to titillate me and my teenage friends.

NEW SETTLERS

An increasing number of pleasure-seekers built cottages, hotels, and resorts along the shores of the lake in the last decades of the nineteenth century. They stayed summer after summer, and they brought their families. Although only a few members of the three camps on the north shore of Higgins may have been millionaires, they belonged to a growing group among America's economic and urban elite who believed that periodic "back-to-nature" excursions were good for both the body and the soul. According to cultural historian Cindy Aron, a camping vacation could be seen as a barometer measuring middle-class dedication to health and work and reflecting middle-class goals of leisure and prosperity.[29]

Camps with the same Protestant homogeneity and middle-class values as Pinewoods were springing up throughout the United States during this period. Some of these camps were close by (the summer settlements of Huron Mountain on Lake Superior, Bay View near Grand Traverse Bay, and East Tawas on Lake Huron), and some were farther afield in the Pocono Lake Preserve in Pennsylvania and the Rockywold Deephaven Camps on Squam Lake in New Hampshire. The Great Camps of the Adirondacks being constructed by wealthy New Yorkers provided them all with models. Reinforcing this arcadian movement throughout the land was the growth and development of national parks; country clubs and sporting clubs; cemeteries emphasizing natural plantings; publications concerning birds, flowers, shrubs, and trees; an interest in horticulture; outdoors movements for youth—Boy Scouts, Girl Scouts, Campfire Girls; and screened-in sleeping porches.

Lakeside's founders, who first came to Higgins in 1875 to manage lumbering operations, began to bring their families to enjoy the experience of camping in the wilderness. The illusion of that original wilderness experience is continued through the preservation of the term "camp" in our reference to Lakeside, Cottage Grove, and Pinewoods. Camps at Higgins never attained the rustic magnificence of the Adirondacks compounds, but like those elaborate and expansive retreats, they provided their owners with the "perfect comfort and even luxury, tho in the heart of the woods" ascribed to the Great Camps by William Dix, editor of *Town and Country,* in a 1903 essay.[30] "Roughing it" was not the issue at any of these camps; a pleasant integration of nature and culture, sustained by the fantasy of a simple life, was the goal. Dix's further comment applies equally well to the Higgins and the Adirondacks camps:

> Few who have not lived this healthful, invigorating life can appreciate its wonderful charm. It is a return to nature after ten months of wearying city life with ceaseless formalities and responsibilities. Here the busy professional man or financier can find real rest and surcease from business as in no other way, and it is an interesting phase of American social life and decidedly significant. . . . As society has grown more and more complex, the swing of the pendulum goes more and more toward simplicity for the vacation.[31]

In the 1880s, Lakeside divided to create Cottage Grove, with Pinewoods splitting off from Cottage Grove to become incorporated in 1920. The first settlers at Pinewoods Camp arrived as guests at Lakeside in 1879. Auntie Helen, my grandmother's sister, discovered Higgins for our family in 1913. Following an initial visit, she returned to tell my grandparents, so the family legend goes, that they needed to get Lucy and Betty, my mother and her sister, off the mean streets of Bay City during the summer. My great aunt would have been impressed not only by the respectability and the camaraderie of Pinewoods, but also by lake water so pure it was used in a baptismal ceremony the summer of her visit. The next year, my mother's family tested the climate at Higgins by renting a cottage, and they continued as renters until 1919 when they purchased and transformed a four-room, one-story cabin into our present capacious, two-story, six-bedroom cottage. My grandmother had the cottage appropriately decorated with rustic wicker furniture and chintz curtains, and my grandfather immediately became involved in establishing the bylaws for a Pinewoods Association and in survey-ing land for a communal dining hall, which had proven to be the hub of social life for the Lakeside and Cottage Grove Camps.

The middle-class vacation evolved and, as it did, the tents of those first campers changed into lean-tos, the lean-tos became log cabins, and the log cabins turned into wooden houses, always called cottages. Recently, some of these cottages have evolved into "summer homes," designed by interna-tionally known architects. As Harvey H. Kaiser has noted in discussing the conscious rusticity of Adirondack camp architecture, designers "followed the rule that building materials possess certain inherent qualities of the forest." Thus, they eliminated "such materials as plaster, wallpaper, or paint—either inside or outside the building."[32]

For the most part, interiors at Pinewoods are unpainted, plain tongue-and-groove paneling, with the natural grain of the wood fully exposed; exteriors are stained in forest colors—pine green, spruce blue, bark brown. Furniture and ornamentation also follow the pattern set at the turn of the century by the Great Camps and evoke their natural surroundings with rough bark left on railings and posts and curiously twisted twigs given special prominence. In the beginning mattresses were pine boughs, and it could be said that the campers truly slept in the beds they had made. (They still nap outdoors in swings and hammocks.) Porches open Pinewoods cottages to the woods and the communal path; pavilions extend them to the lake. At first equipped only with one- and two-hole outdoor "garden houses," lit by kerosene lanterns and heated by fireplaces, cottages are now fitted with full baths and showers, furnaces, and television. For our family, the installation of the first furnace in 1960, a tele-phone in 1980, and a shower in 1988 were arduous collective decisions. We agreed in 1992, after some debate, to put in a washing machine and dryer, but there is only a small TV in one bedroom, and not until 2000 did my niece's fiancé bring in a laptop.

From the beginning of the century, subdivisions and resort hotels proliferated around the lake. Today, Higgins's twenty-six-mile circumference includes two state parks, an American Legion camp, Camp Westminster for Presbyterians, several township parks, boat yards (one in the big bay, one in the small bay), numerous roads leading from the interstate highways down to the shore with free anchorage at their terminus, and houses every fifty-five feet. You no longer even have to go into Roscommon, seven miles away and the village closest to Pinewoods, for the occasional sundry; everything—antiques, bars, banks, beauty shops, carpet stores, insurance agencies, gift shops, upholstery studios, video games—is available out on the North Cut Road.

Stony Point and Huckleberry Point, named at first by the campers for their identifying natural features, have been designated Detroit Point and Flag Point, and other stretches along the lake have been assigned names, such as Evergreen Park, Arrowhead Plains, Sunset Shores, Siesta Woods, Hillcrest, and Almeda Beach, reflecting the visions of realtors. Facing us across the lake are two subdivisions. One, Lyon Manor, a recent development of closely laid out streets, occupies the area once known simply as "The Farm" and marks the opposite shore as a clearing of pale green in the dark woods. Uncle Paul Bruske remembers that in his boyhood, this spot was "a development of a lumber camp" and, except for the three camps, was the only "human habitation on our part of the lake."[33] The other subdivision facing us is called Shoppenagon Lodge.

During recent summers at Higgins, more than a million pleasure seekers assemble every season. Docks, boat hoists, rafts, and beach umbrellas fringe the shore. Strung out from the docks or parked in front of them is an array of boats: canoes, kayaks, rowboats, catboats, pontoon party boats, windsurfers, catamarans, sloops, Sunfishes, jet skis, outboards, inboards, power launches. On a weekend, most of the lake's boats are in action, with helicopters from the National Guard units at nearby Camp Grayling whirring overhead. The sheet of water becomes illegible. It is ripped, zipped, split as sailors, skiers, and racers set their courses. Waves contradict each other, with those formed from the wakes of speeding powerboats slamming against those formed by the wind, and the dome of air above the lake could crack with the shrieking. By Monday, there's a healing. Waves run with the west wind in regular lines of calligraphy; making a quick dip down, a belted kingfisher momentarily punctuates them. Mother and her gang of teenage friends used to walk down to Cold Springs, go huckleberrying at the point, canoe over to The Cut, and hike around the entire lake. Such a trek is impossible now—you spend too much time clambering over docks or maneuvering your canoe around installations; trampling on private beaches, you receive hostile stares from property owners lying beneath umbrellas or tinkering with machinery.

Loons bred in grasses along the shore when Mother was young. She learned to interpret their wild ululations as warning calls, love songs, distress signals. If they turned particularly raucous, she knew it meant rough waves coming up fast on the lake. On an August day in 1991, sailing her Sunfish alone with a mild breeze, she suddenly saw a loon surface. As she sailed toward the bird, it swam toward her. It dove, still swimming toward her beneath the surface. "Visibility," she wrote, "was perfect."[34] She sailed on her way; the loon swam on its way. Whether this lone loon represented the embodiment of memory or desire, a rogue male loon or a young loon feeding at the surface, she sent the news of its re-emergence to the Michigan Loon Preservation Association.

In 1914, when Mother first arrived at Higgins, she has told me the lake was lighted at night only by stars, by moon, and occasionally by aurora borealis streaking up into the northern sky. Immersed in darkness, the south shore opposite ours represented no demarcation, but was simply an extension of the night. Gradually, however, as subdivisions have multiplied, lights have appeared across the water, rimming the lake now like a chrysolite choker. We go on looking to the night sky over the lake for glory: in a canoe in the middle of the lake in August, we can watch the Perseids zooming, one after another, through Cassiopeia across the sky to become embers in Capricornus, those with the longest trajectories still searing in memory.

When you're on shore, Pinewoods is hidden beneath the great pines—those solitary survivors of the timber era—for which it is named. You see the camp best from the lake. From the opposite shore. Or from a canoe in the middle of the big bay where the pines' jagged peaks disturb the smoothly rolling horizon around the lake, thereby distinguishing Pinewoods. Or perhaps the best view is from my computer on the edge of Kansas. I type in the plain fact: incorporated by its first settlers in 1920 with a common dining hall and a common caretaker, the Pinewoods Camp Association has expanded to include nineteen cottages. As Melville says of the island of Kokovoko, "It is not down in any map; true places never are."[35]

Ownership of Pinewoods's cottages, for the most part, goes back to the end of the nineteenth century or to the beginning of the twentieth. Several related families spread out over two or more cottages. Six generations of some families have come to Higgins, and at times during the summer, four generations of a family may be in residence in one cottage. The first settlers were close friends with one another and with people in the other two camps and came, for the most part, from lower Michigan towns prospering from the timber industry—Bay City, Saginaw, Lansing, Detroit. The men succeeded as independent businessmen or as professionals—engineers, architects, doctors, lawyers—and the women testified to their success by luxuriating through the summer at camp.

Through the 1950s, the values and the social patterns set in place by the first settlers prevailed. Wives and mothers arrived in Pinewoods at the end of June to stay for the entire summer; husbands and fathers arrived on weekends, enduring the long hot drive Up North (always capitalized and pronounced as a two-syllable, single word) on two-lane roads, and looked forward to a two- or three-week vacation. They worked hard during the winter, spring, and fall, and they played hard during the summer. As I read over various memoirs and histories of the camp, differences amongst the first generations of campers don't appear. The operant pronoun is the first-person plural. When Grandma Bruske asks after fifty years at Higgins, first in Lakeside and then Pinewoods, "Is there any place in all the world like this?" she answers with assurance, "We firmly believe there is not. Thus it comes that we are bound together in our joys and our friendships by ties that are sweet and enduring."[36]

Long ago, Mother told me that she could never have married a man who didn't appreciate the lake, and when I recently repeated this statement to her, half expecting to be faulted for not remembering accurately, she agreed. Following their wedding in the fall of 1934, my parents had a two-week honeymoon at Pinewoods, and in a memoir Mother wrote about our cottage, I read that my father passed the critical test: "Mac fell in love all over again—this time with a land and a lake. There was ice on the lake that first morning, but no matter, the sun shone every day, and the canoe and our feet took us everywhere."[37]

Occasionally, my sister-in-law, Tammy, points out that it's hard for people who marry into the camp. She usually brings up this subject when we're out on the pavilion in front of the cottage, having drinks before dinner, and she has the support of another spouse who has married in. She is grateful for the public comments made by Jack Wade, who also married into the camp, at the 1995 annual meeting, "that men and women marrying into the Camp have a great deal to give and should be considered vigorously for leadership positions."[38]

Pinewoods is like a large extended family; at any given time during the summer, more than 100 people may be in camp, and many of them are related. Even if they aren't related, everyone knows the elders as "aunt" and "uncle," so it's impossible to figure out who belongs to which family anyway. Even though she has been coming to Pinewoods now for more than thirty years, I think Tammy feels left out when people begin to reminisce. Even my father, who came to be known affectionately to many in Pinewoods as "Good Old Natured Mac," arranged to be gone for part of his summers. Becoming a Francophile and a high-school French teacher late in life, he took to attending Middlebury's summer language school and to traveling in France in July. Mother stayed at the lake. She never joined him; she couldn't bear to leave Pinewoods. Even after he retired from teaching, for several summers running he spent time walking a portion of the Appalachian Trail. Mother stayed at the lake.

In the mid-1960s, I rode a moral high horse into Pinewoods, flinging abstractions about and charging the association with pressure to conform, elitism and luxury, intolerance and indifference. An enclave for the leisured class. An irresponsible, apolitical anachronism. Its routines, its traditions were totally oppressive, utterly repressive. My mother, who was the personification of Pinewoods for me, was on the receiving end of most of my tirades. She bore me out. I had been absent from the lake for three summers, teaching in Japan, and had returned to graduate school, where I found myself challenged to give articulate shape to my values and where I found myself often trembling. Pinewoods was such an easy scapegoat, and I know now I was seeing it only out of a dim corner of my psyche and my eye in those days.

It wasn't until the summer of my father's death, June 1986, that I began to look again. The loss had scooped me empty, and most of what I thought I knew seemed thin tissue. A few days after the formal funeral in Flint, we—my Aunt Mary from New Jersey, Daddy's sister; my brother, Howie, and his family; Mother and I—went up to the cottage. Each of us took a handful of his ashes and scattered them at the base of the perfectly straight white pine behind the cottage, always known in the family as "Grandma's Favorite Tree." Finished, we held hands in a ring around the tree; we sang; we wept; we hugged; we split up and went separately to look at the lake. Both tree and lake returned us to the possibilities for a shimmering life. Their incandescence restored my father to my sense of continuing life and doing so restored me to myself and to my family.

Sometime later, back in Kansas, I heard myself say to a friend, "Because of Pinewoods, I don't think I can ever really be cynical. It's shown me hope for a good life, one where people care, where people grow." Pinewoods remains a privileged enclave, but its vision of a community seeking harmony among its people and harmony with nature also remains a model. Responding to crises, the camp has not been static. Some campers continue to perceive it as paradise as it was perceived by its original founders, but others beg to differ, and the boundaries and traditions of paradise have become increasingly permeable. Each summer, individuals and whole families continue to return to the same cottages which their grandparents and great-grandparents built. Occupations and interests differ widely, and financial variances among and within families have caused changes in cottages and in the camp. In the past few years, without fanfare, Jeff Harman has returned, bringing Nani, his Hawaiian wife, their two teenaged sons, and their adopted Hawaiian daughter, and the camp has embraced Pen, Dave Robinson's Thai wife. Dave and Pen are in camp throughout the summer, and although Pen prefers not to eat breakfast in the dining hall, she has become a regular for tennis, bridge, and golf and has learned her birds and flowers.

Many descendants of the first pleasure-seekers of the nineteenth century are committed stewards of the lake and woods and all that live therein. Members of the camp serve on the boards of the Higgins Lake Property Owners Association and the Higgins Lake Foundation which have, among other endeavors, encouraged a marine patrol on the lake, developed limited zoning laws around the lake, monitored lake water quality, and proposed an endangered species law to protect the black squirrel. No one in Pinewoods hunts any more, and only the occasional visitor fishes. Because the creatures are so much more scarce now than they were in the beginning of the century, we rejoice whenever and wherever we see them and share the news of their appearance. We sport T-shirts advocating support of Georges Bank whales, Antarctica penguins, Point Reyes birds, and the Greens, and our conversation often revolves around conservation.

If I have on occasion felt isolated in Pinewoods, I also realize I have the best of both worlds: I am an individual in a community; my present springs from my memories and those of others and flows into a common future; I stand on the shoreline with the clear swell of lake and sky and the illusion of eternity before me, aware of the dense intimacy of the family cottage and the Pinewoods history and community behind me. On the shoreline tonight with the Pleiades's hissing brilliance overhead, I may miss the conversation at the bonfire and the s'mores, but I'll see everyone at breakfast in the morning. Gratitude for this good life buoys me, and the shoreline positions me to try to see it more fully and to express it more clearly.

SHORE

Sitting on the rocks at the northern tip of Lake Superior's Isle Royale the summer of 1987, I first realized that my place is on a shore. At that moment on Isle Royale, I felt the density of ancient forests pressed at my back while in front of me the pewter gray waters of Lake Superior scrolled endlessly out toward a horizon. I sat on hard rock, lichen-inscribed: paisley patterns of rusts and gold and green beneath my feet to be read in relation to forest and lake. I thought of times sitting on other shores: on Goto's white sand in Japan and St. Vincent's black sand in the Caribbean, on the wharves in Boston Harbor and San Francisco, on the wide beach at Dar es Salaam in Tanzania and the high promontory at Whitby in England. But it's the bit of shore in front of the cottage where I first started keeping watch.

You come down to the shore by stages. Steps lead from the path to the pavilion; from the pavilion to a platform beneath three red pines where my grandmother used to sit by herself and sew, where we set up a newspaper office as kids, where now there are two tall stumps and one tree still standing; from this platform to the lower pavilion; from the lower pavilion to the concrete breakwater by the pumphouse and the dock. You can step off the breakwater into the grass and onto the rocks, or you can go from the breakwater to the dock and then just jump down to the shore.

31

There's plenty to do on the shore: hauling boats in and out; constructing breakwaters; beach-combing for driftwood, curios, trash; stoning. Aunt Betty was the family's most famous stoner; she spent long late-afternoon hours, after she'd arisen from her nap, standing with her legs apart, peering down into the shallow waters which lapped against the shore to see what glacial jewels had turned up since yesterday; she kept her stones in jars of water among the family treasures in Bay City. On top of the bookshelf in my Kansas bedroom sits the squat brown stone on which she pasted two white paper-hole reinforcements to make the white eyes of a Higgins Lake toad.

Everybody looks for stones: pudding stones—aggregates of colorful quartz; Petoskey stones—fossilized colony coral from the Devonian seas 350 million years ago, its polyps, surrounded by tentacles, petrified into distinct hexagonal patterns, and now Michigan's officially designated State Stone; translucent white stones; blood red stones; lucky stones with full circles around them; stones with fossil shells and insects imbedded in them; onyx. After they are lined up on the dock for everybody to admire, the finder tosses them back into the lake or takes them upstairs where they become doorstops or bookends or join other stones in a dish on the windowsill in the cottage living room. If someone throws back your stone before it has been adequately admired, there is quite a protest, although the stone in the lake is always there to be discovered again. (Mother keeps a small bucket of Petoskey stones in the pumphouse which she "plants" on the shore when visitors come.)

I am content just to be on or near the shore. "At the shore" or "at the beach" conjures up a leisured life, a concept that still unsettles me. Sitting, standing, perched on or by this shore, however, I am at home—aware of the steps and pavilions signifying all our known cottage and camp life behind me and the lake and sky signifying all the unknown. Water shapes the shore. With the dam at The Cut open, Higgins's water level has been higher in recent years than it was when I was growing up. A photograph from 1937 shows me in my diapers toddling on a wide sandy beach between lake and grassy bank. Now, stones and only a narrow edge of sand physically define the shore. But the lake, edging into the shore, leaves lines engraved in the sand, often etched with bits of pine needles and twigs, a drowned bee and small gelatinous blobs of fish eggs, always known to us as "jelly-fish." If the line is marked by foam, I know there is a storm in the offing. In any case the line, drawn, is re-drawn in the next instant. As the lake pulls back across the stones, the sand shuffles and there's a soft sucking with small bubbles rising and bursting. A sentimental metaphor: the water kisses the sand,

and with its kiss changes it, leaves it, returns to it again and again, but the two are never one. When the wind rises and the storm comes, all clarity is lost. Still shore waters, which ordinarily reveal snails, clams, schools of darting minnows, the occasional scooting crayfish, and the sand's design of regulated waves, are churned to obscurity and come charging in against the beach. There is no more shoreline. The sounds of lapping and sucking and kissing become sounds of pummeling and cracking and breaking.

I must have been thirteen that diaphanous August morning when I sat at the bottom of the steps leading down from the lower pavilion, looking out to the lake and painting my toenails carnelian. It has been decades now since I colored the nails of either hands or feet, but at that time I had a desperate faith in the magic of body paint, and I was taking great care. But the view of the lake kept intervening as I dipped the little brush in and out of the bottle of nail polish. The lake, usually tricolored with green, turquoise, and cobalt, was silvered and still: no sound, no movement. Its surface gleamed until it dissolved in mist, taking with it the horizon, the opposite shore. With no wind, the boats close in to shore pointed every which way. Those anchored further out floated, featherweight, just above the lake, with an opaque space, like that between the mirror's surface and its backing, coming between them and the water. Way beyond was the island, a nebulous Atlantis, adrift from its mooring, looming. I applied the bright red polish to the nails on my left foot assiduously, but then paused and with the nailbrush wrote out on the dock, "Remember this day: August 24, 1949." Time did not stop. The boards on the dock were gradually replaced, and there is now no sign of my teenage desire to reconcile incomprehensible antitheses. But I do remember this day on the shore, and I keep it holy when in the heat of Kansas in August and the first week of the new semester, I see boats walking on water.

At one time or another, I've mulled over the paradoxical concept at the center of the Chinese *I Ching* that change is the only constant as well as the Heraclitean insight that you can't step in the same water of a river twice. The very brevity of my adult visits to Pinewoods in the summer—two weeks if I'm able—alerts me to changes: I'm the great aunt who sees her young nieces and nephew only twice a year and therefore may be more aware of their growth than their parents and playmates who see them daily.

Arriving at the lake now is the same as it was when I was ten. We enter camp swooping in off the interstate, eagerly reducing speed for the county road blacktops, coming in past the mailboxes lined up at the entrance, at last slowing down to a dawdle on the rutted Stage Road running behind the cottages, shaded by the pines no matter what time of day. Trying as usual to avoid the inevitable potholes, we pass the dining hall and the familiar signs indicating the drive for each family's cottage, each one hand-wrought, several with specific north woods icons—a squirrel, trillium, pine bough. We turn at the sign of the Shaw Cottage's iron sailboat. Unchanged, the same white pine halfway in keeps the same angle, leaning far over the road, a northern sword of Damocles for us to pass beneath each trip coming and going, but leaning no further, to my perception, than it did last year.

Then, with an indrawn breath, you're there, pulling up behind the cottage. You tote the suitcases out of the car, through the back door into the cottage, down the hall, up the stairs, and into the appropriate bedrooms; you usually have to make several trips. If you arrive at night, you move from thick darkness into the cottage's buttery light from the bare bulbs on the back porch and in the kitchen; if you arrive earlier, you move from the day's quick and myriad brightness into subdued light laid out in patches, first across curling blue linoleum and then on smooth pine floors down the hall and on into the cottage. All the time you're breathing a little deeper; you're also listening for pine needles rubbing, boats bumping, water sloshing. Walking through the kitchen, you notice whether grandmother's blue-checked dishcloths are hanging on the three-pronged rack over the sink and whether the basket of clothespins are on top of the breadbox; walking on into the living room, you notice whether the candles are standing straight on the mantle and whether the binoculars are on the coffee table. At last you're out on the front porch where you can see the lake. Glimpsed first through the dark trees and pavilion posts, it shimmers. At last you go on out to the pavilion, to stand and look across the lake: yes, the island is right there, right there where it always is in your memory for ever and ever. Amen.

Only later when I sit down on the pavilion with Mother, drink in hand before facing the annual initiation at the dining hall, will I be ready to listen to the changes. Nowadays, she drives up to camp a month before I manage to arrive, and consequently she has had time to take in the differences. I remember returning to Flint from college to discover that she had sorted through my bureau drawers, deciding that I'd no longer be wearing these pajamas, no longer be needing these scarves. I felt outraged, my privacy violated; when she started weeding through my childhood collections, some sense of my past began to collapse. I sometimes think she responds to Thoreau's imperative to "Simplify! Simplify!"[39] with a vengeance. Whether her mania for discarding and eliminating and simplifying reflects a Puritan ethic, a Depression mentality, or a heightened environmental imperative, it contrasts with my nostalgic instincts, and she and I can still scrape each other over the question of retaining my Auntie Helen's rosewood chair or sending it to the Art Institute rummage sale. I also understand now that because Mother's been watching the camp's comings and goings, the lake's shifting plant and animal life for so long, she can't let some things just go. She saves, rescues, recycles; she also cherishes. She spends an entire summer polishing a small footstool, cast off in a corner of the cottage storeroom, until it glistens; she argues passionately for the preservation of dead trees; she keeps track of the families in each Pinewoods cottage. On the long window sill running in the cottage living room is the bowl of glass bits, lake-smoothed and softened to translucent colors, kept for pure pleasure, and one trout-shaped pineknot, kept for memory as I keep a smaller talisman in Kansas.

Sitting in the pavilion with her on this first evening back, I let my mind go from cottage to cottage, down the path. Mother tells me who's in camp and who isn't coming, who's in the hospital and who has a new job, about variations in the dining hall menu and whether the staff is working out. These are the constant changes; they have the regularity of seasons and of Heraclitus's river water. She goes on to tell me how many ducks are coming to sit on our dock and how many people are complaining about swimmer's itch. She tells me about the devastation behind Cottage Grove due to its "forest management" program and about the gypsy moths and zebra mussels: though the moths aren't staging a comeback, the mussels might be arriving. She mentions, too, that there has been talk of the woodshed behind the cottage coming down to build a structure to house laundry facilities and that Howie and Tammy are discussing buying a motorboat. These are more seismic changes. How will I respond when I hear that a TV has been ordered for the cottage living room?

To avoid the possibility that the path he'd worn between his door and the pond would turn into a rut "of tradition and conformity,"[40] Thoreau left Walden to become "a sojourner in civilized life again."[41] The routines of communal living in Pinewoods and my expectations regarding both the appearance and behavior of its human and natural inhabitants, however, are deeply rutted. By Thoreau's standards, I've turned traditionalist and conformist, for not only am I committed to returning to Pinewoods annually but in returning, I anticipate immutability. I want everything to remain the same, as usual, familiar, known. Yet change always tampers with our desires for eternity, and despite Thoreau, staying in one place or loving one place (substitute one cottage or one boat, one person or one community) proves our vulnerability to time's erosion.

The first-time visitor to camp can see no changes. Stay a week or a month, and Pinewoods continues to appear anachronistic, archaic, a throwback to the nineteenth century, to a more leisured time and place. Spend a lifetime of summers, and it seems that both the community and the environment have adjusted astonishingly to wracks and wrenches of minor and mighty magnitude. For all its old-fashioned wooden cottages, its one dining hall, its docks set perpendicular to the shore in identical places summer after summer, its boats bobbing foolishly in the same places, its single path, Pinewoods isn't static—it throbs. It throbs in response to problems of overpopulation and pollution on the lake at large, in response to demands from Roscommon County for increased taxes and the Higgins Lake Foundation for increased contributions, in response to requests from its membership for new lighting and more vegetarian options in the dining hall, in response to the loss of its great trees to a tornado. I have occasionally thought of Pinewoods as amoeba-like—a basic life form which, within its defining outline, can shape-shift as it encounters water vacuoles or dust motes.

Although the shore has been a defining physical perimeter, the camp's social outline has changed since its 1920 establishment. Most of the cottages continue to belong to the families of the camp's founding fathers and mothers, but death, finances, and shifting allegiances led to departures and to the sale of four of the original cottages. Three other families, all of whom had come to Pinewoods first as visitors and then as renters, purchased these old cottages and remodeled and expanded them. Now, along with the original camp members, they, too, take their turns at camp president and serve on camp committees. They never miss meals at the dining hall, and they participate with wit and whimsy in Hat Nights, with appropriate ferocity in the Rat Race, and competitive spunk in Sunfish contests. They know their birds and flowers better than anybody, and their children have grown up with the sounds and smells and rituals of Pinewoods; long ago embracing Pinewoods, Pinewoods embraced them. There's also a long list of "Friends of Pinewoods" printed on the back pages of the annual *Pinewoods Directory*. Unrelated to any of the property owners in the camp, these friends have been coming regularly to Pinewoods—often for decades—from scattered points on the national compass; they may come for weeks or sometimes just a day to retrieve a family connection or a childhood memory. They are welcomed, and subjected in the dining hall and on the path to the same generous and strenuous series of introductions and queries as everyone else upon their arrival in camp.

With our cottage next-to-the-last at Pinewoods's western boundary, it began my sentence, during my teenage years, with the Loomis cottage being the period at the end of the meandering path which unites all the other cottages in meaningful sequence arranged along it. Not only was the Loomis cottage the goal I set out for so many mornings, but it was then the eastern terminus of camp. Unlike Pinewoods's other cottages, it wasn't built alongside the path, but rose up from the path itself as if to block out both the forest and the society beyond. A Great Wall, keeping us in and others out, or so it seemed to me, swaddled in social smugness during those years. On the other side was Earl Avenue, cramped with holiday cabins owned by local people and used for boat access and boat anchorage. A swarm of as many as sixty ungainly boats could be parked in the shallow water at its terminus. We didn't know who owned them; they seemed to have been dumped there. East of Earl Avenue were several more small roads, equally jammed, and then Gerrish Park, where crowds came on weekends to picnic and swim, bringing plastic rafts and swollen inner tubes. Thus beyond the Loomis cottage was the unknown, and I realize I was as casually indifferent to this very close and real unknown even as I was intrigued by the very distant and exotic unknown.

In 1956, however, the Will family extended the Pinewoods path eastward and pushed into the beyond. Purchasing forest land from the Loomises, they began constructing a series of structures, which eventually resulted in a modern house, a three-bedroom unit, a separate playroom, a paddle-tennis court, and a beach house, all collectively known as "The Willage"; here Jack and Liz Will Wade live eight months of the year, becoming much more than summer visitors and pleasure-seekers. Concerned with issues pertaining to the health of the lake, the land, and the culture around it, they regularly attend Gerrish Township and Roscommon County meetings and sit on the Higgins Lake Advisory Board and the Roscommon Conservation and Development Commission; well acquainted with their neighbors on Earl Avenue, they are citizens of a community larger than Pinewoods, serving the camp as year-round stewards.

Social and physical arrangements in individual cottages also wax and wane. The founders of the camp and the first architects had anticipated visitors throughout the summer. House parties were in vogue from the beginning. The dining hall makes it possible to feed unannounced friends or relatives from anywhere in the world who just happen to be in the Higgins vicinity, and the old cottages come equipped with diverse sleeping arrangements—upstairs bedrooms which multiply like rabbit warrens, lofts, out-buildings, screened-in pavilions and porches, bunk beds, extra cots, hammocks, swings. No one, however, anticipated the expansion of the original families—the layers of generations, the configurations of cousins, the profusion of grandchildren. In part because I have stayed single, our cottage still holds its own. But I know Tammy frets about her grandchildren. Will there be room(s) enough for them?

Families in some Pinewoods cottages struggle with complex summer schedules. Whereas Pinewoods was comprised of Michiganders at the beginning of the century, individuals and families now come from around the world—Japan, France, Switzerland, Indonesia—and throughout the United States—Massachusetts, California, Texas, Washington state, and Washington, D.C. In addition, although a few people, including some grandparents with their grandchildren, see the summer in and out, most members of Pinewoods can't afford the time or the money it takes to stay for an entire summer. Both husbands and wives often work now; their children are engaged in various summer activities in their home communities. To manage diverse demands and divide summer cottage time equally, one branch of a family may take the cottage for July, the other August. Other clans have to parcel out the months in weeks to accommodate their members, rotating the most desirable periods on an annual basis. In a *Town & Country* essay, Barbara Hanson Pierce explains her extended family's arrangements for the summer at their Maine cottage: "There are advance bookings and in-season and off-season rates, and the calendar is divided, almost literally 16 ways to Saturday (check-in and check-out take place on Saturdays at noon)."[42]

Unanticipated family growth is not the only reason for such intricate arrangements: sibling squabbles obviously extend into summer, and all cousins do not see eye to eye. For some families, the Pinewoods cottage is the center of the web, the primary place for family reunions and remembering, for catching up and connecting anew; for others it is an open sore. A Pinewoods cottage has a single living room, a single dock, a single table at the dining hall, and usually only one shower. If the day is dank, there's no escaping the living room; if bright, there's no escaping the dock; whatever the day, the dining hall with its designated family table and its public pleasantry is the only place to eat. It has proven easier for those families who suffer their relations to split the summer or just to split.

For the sake of attaining privacy and peace as well as sustaining kinhsip harmony, some individuals have built annexes apart from the old family cottage. The Loomis elders had TLC (The Little Cottage/Tender Loving Care) constructed alongside the Big Cottage, while Aunt Sally had her own personal cabin down by the shore. The retreat, named the "Grumpus Room," created for Uncle Ed and Aunt Adelaide Taggart behind one of the Taggart cottages, allowed them to have uninterrupted time to integrate James's leisurely sentences or Siebelius's gorgeous measures into bird and wind song. In compact new cabooses behind the rambling old cottages, single members of certain families can let the children and grandchildren of their extended families rock and roll up front while they revel in quietude out back. Marion Foster's back cottage has been a sanctuary for me, too. If the day is chilly, or our pavilion too windy, and we feel the need for dialogue, we retreat to the snugness of her one-room cabin, comfortable with wicker furniture, art books, and light filtered through surrounding trees. It's quiet enough on Sunday here for the two of us to settle into a Quaker meeting.

Fluctuations in the outline of Pinewoods have not all been extensions; there have also been diminishments. Some families left the camp long ago, existing for me now only as names in Mother's stories or names in camp memoirs. In the late 1960s three families, all descendants of Pinewoods's founders, chose to limit their relationship with Pinewoods. The reasons for these decisions seemed shrouded in ambiguities. Since no one in my family remembered how this rift in the camp's communal harmony had come to be, I sought an explanation in the minute books of the Pinewoods annual meetings. There it was: a line drawn in the sand. Threatened by insecure finances and fluctuating attendance, the majority of the camp agreed that membership in the Pinewoods Camp Association made dining hall attendance mandatory at all three meals. Desiring alternatives to this policy, these families withdrew from the Pinewoods dining hall, while continuing to use their cottages. Camp members' responses to their withdrawal have been diverse—anger, hostility, regret, sorrow, acceptance.

In the same year that these families separated themselves from the association, the camp voted to shift from served meals to self-serve cafeteria in the dining hall; now finances are stable and attendance flourishes. At dinner after my long afternoon with the minute books, I said to Mother and our next-door neighbor, "We'd find another way now. We'd talk longer. Try negotiating further. Try alternatives. Considering the crazy worlds we live in most of the year, everyone at Pinewoods knows it's too precious for us to lose now." The lake erases the lines it draws on the shore; the sand above the shore shifts imperceptibly; generations shift. Gradually these families are easing back into the dining hall. There is room for them here.

DINING HALL

Waking up early in Kansas, I hear the first Pinewoods dining hall bell tolling through memory and through the woods; with its faint echo, the Cottage Grove bell follows. If I lie still, I can hear the cottage creaking, wind lifting branches, Howie rushing in through the front door, just up from swimming, Mother on the back porch opening the refrigerator for cat food. She'll call me in a minute or come and knock on my bedroom door. It doesn't take me long to wash and dress, but because she's been up for a couple of hours—checking the boats, taking dry bathing suits in off the line, loading kindling in the box by the fireplace—she goes ahead. We'll go together, then, at lunch and dinner, our arms entwined. We share an umbrella if it's raining. Usually we meet others taking the connecting paths behind the cottages, all of which lead to the Stage Road. Along the road, set back inconspicuously in the woods, is the dining hall, where everyone at Pinewoods meets for all three meals.

For breakfast, lunch, and dinner, the bell brings us together: by tradition it is rung three times for each meal—the first a half-hour before mealtime, the second to open the hall, the last to warn us we have fifteen minutes before food service will stop. The bell, housed in a cupola over the double doors opening into the hall, is a vestige from the days of water pumps and kerosene lamps. When someone pulls its long rope just inside the doors, the bell resonates throughout camp from the past in somber tones, but it calls us every day into the present. Every Pinewoods child is initiated into the community by being allowed to ring the bell. The catch is to get the pulls synchronized with the clapper; when the child succeeds, with or without the help of a supervising adult, it's ecstasy. The bell booms out her triumph, and she scurries back to her table, with everyone clapping for her success. Only on Wednesday evening is the bell silent; this is the staff's night off and an opportunity for some families to picnic together or explore the local eateries.

The Pinewoods histories—*A History of Pinewoods, 1928–1929; Pinewoods, 1948–1966; Pinewoods, 1920–1987;* and Mother's essay in *The Pinewoods Scrapbook, 1992,* titled "The Beginnings of the Pinewoods Dining Hall," accompanied by a diagram identifying which families sit at which of its nineteen tables—all point to the dining hall as Pinewoods's pulsating communal center. Cottage Grove's recognition in 1919 that it could no longer accommodate the Pinewoods families in its dining hall led immediately to plans to purchase ten acres behind the cottages, construct a hall, and form an association. Consequently, in the winter of 1919–20, my grandfather and three other men, after plowing through four feet of snow, staked out the land for the Pinewoods dining hall, measuring it with a trolling line. Through the spring "the demon contractor," Mike Ullman,[43] was furiously at work on the hall, a pumphouse, a screened-in fish house, and a two-story icehouse. When the bell rang on 1 July 1920, Pinewoods Camp Association came to life. If the camp's founding fathers and mothers saw the lake and the great pines as lifting spirit, the dining hall was to nourish body and heart. Although practical people, theirs was a utopian vision of individuals, healthy in all ways, and fed by a community. The dining hall was their means for embodying that community, making it possible to believe that Pinewoods would be idyllic, Edenic, the perfect place to be.

The dining hall, then and now, in releasing us from the labor of purchasing, planning, and preparing meals, gives us—particularly the women—time, gives us the illusion of freedom. In the 1870s when there was no legal association and Pinewoods people were visitors in the Lakeside Camp, with everyone in tents and lean-tos, meals were prepared over open campfires. Pinewoods men used their guns and rods to bring home the bacon and the perch. At that time there was enough wild game to be killed, fish to be caught, and berries to be picked to feed the camp from the fat of the forest and the lake. When log cabins and cottages appeared in the 1880s, housewives also appeared, along with their maids. They came with bags of flour and salt, whole hams and sides of bacon, canned fruit and butter by the crock, all imported by train and wagon. Fishing and berrying came to be shared by everyone and to be regarded not as tasks, but as adventurous outings with specific rewards: first the dazzling string of perch and the heavy bucket of huckleberries, then the succulent fish fry and the oozing pie.

Among "Local Items" noted in the 14 August 1885 *Roscommon News* was the fact that "Quite a number of our citizens are rusticating at Higgins Lake."[44] Rustication didn't last long, however, and camping rapidly became domesticated. Most cottages came to have full sets of silver, china, tea services, and linen. Photographs show our great-grandmothers corseted and in long dresses seated in sailboats, silhouetted on the dock in their lovely hats, or propped up in poses against boulders or logs. My grandmother, Kirty Eddy Shaw, whom I never saw in pants, had the reputation of being "the camper with the whitest shoes." The dining hall, however, shifted the primary burden of domesticity—the preparation and serving of food—to a hired staff. Camping evolved from a masculine sport into a family affair, allowing middle- and upper-middle-class men, women, and children to work and play together.

Mother has been there from the beginning and seen it all. Her essay on the dining hall acknowledges multiple changes. Many of these changes occurred when Pinewoods was electrically connected to Roscommon in 1929, and the dining hall shifted from wood-burning stove to furnace; from ice, sawed from the lake and brought up to the icehouse by horses, to refrigeration; from oil lamps to electricity; from candles to elegant, wrought-iron lighting over each table. She remembers that Pinewoods women sewed the linen covers for the rounded backs of the hall's walnut chairs; cut the oil-cloth doilies, painting a pine-needle and pine-cone motif in each corner and placing the napkins in birch-bark holders; selected the curtains, which go on year after year. In her essay, she doesn't need to remind us that chairs are no longer covered and that place-mats and napkins are now paper (useful for leaving notes, generating lists, making *origami* at the end of a meal). Nor does she need to remind us that formal wear in the evenings and on Sunday noons for men, women, and children is no longer required. She does not mention the switch from waitresses and three sit-down meals a day to a self-service cafeteria line; the condemnation of the dining hall's second floor as unusable for living quarters (some remember that during the 1970s the plumbing began to leak from upstairs through the ceiling into the coffee pot); or the addition of separate quarters behind the hall for the cook and the staff.

Mother might have mentioned the demise of the dining hall store, with its private booth (for the camp's only telephone until the early 1960s) inscribed with names, numbers, hearts, and miscellaneous doodles going back to the 1920s. Since there were few lines in those early days and they were readily clogged, phone calls were not made or received casually; they were pre-arranged, timed, and awaited, and from the moment the phone gave its chortling ring, the expectant receiver felt her heart leap up. This technology connecting us to people and worlds beyond Pinewoods was exhilarating. The store also sold marshmallows, cigarettes, postals, film, candy—Necco Wafers, Tootsie Rolls, Babe Ruth bars, gum drops, licorice—and chewing gum. After desserts—pies and cookies at noon, cakes and puddings for dinner—candy must have seemed an excrescence, but as a kid, "The Store" was irresistibly fascinating to me. To hover over the glass counter, behind which these infinitely desirable sweets were displayed in delectable colors and shapes, was to experience the first anguish of consumerism, and by exchanging a penny for a very long and limber licorice stick, I received my initial lesson in the pleasures of purchase. Gum could be chewed and twisted into initials and cartoons and stuck on the "Gum Tree" out in front of the dining hall to join a history of other gummy mementos. When telephone lines came into individual cottages and the Evergreen Park Stop 'n' Shop opened within walking distance at the end of Lakeside, "The Store" closed. From 1985–95, Paul Brown operated his version of the store after lunch behind the Big Taggart cottage for the camp's kids. Now there's a playhouse for the smallest children, set up in front of the dining hall front door, to intrigue them after meals.

The dining hall cook no longer prepares a platter of bass, caught on the edge of black water by Uncle Paul, to be shared with the entire dining hall for breakfast. Instead, we may pass around a new Kiss-of-Fire salsa from a Traverse City mall or an olive-and-walnut bread brought back from a Petoskey bakery. Summer birthdays continue to be shared. The lights go off, and a blazing cake is wheeled in from the kitchen, with the staff and the entire hall singing felicitations. When the candles are blown out and the clapping is over, the cake is cut into enough pieces for all and taken from table to table. The patriarch still commands the head of some family tables in the dining hall, but at other tables, whoever returns first from the cafeteria line or whoever wants it for a given meal can claim the head. At our table we rotate chairs arbitrarily, with the chosen seats being those from which the diner has the larger perspective of the comings and goings in the hall.

The Pinewoods histories and Mother's essay—"the happy story of a plain, warm, friendly, brown building,"[45] she calls it—all imply that outweighing any changes is the comfortable continuity of a harmonious community which the dining hall has seemed to assure. In midsummer, when the camp is full, the dining hall swells outward. You can hear the clatter and chatter through the woods when you're on your way to a meal. There's a long line when you arrive, and you better arrive early because there may be a run on the raspberries or the corn-on-the-cob. You push your tray along, commenting on the sunset to one person, reaching for the olives, speculating on the number of women in Congress in response to someone's question, asking someone else to pass the Paul Newman, scooping up some spinach casserole, stepping back while a kid darts into line for some radishes, checking with a neighbor on her mother's health, taking one of the last ears of corn, moving the tray off to the coffee table for a cup of unleaded, over to the dessert table for a sliver of cheese cake, a cluster of grapes. Children swirl around the adults as people move from the serving area back to their tables; it's everybody's lookout to see that none of them bumps a head on a table corner. At your own table, you set down your tray and pour water for everyone.

At the time the dining hall first opened, Pinewoods families chose their tables; for the most part they sit at the same tables now and will sit at them for years to come. In the course of a summer, as family members and visiting friends come and go, the tables seem to expand and contract. Three and four generations may crowd around a single table, laughter and food heaped high. Everyone also table hops in the dining hall. It's so easy to shift a place setting, and so important if you're not going to see a camper from California for another year because she's leaving just as you're arriving. You join her and her husband and her brothers and cousins and aunt and nieces and nephews and visiting friends at their table. Or if you've gotten into a long discussion out on the pavilion with a young friend about Iroquois mythology and his experiences teaching Native American high school students art, you invite him to sit with you. Or if you're part of a gang of kids who have been organizing a skit together through the morning and you just have to keep at it through the afternoon, you all have to eat together at the same table. No one dines alone. On weekdays some women may be alone in their cottages, and if one arrives at the hall early in the morning in an actual attempt to have breakfast without social intercourse, usually she will be beckoned by people from another table to join them with her toast and coffee.

In the dining hall, you do more than dine. Over the salad bar, waiting in line for ice-cream cones, leaning over to speak with friends at the next table, you plan a canoe trip down the Au Sable River, commiserate over the rain, inquire about someone's bum leg, find out when another family is due to arrive in camp, arrange to borrow a hacksaw, discuss Jane Smiley's *A Thousand Acres,* speculate on the outcome of water samples taken by the Higgins Lake Foundation around the lake, report on the name of the frilly yellow fungus on the oak out by the garage. Tacked up on pillars in the hall are the courses for sailboat races and the sign-up sheets for paddle-tennis tournaments, golf scramble, and the infamous Rat Race at the tennis court. For many summers, Hat Night brought campers to the hall for dinner in the most outlandish headgear they could devise. The hall has also hosted lectures on such topics as the gypsy moth infestation and fire prevention, slide shows on such exotic subjects as Antarctica's penguins and an odyssey around the Peloponnese, as well as celebrations—weddings with the posts and rafters wound with wild sweet peas and Queen Anne's lace and Hank Taggart's long-awaited return from the Pacific in 1946. His parents met him in Chicago and "brought him straight to Pinewoods," where he was greeted with banners and bunting strung about the dining hall, "costumes, music, and general whooperino."[46] On the last Saturday in July, tables and chairs are rearranged for the association's annual meeting and, following a few moments of silence to memorialize anyone from camp who has died in the preceding year, committee reports are made, and camp business proceeds.

It's impossible to sneak unnoticed into camp. Sooner or later, everyone comes to the dining hall. Your first meal in camp each summer brings with it an onslaught of affection. As soon as you step through the front doors, someone is there to hug you, pat you on the back, pump your hand. When a camp member arrives after an absence of several years, or when summer schedules that have prevented friends from being at Pinewoods during the same two-week vacation period are revised, the meetings and the greetings are effusive. The dining hall makes it equally impossible to be either sick in secret or ornery in solitude, to have either an eccentric eating schedule or a specialized diet. Once you arrive at the lake and have established your presence by appearing for a meal at the dining hall, your absence will be noted by one and all. Family members pile up trays with food to take to folks who insist on sleeping late in the morning or who have come down with a bug. There are always sympathetic inquiries around the central coffee pot. "Where's Martha this morning? What's the matter with Dave? Is Sharkey really ill? She's never been sick before." The dining hall demands a kind of heroism from those with walking difficulties; navigating over the roots and pine needles of our paths and the ruts of our sandy road has necessitated that some elders make the trek to the hall by car. But trek they do, for we all await them.

Whitefish Friday night, hamburgers Saturday noon, roast beef Saturday night, chicken Sunday noon: this basic menu that I remember from childhood persists; like apple pie, it is all-American. By the late-1980s, however, enough people had converted to vegetarianism to necessitate a built-in salad bar and alternative selections at each meal. In the summer of 1993, for the first time, turkey as well as pork sausage was available for breakfast, and rice steamers (one for brown, one for white) as well as the sterno full of carbos—banana bread, doughnuts, or raspberry strudel, all out of cellophane packages—were set up on the counter. (Hall-made blueberry muffins, sticky cinnamon buns, and Parker House rolls disappeared with waitresses.) Contemporary taste differences, specialized dietary requirements, and individual eating patterns point to fractures in the easy conformity and pleasant rituals generated by the "plain, warm, friendly, brown building" and by the camp community. Fractures left out of camp histories.

For me, the sound of the old bell tolling at its regular intervals reassures. It confirms the more elusive hours established by sun and shadow. For others, however, the divisions of the natural day determined by the dining hall's hours are imperious: Aunt Betty, for example, declined to hear the bell. On those pale blue summer days, she told others to go on to lunch without her; she would stay down on the shore. While we trooped back into the woods to congregate over hot soup, she could be alone in the lake's light. Removing her bathing suit, she waded in the shallow water, stoning for a while, then walking out further, swimming, returning, lying flat out, a white shadow, sunning on the warm boards of dock. I know because once, engrossed in reading on the old canvas swing on the lower pavilion, oblivious to the noontime bells, I looked up to see her. Since then, I've learned the word Nereid. She was nude, dancing along the beach, her lovely long legs shining, a gauze scarf floating between her hands. Free for an hour or so. Although it's the pleasure of the company that guarantees we come to meals on time, there's also an element of public shame in being late and, thereby, being a nuisance for the staff: heads turn when the person who has overslept or gotten becalmed on the lake barges late through the doors. The time-honored fine for latecomers remains 50¢ after all these years. Aunt Betty didn't bother with fines; she simply didn't show.

The "Eat It All Club" first made me conscious of dining hall pressure. Internalizing our parents' pity for the mysteriously starving Armenians and their demands for clean plates, Marilyn Schirmer and I, best friends and ages eight and seven created a gang of two with cruel and unusual rules for self-criticism and self-regulation. We agreed, between ourselves, on punishments for failure: she who ate only her Jello salad and her dessert and left all her meat and potatoes would be forced by the other to consume a bowl of sand; she who left any food at all on her plate would be forced by the other to jump off the roof of the Schirmer family's lower pavilion. The pressure mounted in the 1950s, the decade of my teens, when it became evident that I was developing what is euphemistically called "a weight problem." My lithe aunt put it more succinctly when she pointed out at dinner one night that I was the only one in the family who'd "ever run to fat." At the dining hall not only the family, but the entire camp community could count the number of cookies you took at noon from the generous platters on the central tables and the number of ice-cream scoops you ordered from the waitresses after supper. As easily as they added bridge scores, they also counted calories, announcing your grand total publicly at the table. "Boring, boring, boring," I used to shout during these caloric conversations, in defense of my taking just one more piece of Boston cream pie. I binged in private on cans of deluxe salted nuts (lots of large pecans and Brazil nuts) which I purchased in secret at the Cottage Grove store, where no one knew me, and which I kept behind the shoes in my bedroom closet. No doubt I had the makings of what is now called "an eating disorder," exacerbated by the contented chomping mouths at the dining hall.

When, as a result of the wear and tear of graduate school, I lost thirty pounds and assumed the average size of the rest of the family, I picked a private bone with the dining hall. The food was too starchy, too greasy, too oily, too fattening; there was no seven-grain bread, no yogurt, no steamed veggies. Thin is still in at Pinewoods Camp; although a few pudgy babies and pot-bellied gents sit amongst us, the overweight members in a family clan seldom come to the lake. Recipes for dining hall menus continue to come from *Woman's Day* rather than *Gourmet,* and given the all-American quality of these menus, ethnic foods (like ethnicity itself) seem collectively to belong to conversation, fantasies, and the lives we leave behind in cities. We reveled in the Vietnamese dinners that Linda Wade, after a full day's preparation in the dining hall kitchen with the staff and family members, presented to us for two summers.

Sharkey Fink, who for many years served as chair of the Pinewoods Dining Hall Committee, was told by her mother that her primary task would be to keep the vases on tables filled with fresh cedar sprigs. In taking on the responsibility of this volunteer job, however, she discovered fissures in the building's physical structure as well as in the Pinewoods community. Her task was to try to heal them. She had to be the liaison among the bookkeeper, the hall manager, the cooks, waiters, clean-up crew, and all the individual members and families in the camp. She listened to complaints on both sides and talked people down and around. She listened to the traditionalists and the revisionists in camp. It took her five years to find a lighting system to place over tables that was acceptable to everyone and three years to convince people that natural wood tabletops were aesthetically more pleasing than Formica. Hopes persist that menus planned around Michigan-grown fruits, vegetables, and herbs, Michigan-produced breads and cheeses, and recipes generated by Pinewoods people themselves might please more of the people more of the time. Since I am at the lake usually for less than two weeks, I select my greens and keep my peace. My niece Lucy, a vegan, simply loads up with fruit for breakfast, salad for lunch, a bowl of peas and a plate of potatoes for dinner. Since 1990, a "Suggestion" Box has been posted on a pillar in the hall for complaints. I know that one tribe banded together to write notes demanding, "No more carrot bullets." While their protest has been successful, another tribe's attempt to stuff the box on behalf of grilled cheese sandwiches for all three meals has not.

Marion, who believes her health to have been saved by a macrobiotic diet, has been shipping packages of specialty foods from Cambridge to the cottage since the early 1980s. She prepares them herself at the cottage, packing them carefully in her black lacquer Japanese *bento* box, which she then carries three times daily to the dining hall, supplementing her macrobiotic meals with rice and vegetables from the dining hall menus. As she needs our great pines for spiritual sustenance, she tells me she has the same need for the nourishment of the dining hall's rituals of family and community.

PATH

There is a path. It ambles between the cottages and the pavilions overlooking the lake. Both cottages and pavilions connect to it with runners, and from it the glinting lake can always be seen, and its sound against the shore can always be heard.

Here and there the path shows the earth beneath—quartz sand left from glacial deposits. Except for an occasional root stretching across, however, the path is cushioned with pine needles—the short, fine needles from the white pines and the long, coarser needles from the red pines—marking it a distinct, bright brown. When it rains, rivulets form, creating many-fingered deltas among the path's pine needles. In the fall, we gather pine needles from the woods behind the cottages to spread over the path where it seems to be getting bald.

There is no record regarding the path's origin—if it existed before people came from Saginaw and Bay City to set up their summer camps along the north shore, if it was part of a Chippewa foot trail leading from Saginaw Bay to Mackinaw with its major deviation for Grand Traverse Bay occurring right near Higgins, if it was part of a continuing course around the lake. Now the path only connects the cottages of the three camps—Lakeside, Cottage Grove, and Pinewoods. There were no telephones when the camps were first set up, and I assume that the campers wore the path themselves in their peculiar business transactions: plans for a community icehouse, pickups from the stage, the camp menus, a huckleberry outing, arrangements for horses to come to take the boats out of the water, Fourth of July fireworks. The business of the camps remains much the same, and even now most of us walk to offer an invitation or arrange a meeting rather than phone. In addition to assisting with business, the path allows for sociable connections—not only meeting people from the other camps (sometimes even distant cousins whose names and exact relation I can't quite keep straight) but also for meeting Pinewoods people. On the path, we intercept each other. Someone comes out of a cottage, en route to the pavilion or the shore, and we stop, and we chat. People puddle on the path, like the rain among the pine needles. There is always news, even if it's only the weather. By the path, we keep track of one another.

People also use the path for their private purposes. We stroll the path in company, arm in arm, side by side, single file. Many use it for exercise and are out early in the morning so they can jog and not disturb the latter-day saunterers; others walk their dogs on it (scooping poop along the way); most just stroll. A few cyclists have taken its twists and roots to heart as the path has caused them to catapult. But the only other vehicular traffic is a child with a red wagon, hauling another child. He, too, has important business to transact. There have been parades along the path for the Fourth, of course, and also to celebrate the end of World War II. When Marilyn and I were best summer friends, we set up a table alongside the path with special stones and terraria for sale. We added painted stripes and speckles to the already striped and speckled stones from the shore; Marilyn argued that the pink-and-green stones were such treasures that they needed nothing extra. For the terraria, we collected bits of moss with the red flecks of British soldier fungus prancing among it, waxy wintergreen plants, and yellow mushrooms from the woods and arranged them in saucers and jars. I remember Marilyn's sister's comment as she admired our display and paid us with her pun: "Not mush room for improvement here."

During the summer we talk—in families, in groups, just two or three; we talk around tables in the dining hall, in pavilions, in living rooms, at dock ends, becalmed on the lake. There are always the three other seasons to catch up on, and for the newcomer arriving for the summer, there's all the news of the camp. Much of my good talk occurs on the path. Almost as soon as I get to the lake, I say to Mother, a next-door neighbor, or a friend at the end of camp, "Let's walk to Lakeside." Walking means talking. And as your time at the lake lengthens, the talk on the path deepens. Ideas link; we link. We talk on, taking the path itself, the cottages, the woods, the lake beyond into our talk. The specific lingering smell of sweet fern, a jay's scream, a bundle of white fungus on a stump, last year's gypsy moth egg sacks on the trunk of an oak, the lake flickering there in the sunlight—all become metaphors for relationships, for memory, for trouble, for spirit around. Every morning my father and Marion's father walked the path, past the end of Lakeside, all the way to the Evergreen Park Stop 'n' Shop for the Detroit newspaper. It hardly mattered that neither the path nor the news changed. At the end of the path in Lakeside, you turn back to Pinewoods; only the light, no longer in your eyes, has tilted, and that tilts the world.

I think of a friend who, after years in Boston and Munich, returned to Kansas to drive a school bus for the very reason that he wanted to cover the same road day after day. He said he wanted to learn to pay attention along the way. The path at the lake is a beaten track and has taken the impression of many people's feet. Yet as neither I nor my companion nor the day is ever the same, it is never quite the same. When I was twelve or so, I learned to walk the path at night. Staying late playing charades or mahjongg with members of the Loomis tribe at the east end of camp, I had to get back to our cottage at the west end, and usually forgot to bring a flashlight from home. The Loomises had plenty to loan me, but it became a point of pride with me to find my way home without external assistance. Lights from the cottages and occasionally the moon were partial guides, but there were some turns where darkness was an all-absorbing blotter. The outlines of myself disappeared with the path. I stopped and let sounds establish contour. So long dependent on sight, I had to let go of eyes. Then listening to space—lake and trees breathing and myriad other forms that do not sleep—I moved. Trusting to our mutual life. And grateful for the beaten path which permits such shifts of time and light.

I love to walk alone on the stretch between Cottage Grove and Lakeside. Named "No Man's Land" by my mother and her teenage friends during World War I because it lies between two camps, it's owned by members of the Cottage Grove Association, who have been paying taxes on it since the early 1920s, sharing it with all of us subsequently, and keeping it as a legacy for the future. In a city, where potential danger develops a different kind of sensitivity, you walk—with exercise, purpose, destination in mind—and you keep on walking. Along the path in No Man's Land or on the trails in the woods behind the cottage, you can take a walk. For about a half-mile on the path through No Man's Land, there are no cottages. You dawdle. There is only the path, a constant through the diversity of trees and shrubs along the top of the bank. Birch, ash, pine, oak; huckleberry bushes, sweet fern, poison ivy, shooting star, false foxglove, butter and eggs. You pause. A chickadee, a downy woodpecker, black squirrels, occasionally a white-tailed deer, in the past a plumed skunk. Trees fall, develop burls, rot, and moss grows. The eye is the primary instructor along the path, but every sense plays and is played upon. I touch wood. It touches me. The smooth bark of birches is so different from the harsh bark of oak. The crumbling softness of cedar is so different from the compact softness of moss. You amble on. Sounds are also more discrete: the stray birdsong, chattering squirrels, a twig breaking. And I know that I am heard. Overlapping smells, including one strong, pure skein of dead fish from the shore below. How do I smell to the woods, I wonder.

Walking down the Bright Angel Trail into the Grand Canyon, I kept my eyes on my feet for fear of stumbling and missed the scenery. I realized later that sometimes you cannot see the way for the path. In following a path, I've learned that the task is always to watch out for roots and at the same time to give yourself up to the breathing woods and the whispering air.

PINES

At Pinewoods, the great pines are our measure. Their scale is something far more than human. We must look up to them. Beneath them, staring up, they teach perspective as their tops almost dwindle into invisibility. Rooted deeply, each tree, with a midden of its own needles around its base, is drawn toward the sky. On land, they pattern the sky for us; no clouds or night constellations can be seen but through the configurations of their branches. Out in the center of the lake, they mark home; darker green than other trees, taller, and less conforming to the hills, they unsettle the smooth ring of the horizon just where we are on the north shore. No matter how far out I am, I can come home by setting my direction in relation to this disturbance on the horizon. No need for celestial navigation on a lake when you have such trees. Mother remembers being asked by a girlhood friend's mother, when she'd returned to Bay City after her Pinewoods summer, "What did you see?" She replied, "Trees as tall as clouds."

These are Michigan's big trees: the red pines, sometimes called Norway, and the white. The red is obviously named for its bark, a general rufous color, which appears in layers of rough, multishaped scales, dark rust on the outer surface but which, when removed, reveal a pale rose underneath. Paradoxically, the white pine has the blackest bark of any tree I know, and standing beneath white pines in the woods in midday or looking back to them on shore from the center of the lake, I see these trees as darker than night. Fallen or cut down, they show a creamy interior, though, and their pitch runs first translucent, hardening to alabaster. In bright sun, the needles of the white pine have a shine like white steel. Unlike the red pine, the bark of the white does not flake off; it's in ridges with deep crevices between running helter-skelter down the tree.

The most obvious difference between the trees is in their needles, and if I began to learn the significance of contrast by feeling that Mother was not Daddy and vice versa, this lesson was clarified for me by learning that the short needles of the white pine come in bundles of five whereas two long needles are paired together on the branches of the red pine. Set off against lake and sky, the branches of the white pine are feathered, their light green needles soft puffs in contrast with the straight, dark severity of their trunk and branches. Against the same background, the branches of the red pine appear drawn by a *sumi* master; they strike out and turn and twist back on themselves, the needles forming prickly clusters.

As kids, we gathered fallen white pine branches and plucked off the little bundles of dried needles to roll up in squares of toilet paper for cigarettes; from the red pine we lifted off the bizarrely shaped pieces of bark—to create jigsaw puzzles, charts with new continents and countries, and zoos of curious beasts and birds. Because red pine bark has a certain softness, it's possible to scrape it, to inscribe it, to highlight its fantastic shapes with design. When I arrived in my cabin on the *President*

Johnson in 1958, embarking on a three-year voyage to Japan, a package of letters, each written on a piece of red pine bark by Pinewoods friends, awaited me.

Beginning in the middle of the nineteenth century, however, white men found other uses for these big Michigan trees. They made logging and lumbering a terrible art which took the stands of red and white pines in the north woods of Michigan's Lower Peninsula. (My forefathers helped in this endeavor, coming from Maine, where they had already stripped the woods. But in Michigan, they went in deeper, participating in the development of rail and boat systems to move more logs faster, further.) Across the Lower Peninsula, driving up to the lake, you see the cemeteries of the pine forests these men left, the stumps of trees, cut waist high, their rotting tombs. Farmers unearthed their roots in an attempt to convert forest to field, and now you also see these vestiges of ancient life clumped together to form fence-lines.

Taking only their trunks, the lumbermen also abandoned the pines' full tops, which proved to be tinderboxes. Thus, fire frequently followed the massacre. In 1923 Anna Ring Conroy of Cottage Grove, who first came to Higgins in 1875, wrote elegiacally: "We saw our beautiful shores gradually denuded, the island trees laid low by a cyclone, and then a devastating fire swept around and over every green thing leaving only charred stumps and ghost-like masts. For years we looked upon this waste which as we watched slowly came back to green again almost before we realized the change. But no one will ever again behold the glory of the Michigan forests."[47] Grandma Bruske's joy on returning to Pinewoods for the summer, recounted in her 1928 memoir, was qualified by the forests' destruction: "The route to the camps from the railroad was little more than a waste, in which an occasional tall, slender pine looked down from its lofty crown. Yet this sad sight added to the delightful welcome which we always received from our own little plot of primeval forest, against the glittering background of the lake."[48]

In the bottom of the lake lie great logs, sunk during the time when Higgins served as a link in the waterway that took the trees out from northern wilderness into southern civilization to be lumbered. It is estimated that 750,000 feet of logs are at rest on the bottom. Logs occasionally come up onto the shore of No Man's Land, creatures from another age, entwined in seaweed and slime. During the 1950s, a Detroit company decided to try scuba diving in search of these lost logs because they fetch a pretty penny on the market. Wood today has only six to eight growth rings per square inch, whereas first-growth, virgin timber is fine-grained with more than fifty growth rings. Leick Furniture of Sheboygan, Wisconsin, salvages the trees that sank in the Chequamegon Bay area of Lake Superior from the log booms of 100 years ago for expensive, limited-edition, turn-of-the-century tables and chairs. The Detroit folks marked their sites on Higgins with bobbing red flags, and Howie, thinking he would get into the act with his own diving equipment, went down a few times to look for an underwater forest. He found a bronze cowbell, perhaps from an ox used to pull the sleds of logs over the frozen lake in the winter, and four great logs. With block and tackle and help from a Pinewoods buddy, he brought the logs to our shore; two were sawed into firewood, and two are still there, serving as beach breakwaters.

A tree lives—it has trunk, branches, needles, roots; when it is reduced to stump, log, wood, timber, lumber, boards, planks, slats, it can only be used as a part of something else and it has nothing to call its own—it is dead. Alive, the old red and white pines are named "monarchs" and the last "virgins" of the wilderness. Photographs are taken of them from their base, angled upward to show light streaming downward and to suggest that they form the columns for forest cathedrals. Marion designates a certain grand pine west of Lakeside as goddess: her thousand arms stretch out in blessing, and beneath them, lowly bushes and ferns crouch in supplication. Thus we assign our own ancient metaphors of empowerment to these trees. But we know, too, how powerless these trees are, standing solitary; their only sources of strength are their growth, their use of light, their creation of seed and of shadow. Acknowledging the decimation of forests and the difficulty of farming in the upper part of the Lower Peninsula, the state established its first nursery on the northwest shore of Higgins in 1903 to begin the process of producing seeds and seedlings to replenish the denuded lands. The nursery thrived, with as many as 20,000,000 seedlings produced annually; members of all three camps gathered pine cones to help perpetuate the pines. And in at least one state park—the Hartwick Pines near Grayling—and in our camps, some of the old ones still stand tall.

Amazed by the girth of one white pine behind our cottage, I try to link hands with two friends, reaching to encircle it and just barely touching fingers. By the southwest corner of the last cottage in Lakeside there is a stand of five white pines. They're often the goal when we set off walking down the path in front of the cottages after dinner. We seldom say, "We're walking to the end of Lakeside"; far more often, it's "Let's walk to the Five Pines." Placing yourself in the center of these trees and looking up sets you in a cosmic spin. Far back behind Pinewoods, on a firebreak cut through the woods in the 1940s, is a lone red pine. Along Mr. Wiseman's Road, overgrown for years but now part of a network of trails into the woods, is a great white pine, singular because many of its lower limbs are still intact, stretching out to create a clearing around it; beneath this tree I've found great horned owl feathers. Deeper into the woods is the white pine struck by lightning whose trunk deviates from the straight and narrow; by locating this tree, Mother can go on to find "The Porcupine Condominium"—three trees in which porcupines have set up shop, gnawing away at the trees' interiors. Just about any walk back into the woods alone demands intimacy with particular pines. In front of the cottage three red pines take their stand. Straight up they go before their branches begin to jut out, higher than the cottage, higher than the pavilion. First views of the lake come between their trunks. We pose family and camp pictures against their great simplicity. We mark our lives in relationship to theirs.

"Grandma's Favorite Tree" is just behind our new boathouse. She must have singled it out because it seems picture perfect, and in her life, she tried hard for loveliness. This grand white pine stirs the illusion of order in our back woods. Spindly young red pines and bushy young white pines shape up in its presence. And all about it, the aspens and oak disentangle. My father's ashes were not the first placed there. After consultation with Mother and Daddy and her kids, a Flint friend decided that her dear husband's ashes should be buried there. Now she herself and Daddy are beneath this tree. Mother will be, too, and I, and perhaps Aunt Mary, to whom Mother has written, inviting her to join us in nourishing the earth together. Neither monarch nor matriarch, this particular white pine simply sanctifies us.

PAVILION *n.* 1. A moveable or open structure, as a large tent or summerhouse. 2. A related or connected part of a principal building, as for patients at a hospital. 3. A canopy. 4. The external ear. 5. The sloping surface of a brilliant-cut gem between the girdle and the culet. [< OF *paveillon* < L *papilio* butterfly, tent].[49]

Oh, wonderful dictionary, you tell me that the pavilion in front of our cottage, midway between the path and the shore, poised on the bank overlooking the lake, is "the sloping surface of a brilliant-cut gem" and related to butterflies! You tell me that it is "the external ear," projecting out beyond the cottage and ready to catch the sounds of the wind's improvisations, its light rifts, and its regular rhythms. Synonyms I would have come up with first in describing the pavilion are an "open structure," "a related or connected part of a principal building," indeed, "a summerhouse." But these other dictionary definitions suggest its essence: it is an extravagance, a luxury. Unnecessary in the realm of utilitarian affairs, it provides only the barest shelter and minimal storage. Like butterflies and gemstones, the pavilion exists for the sake of beauty, for the sake of interest; it exists to enhance the pleasures of life—that is, if butterflies and gemstones are understood from the standpoint of a human viewer who seeks neither to possess nor to display them. An English friend traveled worldwide with an old and lovely silver-backed brush, about which her lover once challenged her, claiming it to be unnecessary extravagance. She argued that it was, instead, like love itself, a necessary luxury, suggesting unseen possibilities, and remembering Lear defending his extra knights, she pleaded, "Reason not the need" (II, iv, 259).

Architecturally, the pavilion has the outlines of a cube with a high, peaked roof and a wooden floor. Cedar posts, their shaggy bark left on, support the roof, and cedar railings edge all four sides. Benches of pine slats line two sides, and on the bench facing the lake, Captain Howard Shaw, my grandfather, carved a compass rose, which informs all who sit just where they are. An assortment of chairs are set to face the lake; only one, made of bent hickory, its seat of woven slats, remains from the time the pavilion was built; the aluminum ones with plastic webbing reflect Mother's practical attempt to get something to endure the vicissitudes of weather, and the directors' chairs with subdued beige canvas backs reflect my attempt to get something uptown for the cottage or at least for the pavilion. Hanging from the rafters, a heavy chain for each corner, is the great swing made by Mr. Cederburg, one of several talented local Swedes who turned from farming Roscommon's sandy soil to carpentry. The fabric on its cushions has changed from grandmother's flowers to Mother's stripes to Tammy's dots, but the cushions themselves remain scattered in the swing, their arrangement determined by the last reader, napper, group of children, or cocktail-hour conversationalists to use it.

Some pavilions in Cottage Grove and Lakeside are screened in or have enclosed dormitories built in beneath them, but ours stands open. Hummingbirds flit in, and chipmunks, seeking peanuts from last night's cocktails, hesitate a moment and then dart forward. Until evening brown bats are curled among the rafters. When I was about eight, Mother assigned me the task of sweeping the pavilion and the steps going down to the lake. I must have protested, for I was always caught up in my own projects at the lake and begrudged any adult's interference. Sweeping is a morning ritual now, first an examination of what the night has brought into the pavilion—the woods' flotsam and jetsam—and then the steady stroking with the broom—canoeing on land—until all the shattered pinecone petals have been brushed away. There are few mosquitoes and flies to bother anyone sitting on the pavilion, but cobwebs add their fretting to the tops of the cedar posts. It's the weather, above all, which enters here as we look out.

Although extravagant, the pavilion does have its purposes. Cats like to scratch their backs on the cedar posts and railings and habitually find the sand beneath the pavilion especially soft for other needs. One wedding has been held in our pavilion, with wildflowers picked that morning woven through the railings and twined around the posts. The family gathers here most evenings with drinks before dinner; often the neighbors join us, and sometimes there's a real party, with invitations having been issued at the dining hall in the morning, bottles brought out from the cottage and placed on a side table, beer on ice, bowls of peanuts and pretzels, napkins printed with sailboats received from Aunt Mary at Christmas. We talk, but each of us keeps one eye on the sky's changing colors through the pines. On certain hot summer nights when the moon has thrown down shining shards of crockery on the lake's surface, and the air stirs in fits and starts lifting the hair on your arms, the pavilion's the place for secrets. Never mind that it's so open: I wonder if there's anyone in the family who hasn't made love in the pavilion swing, or hasn't pulled chairs over into the corner to gossip or talk about God.

Most often, though, the pavilion is used for watching—for watching birds, for watching boats, for watching weather. The binoculars are meant to stay on the table by the front door of the cottage, but frequently a pair is left out on a bench in the pavilion. It's a roaring wind out of the northwest, whitecaps are up across the lake, and Mother stands there, the binoculars pointed lakeward. She checks the course of as many sails as she can. If one goes down, will it be righted? She is ready to send one of us racing down the path to a cottage with a powerboat should a sail flounder too long. On calmer days, she calls out for us to come see seven ducklings paddling behind their mother.

The pavilion is primarily a vantage point, a perspective, a point of view. Quite unnecessary, but necessarily shaping the scene. The view is always of the lake, framed by roof, posts, and railings; by branches drooping down from the great red pines on the same bank with the pavilion; by the low line of hills which begins with Sunset Beach in the east, goes to Huckleberry Point all around the little bay to Stony Point, is interrupted by the island, but continues onto The Farm, the American Legion grounds, and the western hills into which the sun drops. On a sunny day, these hills contain these waters: near shore a pale gold, and then in a wonderful reversal of the alchemist's plan, they flow from jade into turquoise, amethyst and, at last, into deepest cobalt—our black water. When we were learning how to sail and to canoe, that amethyst line of demarcation where turquoise is transformed into black water was our boundary; from the pavilion it's apparent that most of the lake is black water. I want to believe that this spectrum reflects the lake's true colors. But depending on time, season, clouds, and weather, or on certain days at certain moments, the pavilion may frame quite different colors.

Looking out, I've seen (can "scene" be a verb?) the lake an amorphous mist which, when evaporated, becomes a glimmerglass, a steely plate, a rumpled bedspread, a panoramic stage with lines of girls throwing up their crinolines doing the cancan. I've seen the lake, like Thoreau's pond, an eye of heaven, the sky its brow, the hills its lashes. I've seen the lake change before my very eyes in the process of a storm. First the anticipatory stillness in which the island comes so close its trees stand as separate entities, and the boats anchored out in front appear as precisely outlined and colored as in a child's book of maritime vessels. Except for a gaggle of bugs gyrating just off the end of the dock, nothing moves. Then the air shifts, and the canoe turns slowly on its line, pointing like a compass needle toward the Gold Coast in the southwest. The sky is a boiling darkness, and the first bright dragon claws of lightning slash across it. Needles of rain begin to puncture the shallow waters, and soon, chased by a driving wind, the whole storm comes pell-mell toward us, cross-hatching and slashing all horizontal lines, erasing the lake's true colors. How long can we stay watching in the pavilion? Rain pelts us now. The pavilion offers no protection. We rush to turn over the cushions on the swing, to bring the chairs in closer, to make a mad dash to the shelter of the cottage.

The pavilion: here I see better; I see more. Yet it reminds me that I only see the partial lake. I do not see the lake from the perch's eye, the eye of the fisherman out on the Sunken Island, the eye of the Gold Coast developer, the eye of Shoppenagons who was here first. And when a storm comes, I run from such outlandish extravagances.

ISLAND

This island. In the middle of the lake. In memory it is always there. An aerial photograph shows it to be the shape of a wild goose in flight. When Mother arrived at the lake, a lone hermit lived on the island, and I grew up with stories about this grizzled old fellow who had dug himself a bungalow into the north slope just above the ice-line. If he looked fierce when summer people went over to camp on the island, it was, Mother said, probably because he didn't see anybody for weeks on end. When I was a child, nobody lived on the island any longer, although a house built of round lake stones, said to be that of the island's owner, could be seen out on its southeastern point when we sailed by.

Not to be confused with the two sunken islands, one in either bay and both shallow areas thronged with fishermen hovering over them, the island, which organizes our vision of the lake from the pavilion, always seems to hold mystery. Not just because it was hermit-haunted and called "Treasure Island," but because the ecology of the whole place is different from our shore. The trees are lower—no great red and white pines—and there is far more poison ivy. The west side is all rocks, known to Pinewoods sailors as "The Grand Piano Ledge," but on the east side is a cove with a perfect curve. The sand seems finer here than on our shore, and the water a deeper, more tropical turquoise. Protected a bit, sometimes the water in the island's cove is so smooth that you can see from your canoe down into its depths; you can see the hieroglyphs left by snails and clams wiggling across the waves' regular inscriptions. The spit forming the curve makes a fine place for gulls to stand and have their feet tickled by waves. The island, our own Galápagos, also has its own special bird and bug life. Once while canoeing along its west shore, I saw a sudden effervescence of yellow butterflies lift off, a halo of sun motes. On another day, I saw a glint of warbler on the south shore, unseen around the cottage, quick in the overhead low shrubs. I've wondered if this could also be the rogue loon's hideaway.

During my teenage years the island's mystery intensified as its cove became the hangout for the kids with speedboats. Because of the cove's calm waters, they congregated here to begin their water-skiing, and after skiing they'd come back to swim off the point, where the water went from ankle-shallow down quickly to a thrilling depth. I was envious, for we didn't have power in my family. Only canoes and sailboats and a low-speed putt-putt. But learning to sail during those years, I made the island a feature on my map. Setting out in my Sunfish, I navigated depending upon the wind shifts against the island, its shallows, and the tacks I would have to take around it. These days I wait for a calm day and take my time canoeing over. As a goal for sailing and canoeing, it retains its elusiveness. Trying to get to sleep here in Kansas, I swim to the island, hand over hand, keeping it in front of me steady, believing the point where the gulls stand is just within reach.

Electrical and telephone cables were laid under the lake to the island during World War II, and it was divided into lots in the late 1950s. I remember the summer the developers were burning off the ivy: a thick black cloud hung over the lake, and we worried that poisonous sap might be wind-borne. With the jungle of poison ivy and wild blackberry bushes gone from its interior, the island's secrecy seems rent. The Higgins Lake Boat Club now commands the cove, and more than twenty small cottages have been built along its shores, each with a chemically fertilized lawn, a stubby dock, and a powerboat canopy.

Yet the island mysteriously is still there. Yet and still. It is still. A comma in a sentence, a pause on the line of Higgins's horizon. And like a comma, a pause is a place where you take a breath, a place where temperature intensifies. The island on the lake's horizon catches my breath, focuses my sense of time and light. Before me, gazing from the pavilion, haze erases it; rain slashes across it, distancing it; with early morning fog, it levitates above the surface of the lake; autumn makes it appear as fire on water. But in dreams the island is definitive summer green held within a ring of water beneath an infinity of sky. It is still life.

Higgins Lake

Higgins Lake, Clear Day

Higgins Lake, Single Sail

The Island

Clouds over Pinewoods

Shoreline, Raccoon Tracks

Shoreline, Stone Breakwaters

The Pinewoods Path

Outdoor Fireplace

Red Pines

Jane Kohring

Red Pine Bark

White Pines

Elizabeth A. Schultz

White Pine Needles

Shoreline, No Man's Land

Elizabeth A. Schultz

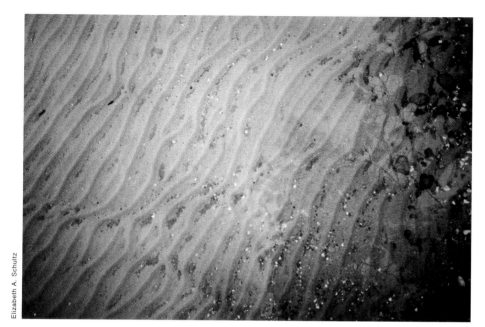

Inshore

Outdeep

Mother Pausing

Elemental

The big trees go on falling in our forest—that's certain. People organize their demise in the name of commerce or management. Lightning strikes more quickly, more erratically, blazing a single tree or blasting it into shards and spears; tornadoes tear trails through forests; age works more slowly. Weighted with snow, punctured with woodpecker holes, riddled by insects, eventually trees come down. Someone must hear them when they do, for they fall hard, smashing all smaller trees in the path of their dying, their roots forcing the living forest floor to tilt upward. Surely there is crashing and screaming, for in such an upheaval the slender backs of young trees bow down beneath the fallen tree's dead weight. Shattered bones break through bark; trunks are scraped and gouged, their sap beading unbandaged. Thin, pale roots, exposed to alien air, surely whimper, crying to return to earth's warm gaping hole from which they were torn. In a few years' time, although the dead tree's diagonal still interrupts the forest's verticality, any distinction that it gained in dying is absorbed into new life. There's a complexity of new growth: some of the young trees felled spring upright; others take root, including two or three that wave their green pom-poms in the moist body of the dead tree with almost too much adolescent aplomb; moss lays its diversely colored hands all over the trunk; bark scales off, showing the vermiculated tracery of carpenter ants; on the sandy rim of the gaping hole are raccoon tracks.

There is power in this dying. So different from the systematic and often careless slaughter of lumber companies and forest management programs. One white pine falling near the cottage took out both the Cottage Grove and the Pinewoods power line for a few days one spring; another smashed the roof of our boathouse. Mother and Daddy argued about the two red pines by the steps on the way down to the shore from the pavilion: they had to go before they disrupted the whole bank. Daddy thought they should come all the way down, but Mother insisted on tall trunks being left for woodpeckers: one came down, the other partially stands. It took all of a day for the professionals from Grayling with their chainsaws growling to bring them down, section by section, column drum by column drum. Shadow, Mother's cat, uses the stump; it's her post for observing all movement on the steps, and we imagine that out of season an eagle might survey the entire lake from the vantage point of the tall trunk which continues towering over us. Something continues.

Something remains: pineknots, known to lumbermen as Rich Pine, the aggregation of pitch that occurs in a tree at a branch's juncture with its trunk, a hard ganglion of arteries containing richest tree blood and, incidentally, the best fuel with which to start a fire. Some afternoons when everyone else was on the lake or by the shore, Daddy would be by himself back of the cottage splitting logs or in the woods seeking pineknots. These were chores he assigned himself; he chose to do them, I think, because he could. When he went into the woods, he took an old bushel basket from the woodshed behind the cottage. I never went with him, but I saw the full baskets he brought back. Whenever I go into the woods now, I look for pineknots he might have picked up and wish I had asked to help him with his appointed tasks. (I'm glad Howie has taken up his task of splitting logs.) Trapped in the soft, decaying wood of rotting stumps and logs, the solid pineknots are easy to spot. Their sharp, wing-like flanges, remnants of the tree's desire to stretch, to lift, to rise, project forth from this decomposition. Reaching down into a log's crumbling cradle, I've pulled forth the image of a russet-winged bird, but then decided to let it lie to fuel the forest.

The wings are worn from pineknots pulled out of the lake, however. These pineknots—remnants of trees that fell into the lake before the lumbermen came, remnants of the whole forests they sank—are smoothed by long years in the water. They resemble waterlogged fish without fins, without eyes. Though tree lines are still apparent on these pineknots, the lines have come to resemble ripples of waves in the sand or concentric circles spreading when a feather lands on the lake's calm surface. They turn into the whorls of fingerprints. Daddy added his harvest of shaggy pineknots from the woods to those gathered from the lake and piled in the woodshed by my grandfather.

Mother followed her father in searching the lake bottom for these sand-smoothed, water-rubbed pineknots. She paddled alone at sunset beyond the east end of camp, beyond the stony bottom in front of our dock to the shallow sandy stretches below Pinewoods. Nothing stirred except her canoe as she let it drift on the calm surface, except the rose-colored streamers reflected on this surface as the canoe moved across them. She stood up in the center of the canoe, scanning. Where was I to observe her? Sitting up in the bow too small to paddle? Left at the end of a dock? She is, as I see her now, perfectly balanced, allowing the paddle to trail in the water when the canoe glides forward. She lowers herself down into the canoe, backwaters, rests the paddle across the gunwales, reaches down into the still, roseate waters to fish out the pineknot. She rises and moves on forever.

I don't know how many pineknots were collected. The special bin for them in the woodshed always seemed full. But in the summer of 1992 the family decided that the woodshed had to go, that in its place we'd have an outbuilding for tools and a washer and dryer. Mother tried to decide where the pineknots would go. Into the fire, of course. But one particularly large, trout-shaped one, solid and simple, she reserved for the long windowsill in the cottage living room. And I have a small one before me on my desk in Kansas. Against erosions of time, we choose carefully the tokens which will fix our memories.

RELIGION

Sitting around our table in the dining hall after lunch the day before I depart for Kansas, a neighbor talks of her Indianapolis church. She concludes by saying, "Yes, I'm a Presbyterian." Aunt Mary, visiting from New Jersey, also identifies herself as a Presbyterian, as does Howie at the end of the table. In these communal conversations we feel driven into definitions, and Mother says, "Well, I'm nothing." In other such discussions, I've heard her declare, "I'm an atheist."

For years, she kept posted in the corner of the mirror over her dresser a clipping that quoted from the opening book of Genesis: "And God said, Let us make man in our image, after our likeness: and let him have dominion over the fish of the sea, and over the fowl of the air, and over the cattle, and over all the earth, and over every creeping thing that creepeth upon the earth" (1, 26). For Mother, this statement was not inspirational. Rather, it was a warning, reminding her of the religious and historical basis for western environmental imperialism. It became, I think, the basis for her "atheism"—at least for her rejection of organized religion. Far from being "nothing," and long before the words had cultural resonance, Mother was an ecologist, an environmentalist, the Earth's outspoken advocate; if she no longer accompanied my father on Sundays to Flint's First Presbyterian Church, her religious institutions became the International Wildlife Federation, the National Wildlife Federation, the Environmental Defense Fund, Defenders of Wildlife, Greenpeace, the National Humane Society, and Planned Parenthood. She read Thoreau, Anne Morrow Lindbergh, Rachel Carson, Aldo Leopold, Edwin Way Teale, Lewis Thomas, John McFee, Barry Lopez, Loren Eisley, Annie Dillard.

Mother campaigned for the Michigan Bottle Bill, helped to organize the Flint Environmental Action Team (FEAT), wrote frequent letters to the Michigan Department of Natural Resources, announced her predilections with bumper stickers—"I Brake for Animals" and "Every Fur Coat Hurts." In her backyard in Flint, she made a compost heap, banking it with old shutters, and lets the grasses and trees take their own course. She proselytizes everyone although the members of her bridge club continue steadfast in wearing their fur coats. Before recycling became a household word and a national necessity, her New England impulses led her to save string and rubber bands, iron Christmas wrapping paper, darn the heels of all our stockings and the elbows of all our sweaters, wear out her own clothes, pile up old boxes in the guest bedroom closet, repair the coffee pot herself rather than buy a new one. If she still can make me feel guilty for discarding paper that could be cut into useful note cards or for purchasing a new sweater only because I think it's pretty, hers is the moral imperative. I, too, have a basement full of empty boxes, and together every summer we canoe the shoreline, gathering up beer cans and plastic flotsam and jetsam.

After Mother's statement at the lunch table, I felt the eyes corner me: I didn't know my own religion until I heard myself say, "I'm a naturalist." Mother's response followed, "Well, I'd like to know what that is. Maybe you could just give me a definition in a few sentences." The tasks our parents set for us may take a lifetime.

In her memoir, "Fifty Summers of Higgins Lake," Grandma Bruske describes "the simple religious services" her husband, the Reverend August Frederick Bruske, a Presbyterian minister from Saginaw and a Pinewoods founding father, conducted from the first Sunday he visited the camps and every Sunday thereafter, preaching from the porch of their cottage or on a pavilion "to an audience sitting on benches and cushions in the open air, under the pines":

> The services were a magnet which drew devout persons from all camps on the lake. The music was inspiring, as well as the brief, sparkling sermon which my husband always drew from some subject in the great outdoors in which we lived so pleasantly and so simply. . . . The collection was taken by the little children, and was always devoted to some specific purpose close to us all. Nearly everyone in camp attended.[50]

Reverend Bruske's son, Uncle Paul, in another essay on Pinewoods, called his father, "a sincere naturalist," explaining his understanding of this term by describing his father's interaction with nature: "With a single-shot Winchester he carefully collected a specimen of each type of bird the region afforded, and mounted the wings on the front of our log house. The display included an amazing variety of woodpeckers and ran from little sap suckers to a giant hawk almost as large as an eagle. Blue jays were then our most numerous bird."[51] It seems dubious that the Reverend Bruske felt any contradiction between his objectives as naturalist and preacher, but pursued the killing and classifying of northern Michigan's birds and a pleasant Christian transcendentalism with equal sincerity. Through the nineteenth century and into the twentieth, knowing nature necessitated hunting and gathering, pressing flowers between pages and birds behind glass so that they might be scrutinized, categorized, and counted. Perhaps the Reverend Bruske could not imagine today's woods and lake, for the parameters of his categories no longer exist: while blue jays may yet be "our most numerous bird," sapsuckers are now gone from the woods, and the giant hawk-like osprey is gone from the lake. The sight of birds, diverse in size and color and nailed by their outstretched wings in rows on a log cabin wall is, for contemporary naturalists, Golgotha.

Such naturalists, like the Hopis, have a Spider Grandmother, who has only two commandments for Her children, both equal in importance: "Don't go around hurting each other, and try to understand."[52] They assign value to all life, and while appreciating infinite variety, try, like the Sioux, to recognize similarities, calling the porcupine four-legged and the human two-legged, reading the same wind as unifying the grass and the sky. Like Michigan's Chippewa, who perceive the relationship between the newborn child and its mother to be identical with the relationship between the people and their mother, Aki, the Earth, they see the possibilities of connections. A ceramicist friend discovered a spatial connection in just a brief visit to the cottage some summers ago: her experience sailing beneath the domed blue sky over the lake linked her with a multidimensional, holographic spider's web suspended in a young white pine back in the woods and our small circle of Sunday morning meditators in the Loomis's little cottage. Such naturalists, I believe, also praise mystery, perhaps like you, Mother.

On my first morning in camp in 1993, Mother, you and I paddle west, going out along the shore of No Man's Land, but then head south for black water to follow its edge back home. The water, so smooth that morning, seems glazed with brightness, all colors diminished into shining as we look out across it. Yet looking downward, we see the lake's mercurial colors, the fluid gems of its depths— pale jade, turquoise, deepest lapis, obsidian. Paddling close to shore, we see how the sun spreads patterns of brilliance, gleaming nets of light over rippled sand, while out on the edge of black water, this same sun forges long lances of light, plunging into that darkness. As we cross over the drop-off, aware of a soft slope of green on one side of the canoe and of impenetrable deep water on the other, you say, "I still can't help it. I get a thrill being in black water." You tell me about paddling back from the island after a picnic with your gang. Leaning over the gunwale to wash the dishes when you were just entering black water, you dropped one of grandmother's favorite plates. "I looked real hard for it then, but couldn't see it. Even now I keep on looking for it every time we paddle to the island."

Like Walden, the depths of Higgins have been hard to sound. There were the Chippewa legends of a secret passageway and unfathomable holes. Lumbermen, moving their huge booms of logs across the lake, also tried to measure it. Their locomotion was dependent upon an anchor dropped from a small boat, connected by a 1,000-foot chain to a much larger raft, to which the log booms in turn were connected. With horses working the massive windlass on the raft and, thereby, drawing up the chain to the anchor boat, the booms inched across the lake. In 1887 John Colemen reported that his men could not find the bottom of the lake, although they had let out 900 feet of anchor line. In 1895 the Michigan State Fish Commissioner recorded a depth of 300 feet, and in the 1930s the Institute for Fisheries Research at the University of Michigan, the Michigan Emergency Conservation Work Organization, and the CCC took soundings through a grid of 11,000 holes spudded in the ice to discover the lake's maximum depth to be 138 feet in the big bay and 100 feet in the small bay. A third of the lake is very shallow—two to three feet, with an average overall depth of ninety feet. The shallow water, which goes out from our shore for 100 feet, makes the lake a delight for parents who feel at ease letting their kids experiment with swimming and boating in such waters. But as soon as I moved off the inner tubes and boat lines on which I learned to swim, I yearned for black water. Once as a kid, I wanted to take samples of black water home at summer's end to show in school and so brought several small bottles out with me on our final sail of the year. The black water, dipped up in my bottles, proved to be not ink, but was instead as clear as any tap water. I was flabbergasted by the lake's protean powers.

Mother and I drift on the gleaming surface. A shiver passes across it. I observe, "Isn't it amazing—only the surface and the edges of the lake move? Underneath, it's so steady." A fish jumps, arching high. Mother sees it. Another jumps. A flashing of bright scales in the air. I see it. It dives silently back into the water, leaving expanding rings. We glide over the rings and over the invisible fish. A fine spray of silver bubbles appears rising up from the darkness, sequins and spangles enlarging, one after the other, as they approach the rings and expiration on the surface. "The springs which fill the lake," Mother explains, and I realize once again the depths of her knowledge of this lake. I rejoice in the reality of these unseen springs and in the mystery of their bubbles, which rise and sink to its pulsating surface as if the lake breathes.

At Higgins, earth is sand. At Higgins you cannot build your house on a rock. This is not to say that the bank on which our cottage sits is like the Sleeping Bear Dune just north of Traverse City in the little finger of Michigan's mitten. There wind, water, and glacier have worked to push sand up from Lake Michigan so that it towers over all other life. You can slide down it on your bottom in a few seconds, but the climb back up, your feet sinking and slipping with each step, leaves you breathless. Inland, in Roscommon County, glacial moraines packed together a denser, more loamy, sandy soil around Higgins. On the lake's shores it's golden in stretches, interrupted by multicolored stones and rocks and an occasional patch of black where iron deposits run; in the woods, it's masked by layers of decaying foliage. The soil is superb for producing pines, but not potatoes, as the lumbermen and the farmers both discovered after the Civil War.

Soft, it's a soil you can dig in. In the woods, you'll find a fox's den, with the yellow earth thrown up in front of it as a porch. Assorted holes in the earth—scooped out as small caverns, drilled out as narrow, dark passageways—hide the secrets of other creatures throughout the woods. In front of our woodshed, moles lay out elaborate subway systems, and chipmunks develop catacombs. Even though the garbage truck now comes roaring and teetering down the Stage Road on Monday mornings to collect our black bags, we still dig holes behind the cottage for our biodegradables.

Most Pinewoods cottages, however, were not built over holes. They stand elevated above ground on cement piles or wooden posts like short stilts. Until recently, basements were not included in cottage blueprints, perhaps because a basement testifies to a more serious structure than these summer homes initially suggested, or perhaps because a basement is necessary for food storage or a furnace, which the Pinewoods summer rendered irrelevant. (When families began to go north for winter holidays and furnaces were needed to supplement fireplaces, cottages were excavated from within by hand for furnace rooms.) When you see red pines tipped up after a tornado, you wonder what kind of foundation could ever anchor a cottage in sand. No matter their depth, a tree's roots can be yanked up from the soil, their intricate, pale mass exposed to day's cruel light. The sandy earth, which for years had provided a nourishing placenta for the tree growing above it, can appear beneath the roots a gaping grave.

Sandy beaches, so central to summer, do not come easily to Pinewoods. People at our end of camp have to work for them. Shortly after camp opens, someone from each cottage goes down to the shore to begin the work of beach construction: drags down the pine log that was pushed up on the bank by the ice, places it perpendicular to the shore, secures it with rocks, heaves other rocks on top, alongside. For our beach we start with the big stones grandfather brought over from the island for the cottage fireplace and which, unused, remain on the shore. All summer long we keep tossing rocks in the log's direction until gradually a curve of golden sand begins to emerge from the base of this submerged pier. Each winter the ice forces the stones and the log back against the shore, and each summer we begin again the construction of a beach.

In our family, beaches have been primarily for children. The differences between warm and cool, dry and moist, hard and soft first became apparent to me on our small sand spit as I sat on it and dabbled in the water. The sand by the bank was shapeless, whereas with the firm, damp sand by the water, I discovered the pleasure of patting and molding and eventually shaping entire fantasy cities. I sat at the water's edge as long as Mother let me, sometimes alone, often with Marilyn. Our architecture of choice was the drip castle, erected by letting the proper mixture of sand and water dribble onto a cake of sand. With this method, we could fashion turrets and towers of Gothic complexity to rival Gormenghast. One castle always led to another more labyrinthine, and it would become necessary to design moats and roads as well as ponds and pastures. Our beaches always supplied appropriate ornamental paraphernalia: gull feathers for flags, tiny stones for crenelation, waterlogged twigs for forests.

At the Loomis cottage the beach was much wider, and we spent days developing more cosmic landscapes, naming the sites and giving them histories. Suddenly, when we turned into teens, we realized that with sand we could reshape ourselves. On the Loomis beach, we could assume a mermaid's tail or swap genders. Buried completely in sand, for a few seconds you could also entertain the unbelievable: you could be eradicated from the world just when it seemed most gleeful. But with a breathing tube in your mouth and a bathing cap on your head, you knew you were playing possum and planned the moment when you would rise from the dead with grand commotion, scattering sand everywhere.

We need the beach for pulling up the boats—the canoe and Sunfish—for draining and cleaning. But mostly we need to feel the grit of sand between our toes. We leave our shoes on the dock and hop down onto wet sand, firm and resilient. Our feet leave their mark which water, instantly pressing up on the shore, erases. We wade into the shallow water, and sand slithers across our feet. Like Antaeus, we can't get enough of it.

We take sand upstairs from the beach into the cottage. On the way up, bits of broken bark, leaves, and pine needles also cling to our wet feet. A bucket stands at the back door of the cottage and there is a faucet for rinsing off this composite Pinewoods earth. We can count on being scolded if we come through the front door of the cottage with wet feet rather than going round to the back and using the foot dip. Despite all our best efforts, sand, mingled with bark and pine needles, always makes its way into the cottage. Sand creeps in invisibly, silently, from shore and road. Corrugated rubber mats, coconut fiber mats, steel mesh mats, and extra rugs are placed as border guards at all doors, but sand crosses thresholds easily. It sneaks into the crevices of Topsiders, those boat shoes that many of us continue wearing although we're no longer sailing boats with walkabout decks and cockpits; it arrives in pant cuffs and stuck to knees and elbows; it travels lightly in the fur of our dogs and cats who roll and dig in it with delight. Ubiquitous, sand is invisible until rugs are lifted and the cottage floor is swept. It is never "dirt." We sweep it up by the dustpan to place back out on the path. Jens Peter Jacobsen tells us, "Every palace of happiness that rises up has sand mixed into the foundation on which it rests, and the sand collects and runs out beneath the walls, slowly perhaps, imperceptibly perhaps, but it keeps running, grain after grain . . . And love? Love is no rock either, no matter how much we want to believe it is."[53] Though sand at Pinewoods may give us grit, its shifty ways keep us from ever letting down our guard.

ho has seen the wind? / Neither I nor you."[54] The poems of childhood—I know them by heart. "Where does the wind go?" The riddles of childhood remain unsolved. In showing me the wind, Higgins introduced me to poems and riddles. Waves with whitecaps. A fluttering flag in front of a cottage. The scarecrow flapping on the raft to frighten the gulls. Our canoe turning peacefully on its line at the dock. An oak leaf airborne. Boats under sail. Shadows of tree limbs shifting across my bedroom ceiling.

In time, wind on the lake showed me extremes: too much and too little. Too much wind, and the great pines cannot stand. Rooted in sand, they fall, masses of roots thrust up pitiable into the bright air. Smaller trees acknowledging their sovereignty bow down with their demise. Garages, cottages, bird nests are equally vulnerable when the big trees sway. Too much wind, and everything human beings set on the lake is at risk. Walking the No Man's Land shoreline after storms, we've picked up a box full of sand toys—shovels, scoops, small pails, sand molds shaped like crabs and sailor boys—as well as aluminum cans, Styrofoam cups, a plastic owl for scaring gulls, soggy tennis balls, a duck-billed cap that Howie still wears, and a life jacket for water-skiers. All are the detritus of a leisured shore society, blown off docks or boats. Occasionally whole dock sections are up on the shore.

The boats take their share of abuse from the wind. They pound on the waves and pull on anchor lines out in front of cottages. Water sloshes into canoes, rocking and tugging on dock lines until they break free and crash up against the shore. You leap instantly into the water to the rescue. You grab the boat's gunwales to try to move it out into open water, put it on one of your lines, note the license number, and call the Roscommon sheriff to find the owner. You are grateful for the courtesy of lake people, and know that there but for the grace of God goes your own Lightning. Once it was a glittering powerboat, unmanned, which had drifted over from the other side of the lake and lay pounding on our rocks, but more often it's our own canoe. I have always thought that Mother's insomnia, like her father's before her, derived in part from her anxiety for the boats. Growing up, I slept most nights when she was down on the dock checking the lines, bailing the canoe, walking out to the Lightning to make certain the anchor was secure, with the waves hitting her in the chest. No matter how cold and rough the water is, you don't hesitate to jump in to rescue a boat that is up against the breakwaters. A boat, sure in water, is helpless on shore. Only young robins, tipped, nest and all, out onto the ground by a gale seem more helpless than a boat floundering against rocks in a high wind.

We have specific nouns for a great wind—gale, storm, hurricane, tornado, cyclone, squall, tempest—and the Greeks had a god—Aeolus. But windlessness seems a condition for which we have only adjectives—calm, peaceful, still—or for which we seek metaphors. In Kansas where wind seems a constant, a day without blowing comes as a blessing. On these wind-free mornings, birdsongs plummet like gifts from the trees, and spider webs lace trees, flowers, grasses into a shimmering whole. In the woods behind the cottage, in back of the Stage Road, windlessness seems the constant. Even when there is a hard blow at the lake, the back woods are hushed. The roar of the shore can be heard only as a faint echo in the tossed treetops, distant like the sound of the sea in a large shell. The tornado that ripped through our woods in 1995, however, took solitude with it. Leaving gaps among the trees, it made room for lesser winds to rustle the ferns and to rattle the lower limbs of the remaining pines, replacing hush at times with a mall's cacophony.

Like never being too rich or too thin, windlessness on Higgins—so appreciated by bathers, beachcombers, water-skiers, canoeists—would see the most desired condition. No storms touched Walden. Calm was best for watching water-skaters, for checking depths, for keeping track of a laughing loon, for letting the canoe drift while playing a flute—for meditation. Higgins on windless days, shining and calm, misty and mild, leads to meditation on Thoreau: on his vision of unity, his sense of mystery, his sense of a renewal. In the nomenclature peculiar to Pinewoods, however, another metaphor is used to describe this windless state: "a dead clam." It connotes the disgust of some sailors and the humorous affection of others, always amazed by the air's facile ways, for what Melville designated, longingly, as "a mild, mild wind, and a mild-looking sky."[55]

Learning to sail, I came to regard the absence of wind as a loss. "Never set sail without a paddle," Mother always says. I have committed this sin and have ended up stroking home clumsily with the daggerboard or kicking like crazy from the stern to move the Sunfish awkwardly toward its mooring. Or I have drifted. I spit over the side to see if the boat will pass my little cluster of bubbles;

the bubbles dissipate. I keep pace with a drowned grasshopper. Nothing as pretty or as futile as a painted ship upon a painted sea. Lacking patience and a willingness to give myself over to process, I am weary of all the songs I can think to sing. (Unlike these windless occasions, sailing in a gale allows no time for song or petulance.) Above all I am weary of windlessness expressed by blank sky and blank lake surface. The imagination seems stymied. Eventually the rhythms of drifting lull the mind into drifting as well. With no hint of breeze to make me sit up and take fresh notice, my mind becomes bubbles. Fragile, iridescent, the bits scatter, floating separately, eddying about, until they all vanish, absorbed by the lake.

As Pinewoods kids, we learned to play our grandmothers' favorite game, mahjongg, and if I was fascinated by the Chinese box with its multiple drawers and the tiles with their exotic markings, the concept that each player could be named for a wind seemed wondrous. The royal hierarchies in European cards paled in interest, for the Chinese winds, of course, were mightier and more marvelous than any king or queen. I always figured that my grandfather had carved the compass rose on the pavilion bench and my mother had hung his gyro-compass in the living room so that we could be sure of our relationship with the winds and of our place in the universe. Equally powerful and evocative of the winds—north, south, east, and west—when I was growing up were such phrases as "offshore breeze" or "prevailing wind," which Mother would pronounce after she'd gone out to the pavilion to see how the wind set. The one could take you with deceptive gallantry over into the lake's little bay and force hard beating all the way home; the other gave you a triangular course with a neat tack, a reach, and a downwind run to home. It doesn't do just to wet your finger. Look at the clouds swishing overhead and remember: "Fish scales and mares' tails are sure signs of storm." Check the direction the boats are pointing on the dock lines close to shore and out on their anchor lines. Notice that the gulls on the raft are all standing into the wind. Keep an eye on your tell-tails. Watch the luff on the sail. Be ready always to adjust the mainsheet. If you have faith enough, Toni Morrison says, you may ride the wind.[56] But you have to catch it first.

When a breeze comes, you see it, then feel it. The water darkens and wrinkles. The sail fills and stiffens. The tell-tails, listless, now fly. This is more than a cat's paw, more than a capricious swipe of air at the water surface. I reassemble my mind quickly. It's a practical matter: how to take proper advantage of this riff of wind to make up for lost time? Let the sheet out, raise the daggerboard, sit center: that should do it. Like the sky, like the weather, the wind humbles the person alone in the middle of the lake on a small sailboat. Its whims and schemes create the context for a sailor. Again and again I am instructed in respect, realizing that in the degree that I can see the invisible air and interpret the wind's ways, I'll get home in time for dinner.

FIRE

Fire controlled, and fire wild. Fire giving, fire taking. In my academic, city life, I hardly ever see fire at all. Almost no one smokes any more, so even the quick flash of a lighter held up to the end of a cigarette seems a thing of the past. My Kansas fireplace has been capped off to keep squirrels from nesting in the chimney, and I've never gotten into the backyard barbecuing scene. Candles are about it now, lit on a birthday cake or for a dinner party: flickers of wilderness among silver place settings and crystal glasses, throwing long shadows into a room's corners when the overhead light is dimmed. Living downtown in 1975, I witnessed fire that shot up like a geyser from a nearby building and sent flames sprawling out across the main street; a subsequent gas explosion killed two students and gave me insight into why medieval Christians saw Hell as a fiery inferno. Great flakes of flame kept drifting like Satan's minions toward my roof, and until the cherry pickers from the fire station came in to shoot water down from above into the blaze, there was no containing this rage. Arson is another matter in my town: during a recent winter, two girls were burned in an apartment building, their mother hospitalized at length for smoke inhalation, and posters were put up all over town requesting information about the person who left the empty oil cans in the driveway outside.

But we go on living with fire at Pinewoods, even playing with it. We know it as pure color— yellow, red, and blue; as sound—snapping, crackling, and roaring; as smell and touch and taste—

scorching in the nose, its embers searing on the palm, its smoke acrid in the mouth. Fire does not exist in isolation or as abstraction; wind fans fire, water douses fire, and fire blackens earth in an eternal game of "Paper, Scissors, Stone." Ash is static; fire is not: it burns, blazes, glows, flames, licks, flickers, sizzles, dances. Fire is upward and outward; in ceaseless motion, it changes colors, changes shape, changes direction, changes everything it touches. Not a single thing, it is flame, spark, smoke, ember. It is both transitive and intransitive.

In front of the cottage, between the path and the pavilion, is a circle of stones: the fireplace where we roast hot dogs and marshmallows on the staff's night off at the dining hall and out-of-season, burn trash, and sit long into the night mesmerized by flames. Almost every cottage has a similar circle of stones with wooden benches and chairs pulled up around it: vestiges of early campers at the lake, of the Chippewa who came before, of all first peoples. A circle of light in the darkness, a circle of warmth in the cold, as sparks snap high over the flames into the night, a connection with the distant stars. Food cooked, and creature comfort assured with a couple of oak and pine logs and enough kindling, there's time for memories, stories, questions. "Why did we come here? How did you get here? Was anybody else here? And what did you do at night?" One Pinewoods memoirist muses, "You would think that the lack of electric lights would have been memorable but I don't recall missing them; however the smell of 'coal oil' and the need to handle the kerosene lamp chimney with great care and delicacy when cleaning them will always be with me." She remembers that as children she and her sisters spent their evenings "sitting in front of a fire. . . . Very few candles or kerosene lamps were needed with all the fireplaces and campfires ablaze in the dark of the evening."[57] Someone takes a stick and pokes the fire; a log breaks, sparks exploding and cascading; embers glow and wink, but in an instant, the shimmer and simmer of flame steadies itself again. A late-night walker passes alone on the path; the circle around the fire expands to embrace him. The evolving narrative will include his story. It's easy to speak at night in a circle around a fire, and it's easy to listen. Against the shadows, our faces glow.

Presiding over the living room in our cottage is the great fireplace on the west wall. In the summer of 1918, before the transformation of the old Stanley cottage into the new Shaw cottage began, my grandparents invited their Pinewoods friends to bring stones from their shore to a party. From these stones and the other, larger ones that grandfather and a neighbor brought over from the island, the fireplace was built. With a chimney two stories high, a long mantle, and a depth of three feet, the fireplace required stones too numerous to count. Made of earth, these stones reflect the lake—the water's colors, its persistent smoothing—and yet now these stones hold fire. The biggest stone, a conglomerate pudding stone, with its bits of red and golden agates set in alabaster, is the keystone in the small arch over the mantle. On the mantle we place small things we all use and don't want to lose—flashlights, an axe, a fan, cans of tennis balls, matches, candles, Mother's glasses, fudge from Mackinac Island. The mantle is also the spot for the only things that could pass as icons in the cottage, their iconic status attained only because they have been left there summer after summer: the bronze cowbell Howie brought up from the depths; a plate wishing the Schultzes "Happy Sailing"; a photograph of grandfather before he distinguished himself as the youngest captain of a major Great Lakes shipping line and the first captain of a steel vessel; a photograph of Howie and his winning team in the Rat Race of 1989; a tin cup Mother won in a camp sailing contest; a Yoruba woman, carved from a thorn tree, stirring stew; and a Japanese memento—an elderly couple painted in bright colors and signifying 1,000 years of good life. Grandfather's gyro-compass hangs from the ceiling in front of the fireplace. Other penates and lares, remaining through necessity and familiarity, preside over similar fireplaces in all Pinewoods cottages.

As benches are pulled up around the outside fireplace, chairs, stools, and sofa are arranged inside to face the fire. Even when there isn't a fire, we relate to it; it's as if we need it, want it, wait for it—our remembered center. I always read facing the fire. During cold, damp summers, the woodbox is constantly being filled, and Monopoly games go on for weeks before the fire. It comes to substitute for the sun.

To lay a fire: Jack London told us how in a seventh-grade English class, but I learned the ritual better by watching older people do it at the lake and then by trying it myself. Move ashes and charcoal to make room for crumpled paper, next a pineknot to keep the flame bright blue, then twigs and kindling constructed over it like a tepee for the circulation of air, and on top the split logs set at angles. Matches touched to the paper first on one side and then the other. By the fireplace, the tools—bellows, shovel, tongs, poker—stand ready inside for readjustment of the fire, but if you're outside, you find a big stick, use your foot, and just let it burn. If you're outside, watch the wind; if you're inside, check the draft. Beware of cedar and spruce that spark: in any case, beware of sparks. When you leave the outside fire, stamp out embers, pour on water; when you leave the inside fire, take care that the screen is set up close.

Pinewoods's first fire marshall, Ted Lawrence, recalls that "during his tenure the only reported fire was in the cuff of his pants, the result of a careless emptying of his then ubiquitous pipe."[58] Bambi taught me fire precaution. In a flash, I can conjure up my childhood horror at the forest fire roaring across the whole screen, transforming green into screaming orange. The great stag's antlers rise up like flames as he dissolves back into the fire, unable to protect Bambi and his mother. Now Ted's daughter, Jean, working through the year with the Gerrish Township Fire Department, reports to us on its concerns. Cottages, by law, have inspected fire extinguishers and, as of 1996, have numbers, five inches high, at their entrance and in contrasting colors near their back doors for ready identification. A large cistern, buried near the dining hall, has been prepared for emergencies.

Several summers, we've watched fires around the lake from the pavilion—billowing smoke, like the earth's exhaust system, spewing up over Lyon Manor or over The Cut, assigning dusk to half the sky. Around the lake the horizon shows nicks where firebreaks have been cut to prevent a blaze from spreading, but I know from walking the firebreak out in our woods that this is no protection. Who can break fire? The dried ferns and moss growing over the firebreaks would ferry it across, and the lone pine in the middle would quickly turn torch to light its way.

Sometimes called the firebird, the Kirtland's warbler, whose northern habitat is now limited to eight Michigan counties near Higgins, must have fire. The female builds her nest on the ground under young jackpine, whose branches, low to the ground, shelter her. Mature jackpine, with its branches projecting higher up on the trunk, will not do. Once lightning's flash fires could be counted on to burn off old jackpines, allowing new jackpine growth and providing the warblers with their desired nesting conditions. Now to save the bird and its melodious song, the Michigan Department of Natural Resources sets fires to old jackpines in designated areas. It's a risky business, and some houses have recently gone up in flames. As a child, I saw Aunt Betty, graceful in the drunken pose she had assumed against the fireplace mantle in the cottage living room, but unable to light her match. She tries repeatedly, holding the paper matchbook in one hand but striking air each time until at last, she holds the small quivering light up to her eyes. It goes out in her fingers. Her elegance and her despair burn a bright hole in the air before me. Though we may survive our fires, the phoenix form we assume is never certain.

RAIN

Recent medical studies argue that "cabin fever" is a physiological disease, caused by light deprivation and manifesting itself psychologically as depression. As such, it's common among people living in areas where the winters are long and the possibilities for being out-of-doors consequently limited. But the summer variant of this disease, "cottage-fever," can also prove harmful, especially because we expect to be outdoors in the summer. The entire summer holiday is predicated on personal memories and commercial images of sunbathing beneath blue skies, sailing over turquoise waters, running blithely across tennis courts. When the rain comes to Pinewoods, and when it stays day after day after day, woods and lake, path and shore become inaccessible, the holiday mood vanishes as we are forced into our cottages.

We are forced in upon ourselves as individuals. Some are grateful for repose. Others, disappointed that a golf game cannot materialize or that a sailing date must be postponed, turn grumpily to reading books, writing letters, tending to postponed chores. Families are forced in upon themselves. If it's possible to be gracious or ironic or indifferent three times a day at the family table at the dining hall, it's more difficult to develop convincing social strategies for an entire day. When the sun is shining, Pinewoods provides such a diversity of tasks and activities that the irritating members of one's family can be avoided or engaged in passing pleasantries—impossible options when it rains, and everyone must share the same living room space. For families with small children, rain creates havoc.

Games and stories must be devised; noise and hyperkinetic behavior must be monitored. Rain tests our privileged Pinewoods community.

We must go out to eat. Rain turns the paths into fast-flowing rivulets, complex veins and arteries, carrying twigs and pine needles. We negotiate puddles and maneuver umbrellas away from those branches drooping with raindrops. At the dining hall, a quantity of umbrellas of various vintages and styles leans in disarray against the porch. Kept from year to year and generation to generation in cottage closets and storerooms, along with ancient jackets and hats, they are beyond fashion, and include a 1920s bamboo parasol, a striped golf umbrella, a kids' plastic umbrella patterned in gaudy shades of fuchsia and chartreuse, grandfather's castoff rusty black bumbershoot. In the cafeteria line, it's a relief to complain with someone, other than family members, about the weather. Home again, the umbrellas are opened out on the back porch to dry like stiffened flowers, and we hang raincoats and ponchos on the clothesline that runs down the long central hall of our cottage, which was installed, primarily, for drying sails. Soggy shoes, mostly sneakers and tennies, are placed in front of the fireplace. Coming in, we wipe our feet, but pine needles and sand persist in littering the floors. Dampness seeps into and through the entire cottage. Between the pages of books, between bedsheets, between the penalty cards in the Monopoly set, between cousins.

The line between ripe and rot becomes difficult to discern as the roof over the back bedroom begins to leak. Mother is furious. The back bedroom, the kitchen, and the back porch, remnants of the old Stanley cottage, share a roof which keeps on leaking, and she has had a series of carpenters, roofers, contractors, and caretakers out to look at it. We lay out papers; we sponge; we place the old enamel chamber pots beneath the drips which begin to "ping" into it with regularity, each one reminding us of our imperfect attempts to create shelter and of our vulnerability before a drop. Tammy is doing a puzzle on the table in the alcove off the living room; from an Endangered Wildlife series, it pictures an Arctic polar bear, and she has started fitting the border together. Passing Tammy's puzzle, I look over the maze of white shapes that have been spread out, befuddled as to how I can make a concrete contribution.

Rain tests us. Enduring it, we discover forgotten resources, finding unexpected time for each other. It need not be rationalized. It makes the plants to grow, the lake to fill. It prompts the senses. Pounding on the roof, dripping in the eaves; shrouding and dissolving the tops of the great pines, misting through their lower branches; slashing across the lake, dimpling the water near the shore; moistening earth, freshening skin. After all, I'm always looking for an excuse to read a book. But without the drama of thunderclap and lightning, without the surprise of cloudburst and rainbow, rain can be tedium: the gray, we fear, might be the only medium. Walking in the woods after a rain, I feel gray dissipate and diversity return. The air glistens. Light glints from myriad leaves, and in the crystal beads suspended at the tips of countless single pine needles shines the world made new again and again. Lengths of spiderwebs, otherwise invisible, can be seen, connecting fern and bush and tree with glittering droplets. I am bedazzled. A vireo calls, giving away its place in the top of a high oak and its cheer. I stop to watch it cross shafts of light to come down to a lower branch. It settles and creates a little cascade which slips down from branch to branch, showering a series of leaves. The bird rests easy. Walking on, I begin to see the mushrooms, the fungi, the Indian pipes, roused by the rain out of the woods' dark undergrowth into bright being. I can live with wet pants, wet shoes.

Camping

MAINTENANCE

*S*everal times a year I hear from Mother that the cottage is falling down and that no one else ever seems to worry about it. She's right. I've never made arrangements with a Roscommon plumber to move the septic tank, with a Grayling lumber company to have the dying Norway in front of the cottage lopped and topped, with a Houghton Lake business to bring gravel in for the back road. I have never contacted the Pinewoods caretaker to replace rotted boards in the dock, to lay the concrete breakwater, to re-canvas the lower pavilion, to realign the supports for the upper pavilion, to re-roof the back of the cottage, to install new lighting in the upstairs bathroom. I need the cottage to be there, the pavilion to be out in front, and the dock in place, and summer after summer assume it will be. Lake and trees, shore and path so organize my interior space that changes feel like all the loaded cupboards in my psyche falling.

But time and weather demand changes. Weather affects not only the temperature and the quality of light, but imperceptibly in time it also wears away edges; it creates fine crevices; it softens, moistens, decays. So I have seen Mother kneeling on the roof over the cottage front porch plucking the tufts of bright moss out from between the shingles. I have heard her going downstairs on a storm-blasted night to close living-room windows, to pile up the cushions on the pavilion swing and turn the pavilion chairs in toward the swing, and always to check the moorings for the boats. I have helped her drain the Sunfish, scrub black gunk from the bottom of the Lightning, sponge the bilge out of the other boats. On some occasions I've felt whittled away by my failure to perform a task

91

with the precision and speed she perceives as necessary, while on other occasions I've felt smug at the shipshape condition of our cottage.

Standing round-the-clock watch, Mother looks after the neighbors' cottages—their roofs, their roads, their docks—as well as ours. She looks after the camp as well: sweeping the front porch of the dining hall, rolling the tennis court dry, planting new trees along the path to the mailbox following the tornado. Hers has been a life of caretaking, of taking care; she appreciates the value of careful attention. From her I've learned that to be careless is to have no care. Out paddling her own canoe, she sights a Cottage Grove canoe, swamped and dragging at its moorings, water sloshing heavily between its gunwales. She takes it personally that this lovely boat cannot float. In a flash, she has tied up her own canoe and found help for the floundering canoe of her unknown neighbor.

Boats, immersed in two natural elements—water and air—are especially vulnerable, necessitating ceaseless vigilance. Even in these days of plastic boat furnishings, fiberglass hulls, synthetic sails and lines, a boat weathers. If you're not repairing a sprung tiller attachment, a loose grommet in the sail's clew, a dislocated track on the mast, a frayed halyard, a snapped batten, you're working to prevent a break, a tear, a loss. After a sail in *Lemon Drop*, Howie deposits us at the dock and spends the next hour lovingly putting the boat to bed, securing it against the vagaries of night. Stays must be checked and tightened, sheets coiled and cleated, centerboard hoisted and made snug, sails properly folded and bagged, rudder brought aboard with its pins in place. Only then can the boat be tucked in—the yellow canvas cover stretched over the boom, its corners tied down fore and aft and its snaps attached all along the gunwales.

Filling boxes, hanging from a peg-board, crammed on shelves in the pumphouse are assorted tools and spares for any nautical necessity—cleats, blocks, S hooks, cringles, marline spikes, clamps, cotter pins, turnbuckles, oarlocks, lines of all sizes and lengths dangling in coils, several anchors—many my grandfather's sturdy legacy. Though he is gone, the need for maritime maintenance persists. With his Dacron sails, Howie has no need for the sailor's palm of hardened leather, the awl, the spools of heavy waxed thread, but they, along with grandfather's dented wooden mallet, his riveting and his claw-footed hammer, his cumbersome drill with its precise little wheel, his auger scissors, his sets of iron files and wrenches, are stored in the pumphouse, always accessible for diverse shoreline projects. My father's watch, with its yellowing dial, hangs from a nail by the pumphouse door, put there by Mother after he died to help anyone who is interested keep track of the time down by the shore.

Laid perpendicularly across the pumphouse rafters are extra Sunfish masts and tillers, oars and paddles. On high shelves are stored the faded calico canoe cushions, life jackets, swim fins, a peach basket full of Petoskey stones to polish one day. Setting out for the first paddle of the season with Mother, I notice that the paddles we're to use are splitting and suggest we haul down some of those stashed on rafters overhead. Dust and spider droppings come down with them. We notice that several display the talismanic marks of my grandfather's repair work—copper plates neatly nailed over cracks, rivets still holding firm, waxed thread perfectly wound around splintered handles. We'll take two out. Mother in the meantime is unwrapping the cushions. So mice and squirrels won't invade, she swathes them every year in plastic bags, with each edge sealed tight with masking tape. It takes a while to peel off the tape for this season, and I laugh to hear her say, "I might have overdone it this time." Later in the day, returning from my woods walk, she's sitting on the stoop of the woodshed with an axe splitting the extra paddles, oars, and tillers we lowered from the pumphouse rafters. She tells me, "We can always use more stakes."

Maintenance—of body, house, job, friendship, community, trees, lake, garden—occupies us. It demands careful attention. It may become obsessive, routinized, exhausting, which Thoreau well knew. Concerned to maintain a principle or a search for the mystical hound, bay horse, and turtle dove,[59] he excused himself from maintenance duty in the workaday material world. An advocate of "voluntary poverty,"[60] he excused himself from caring for those things that he could hold in his hands. I can't. The cottage stands because my mother glued, sanded, varnished, patched, pasted, nailed, saved, and the cottage holds me. Pinewoods has taught me to tell time and weather, and consequently I know I now must learn to be so very careful of the turtle dove in the hand. In the pumphouse, while we searched for usable paddles, I discovered a Sunfish rudder which could replace the warped board serving as a shelf beneath the little pumphouse window. Both Howie and Mother are pleased with the exchange. Maintenance helps us to shore up a few fragments against our ruin.

From the beginning we couldn't have managed without help. Shoppenagons was there first to help. He and his Chippewa associates broke the trail and the ice for the early pleasure-seekers in Michigan's northern woods. Those scores of anonymous lumbermen and railroad men who came later also helped although, given their rapacious use of the land, it's hard for me to be gracious and grateful for their assistance now. But I realize that the middle-class vacation rested on the backs of thousands for whom not even the Sabbath was a day of rest, only a few of whose names are ever remembered. Who dug our septic tanks, ran our electric wiring through the trees, set our pavilions into the lake's high banks? Was it Harold Ogrum or Carl Cederburg who built our cottages or, fine Swedish carpenters, did they build only the cupboards? Like my grandfather, these American workers undoubtedly plotted and planned so that their children and grandchildren would be able to take a few days off in the summer to fish for pleasure rather than for a living.

In general, because the very concept of vacation entails letting others do the dirty work, the summer leisure of the middle class is purchased at the cost of hard work and long hours by numerous people. A degree of reciprocity, however, has characterized the relationship between the campers of Lakeside, Cottage Grove, and Pinewoods who needed serving, and those who served. In the wake of the boom days of lumber and the depression days of farming, northern Michigan became one of the nation's most economically depressed areas. Consequently, for many of those who served in this area, making ends meet was a struggle, and visits from those like the Higgins Lake campers—pleasure-seekers, rusticators, resorters, tourists, summer people, strangers—proved a bonanza. Arthur Rosenau records a conversation from the 1880s: "William Donovan [of Lakeside] asked George Cheney [the spokesperson for Pere Cheney, the lumbering center and a major jumping off place for development in Roscommon County] what the homesteaders raised and on what they subsisted until their crops were harvested. Cheney's answer: 'They raise hell generally and subsist on fish and strangers.'"[61]

Most people get to the lake nowadays under their own steam, by car or with a little assistance from the airlines, coming into the Traverse City or the Tri-City (Saginaw, Bay City, Midland) Airport, renting a car or arranging for someone from the lake to pick them up. But before the 1920s, before American expression of self-reliance became bound to the automobile, the campers needed considerable help in reaching the lake. The journey, gleefully recalled by several memoirists, consisted of several stages and depended at each stage on assistance, in and out, up and down, hand over hand. At first they came from their cities in the south by train, traveling in parlor cars equipped with overstuffed swivel chairs and served planked whitefish in the diner, arriving at either Pere Cheney or Roscommon. Here they were delivered to the lake, with their steamer trunks, hampers, and miscellaneous hand baggage, by stagecoach, carriage, farm wagon, and in later years by auto taxi. The individuals who managed the luggage, the horses, and the corduroy roads were fondly remembered for their help. Rosenau quotes a visitor's 1891 account of his trip with James McGillis between Roscommon and the camps:

You are met by a stage, [which] although intended to accommodate ten persons, will, like all stages, carry double the number. The driver of this van is Jim McGillis, or "McGinty," as the campers have found suits him better. He is as odd a character as you will run across in many a day. He no more discovers you want to go to the lake than he knows in some unaccountable way your name and nature. He loads you into the stage and after stopping at the post-office and all the stores in the village to do a thousand and one errands with which he has been commissioned, you start on a drive of nine miles through the pine woods of Michigan and over roads where sand abounds and where horses seldom trot. You listen to McGinty talk for about an hour, when you begin to get tired and dusty and wonder why you came. But a few minutes later you reach a high hill and "Mc" points out the lake. You immediately become interested and again listen to McGillis, who, during all this time has never dropped the thread of conversation except to say, "get up, Dan," and "get up, Charlie," which is woven into his stories with such grace that they remain uninterrupted. You reach the camp after a two hours' ride and having removed the dust and enjoyed a hearty meal the displeasures of the ride fade from memory like pancakes before a hired man.[62]

Pinewoods travelers also remember James Gallimore, who started out with a four-horse stage-coach seating fifteen passengers in 1905, but who by 1911 was meeting them at the Roscommon station platform with his Model T. His wife served hot meals to tired campers at the Gallimore home in Roscommon either before or after the exhausting trip to or from Higgins, and his daughter, Mrs. Barber, assisted her father by driving her car when a large group of campers arrived needing transportation from town.

When the Shaws first arrived at Higgins in 1914, they were accompanied by Marie, a maid of all trades. Coming to the lake, she rode with the family on their three-hour train trip from Bay City to Roscommon in the chair car of the Michigan Central Railroad, but after arriving in camp, she did not eat with them. In the years before the construction of their own dining hall, Pinewoods's families ate at the Cottage Grove dining hall; their "help," however, were relegated to eat at the "Ordinary," an outbuilding behind the dining hall. With our own hall, unless they were back at the cottage caring for children, nursemaids, babysitters, and nannies were included at family tables. We noticed them. And they surely noticed us, noticing them. They sat at the end of the tables, feeding the babies in their high chairs; we greeted them, passing in the dining hall or on the path pushing strollers, and they responded brightly, but conversation never evolved easily. Recently, however, no one has had to hire live-in help; machines do the washing, drying, cleaning, and entire families—grandparents, aunts, uncles, cousins, and both parents—are engaged with child care.

If the dining hall keeps the Pinewoods community together, the help keeps the dining hall together. Usually living in quarters at the dining hall, at first in rooms over the dining room and later, when these proved unsafe, in comfortable bungalows behind the hall, they share summers with us. They are individuals within a summer community as much as the campers are. Perhaps by using terms such as "the help" and "quarters," Pinewoods perpetuated a system of dichotomies—upstairs/downstairs, inside/outside, summer/winter, consuming/producing communities. Perhaps some dining hall people collectively categorized the campers as carefree rich folk, while some campers regarded the dining hall's cooks, managers, waitresses, chore boys, and salad girls as anonymous.

Since the founding of Pinewoods, however, not only have members of the camp served in the dining hall, but friendships spanning seasons and homes have also evolved between the dining hall staff and the campers, as Ted Plum's memoir testifies. Working as a chore boy in the dining hall from 1920–22, Ted, whose family was among the earliest Pinewoods campers, was assigned the job of escorting the kitchen staff, most of whom came from farms close to Higgins, to and from their homes: "These ladies were mostly Swedes, Irish or other foreign people who were very fine and wonderful. I got to know them very well and we became good friends."[63]

As a kid, I idealized our waitresses. They were local high school girls with terrific hairdos and flaming fingernail polish; their snappy way of carrying trays and their sassy way of whisking about among our tables suggested an enviable and sophisticated savoir faire. As a young teen and almost their age, however, I indulged in table-torment with members of my gang: setting minnows swimming in drinking glasses, dumping all the olive pits onto a single plate, standing up all the silverware in the glasses, playing interminable rounds of "Pass the Spoon." The waitresses turned the tables on us by serving up the minnows the next day fried and by setting all our place mats upside down. Occasionally, we would ask the dining hall folk to join us out at the raft in the afternoon or to go sailing. But they always had to leave early, and in the sailboat they sat uneasily on the windward rail, hands clasped between their thighs, awkward, as they weren't in the dining hall, as they scrambled under the boom when the boat swung into the wind. I remember, however, how thrilling it was one winter during these years to cross paths on the slopes of Skyline, a ski resort outside of Grayling, with Erma, our waitress of the summer before. She was laughing with a gay group of friends, tossing back her head of fluffy yellow hair with an abandon I'd never seen before. And I've subsequently heard that another of our waitresses helped to read the riot act on Jim Bakker's philandering. Their lives and stories from the beginning have been their own.

Although recently we've hired professionals from around Michigan as cooks and managers, Pinewoods people have always worked in the dining hall. The camp's own Edith Plum Thomson, related to several camp families and known to everyone as Aunt Edie, managed the dining hall for its first decade. Ted Plum cites his summers as dining hall chore boy as "some of the happiest times of my youth,"[64] and numerous other Pinewoods people have discovered that by serving the camp, they could serve themselves. Among family and friends, with swims, sails, and sing-alongs by personal initiation rather than by invitation, they discovered that an interlude of work at the dining hall could be a lark. Paul Bruske and Al Taggart were hired to help Ted hook and hoist the 200-pound blocks of ice that kept fruits and vegetables cool in the icehouse. In the 1930s Richard Lawrence and then Patty Taggart minded The Store. In the 1960s Ann Cochran was a waitress. Harriet Sinclair met her first husband, Bill Brown, at the dining hall when she was a waitress and he a dishwasher. Danny and Joyce Wilson, following their June marriage in 1958, spent a summer-long honeymoon serving at the dining hall. Recently, several high school teenagers from Cottage Grove and Lakeside have had a ball doing cleanup at the Pinewoods Dining Hall.

The proximity of the Sisco farm to Pinewoods—just at the jog where the pavement vanishes and the road narrows and ruts to become the Stage Road—meant a close connection from the beginning. Whereas Lakeside had thirteen caretakers between the mid-1880s and 1969, until 1975 when Roger Rasmussen was hired, caretaking at Pinewoods was done only by Ed Sisco and his son, Marshall, who followed in his father's footsteps in 1946. For Ed, working at Pinewoods was a way of supplementing his income from the farm; his farm team pulled in our boats when they weren't in the fields, and he cut ice and wood in the winter for the dining hall when his fields didn't need tending. Marshall applied his knowledge from previous experience in Detroit's Cadillac machine shop and in electrical maintenance to the diverse tasks needed by Pinewoods cottage owners. Docks, with their steps and boat lines, go in at the beginning of every season and come out at the end of every season. Left to stand, these wooden protrusions would be smashed by the thick ice which moves like glaciers across the lake every winter. Marshall put on his high-top waders, took up his sledgehammer each spring and autumn, and went forth to care for these docks. When he was not chopping ice and wood, he was wiring our refrigerators, roofing our woodsheds, installing the plumbing in our second inside bathroom, hanging the cupboards in the kitchen, setting up the furnace, digging the hole for the septic tank. As his father had assisted in the transition from camp to summer cottages, Marshall helped convert many cottages into modern year-round homes.

Marshall's wife, Esther, took up the dining hall's management in the 1940s and continued to do the billing through the summer of 1996. At the end of every week, on every dining hall table, we found a statement drawn up in her precise hand tallying the meals for each household. Following Marshall's death, Esther had her own snug home built on the old Sisco farm where, throughout the year, she watches out for wildlife, feeding raccoons, foxes, deer, and a multitude of birds. She has visited some Pinewoods people in their winter homes, and if you are in camp out of season, Esther invites you to dinner and Chinese checkers afterwards. In a 1966 tribute to Marshall and Esther, Phil Will wrote, "More important by far to the enjoyment of our quiet Utopia and the warm tone of our personal relationships are the human qualities of our Caretaker and our Manager. Because Marshall and Esther are able persons of dignity and pride, because they have given generously of their skills, they have a responding friendship and respect from all members. It is their personal qualities which, as much as anything, have created the atmosphere at Pinewoods which brings us back year after year."[65] With Ed and Marie, Marshall and Esther, and now Roger and Kay Rasmussen, dichotomies dissolve. They are there with us, and even when we leave, we remain there with them, taking care together, in expectation of return.

In discovering the devious ubiquity of sand and spiders, Pinewoods ladies realized their reliance on the cleaning ladies of Roscommon. These women were hired to come for two entire days at the beginning of the season to open the cottages—to remove dust covers from furniture, wash windows, shake rugs; they returned intermittently throughout the summer and they appeared at the end of the season for a final sweeping, dusting, scrubbing, tucking in. During their cleaning hours, they took charge of the cottages and our lives, turning both topsy-turvy to check our intimate cracks and creases and to apply appropriate spit and polish. On cleaning days, I fled the cottage. Ashamed of my clothes strewn helter-skelter about the room, I first stuffed them under the bed covers, forming telltale lumps.

Unfortunately, however, familiarity can breed contempt. Mrs. Martinson is remembered by one family as going about her cleaning "shyly with her high voice and halting English, always returning furniture and table covers to where they 'belonged,' not where Mother had moved them."[66] Mrs. Garland used to pause in wiping the windows of some cottages to press her face against the pane in hideous grins and grimaces to scare the little kids passing by on the path. In recent years, she's lost all interest in sweeping sand and wiping windows for summer people. Although Mother now hires Kay to clean the cottage, she sends Mrs. Garland a subscription of *National Geographic* every Christmas. She receives a letter back in thanks, with news of her health, her garden, and her bowling league. They address each other as "Lucy" and "Evelyn." I last saw her the final summer Daddy was alive. Driving to a bit of woodlands known to have quantities of huckleberries which we planned to pick and eat to our hearts' content, we saw her sitting on the ground at the juncture of the county road into Pinewoods and the blacktop to the expressway. Spread out all around her were assorted buckets, baskets, and yogurt and margarine containers filled with huckleberries, each priced for sale. She waved wildly at us and we waved back, but passed her by, leaving her to her own pickings.

Although sand and spiders go on settling in our Pinewoods cottages, the ritual of covering the furniture at the end of the summer with white muslin cloths has passed. We may try to keep up with our own sand through the summer, but invasions by dust and time throughout the year continue to cause us to seek help. We may try to plan our summers for carefree pleasure, but out-of-season fear of fire among the cottages, concern over heavy snows upon the dining hall roof, and dread of vandals continue to cause us to acknowledge our dependencies. Idyllic summers, after all, are the province primarily of children. Beauty, grace, and ease—life-enhancing luxuries—seldom sustain themselves. They wither if they are not shared; they disintegrate if we can't appreciate how much assistance is necessary to support their fragility.

GANGS

nglish has devised a diversity of nouns to describe our fellow creatures in the aggregate: a gaggle of geese, a pod of whales, a jubilation of larks. To describe ourselves in different collective arrangements, we have perhaps even more words: party, club, band, gang, family, committee, company, community, congress, association, society, state, nation. Most of these collective nouns, from the sociological standpoint, are value-free. According to the *O.E.D.*, however, a "gang" is any group of persons "who go about together or act in concert (chiefly in a bad or depreciatory sense, and in mod. usage mainly associated with criminal societies)."[67] Even at Pinewoods, which in itself might be considered a "gang" in distinction from the Cottage Grove or the Lakeside gangs, the gangs that have existed with every generation of kids have had just a taint of the criminal.

"Gaggle," "pod," and "jubilation" certainly describe the buoyant and boisterous composite energy of preteens racing down the path or paddling pell-mell in several canoes out to the raft as well as the combined activities of certain birds and beasts. Yet these innocent Pinewoods gangs, my own and my mother's, about which I couldn't hear enough when I was growing up, seem to me in retrospect not completely unrelated to their inner city counterparts. Tom Sawyer had a gang, committed to secrecy, even robbery and murder, in addition to making mayhem of Sunday School picnics. He also made it darn hard for Huck Finn to join. A number of Twain's readers have wondered just how much was make-believe and high spirits and how much imitated and prophesied oppressive grownup behavior. Even if the gang exists for camaraderie, for fun and games, for communal identification, it always defines itself in opposition to another.

In the 1928–29 history of Pinewoods, there are accounts of the antics of three early gangs. Shrouded with secrecy, the boys organized themselves against the girls, who did likewise, declaring defensive "warfare" on the boys. This gang of girls, in which my mother participated with glee, drew up "International Laws," which pronounced that "the boys should pay a ransom of 10¢ as they were much harder to capture." A memoirist of Mother's gang notes, however, that "we only once came near obtaining a prisoner by calling Pete out in the woods to see a snake, and even then we escaped with a bloody nose or two instead. But there were many memories of [our] being marooned on rafts, or having to dig our way out from under the Plums' house or stand the mosquitoes while tied in the woods." Nonetheless, "The war was continued in hare and hound races, duck-on-the-rock, prisoners' base, and 'push-off' the raft."[68]

In memoirs detailing the further adventures of her gang, my mother is revealed to me as a girl. With her bosom friends, she made woodpile houses and secret mailboxes, sold candy and painted candlesticks, broke into closed cottages to tell ghost stories and play strip poker, gave shows which blossomed into plays. Unlike the boys who turned their energies toward putting porcupines down wells and dropping lighted firecrackers through knotholes, I see this girls' gang as investigating the natural and social dimensions of their northern Michigan world. The gang gave them all freedom to explore endlessly, to swagger fearlessly, and to cavort joyously. Although they moved into spaces with an abandon alien to their own mothers, on their most audacious adventures, such as a canoe trip through The Cut to Houghton Lake, in the interests of respectability, they were always accompanied by chaperons. In their bloomers and middy blouses, my mother and her gang did not identify themselves as tomboys, however, and gender boundaries were as irrelevant as geographical boundaries as they set off to test possibilities:

Bit by bit, we emerged from under the family roof, and our horizons widened. First we slept, six or so in a tent behind Wentworths'; soon we were sleeping in pavilions, on swings, on docks, on roofs, on the ground—everywhere but on the raft. . . . Our hike distance grew from the haunted house at Clayball's, the forestry, and Huckleberry, to Roscommon and Grayling, which proved to take less time, when free rides were available on anything from oil trucks to trains. In Roscommon we discovered the joys of dining at Jimmy's, of mixing our own drinks at Pattie's, of staging a mock trial in the courthouse, and of talking to men through the bars. ("Naughty man," said Addie to a bootlegger.) In Grayling, we looted the Opera House, climbed the railroad tower, and hooked the train back to Rosc. . . .

We paddled around the lake in three days in 1921, sleeping out in the worst storm in years when so many trees blew down in Lakeside, and two in the field we were sleeping in, and the canoes kept blowing off our heads, and our blankets blew around, and the puddles filled our hollows, and Marlo kept dry in a duffle bag, and RB cheered us with, "But think what it will be like when the dew falls!" The next year we walked around the lake in two days, sleeping on a boathouse roof at Stony Point which went through under RB, who was dancing with Luke [the nickname given to Mother by her gang], even though it was Sunday morning. Later we were circumventing the lake in twelve hours or so, by land or sea, by day or moonlight night, and were tripping on to Houghton for further fields of conquest.[69]

The third gang called themselves Pirates; these were the little kids, and being primarily younger sisters, like my Aunt Betty, they, too, organized defensively and continued the traditions of warfare with gusto and glee. In their first year they revenged themselves on certain "dastardly clubhouse attackers" by surprising them in their beds and throwing them in the lake over "the cries and protests of their mothers." Money for their pirate feasts was earned by singing songs throughout camp and passing the ukulele. Membership, of course, demanded walking the plank.

Thus there were precedents for the gang that the kids in my age group initiated. We had our name, the BOA Club, its initials an acronym for a phrase so preposterous we were sworn forever never to reveal it. Our clubhouse was the garage behind our cottage built for grandmother's LaSalle, empty since she had stopped driving. Its furnishings came from Pinewoods rummage sales, camp boathouses, and the Cottage Grove dump, to which we went on BOA foraging trips in search of cast-off beach chairs, card tables, bottles, and shoes. Given that a primary activity of the club was smoking pine needle cigarettes, old shoes, despite their inflammatory and olfactory nature, were to be our ashtrays. Because one BOA member excelled at blowing smoke rings, we came up with a play of knights and ladies, never produced, in which she would star as a fire-breathing dragon. We had a bench with a secret compartment, and into a two-by-eight plank a talented gang member carved the awesome initials of BOA so that candles could be set in them to illuminate our meetings. Candles in bottles, over which wax of every color had been lavishly dripped, gave us further light when the garage doors of the clubhouse swung shut. (Playing fast and loose with fire, how did we keep from burning ourselves and the whole camp down?) We had our oaths and potions, such as BOA venom, concocted from the dregs of drinks left on the kitchen sink in our cottage after the adults' cocktails, maraschino cherry juice, ice tea, and spit. The membership distinguished the BOA from earlier gangs: we didn't discriminate by either gender or age, and siblings were welcome (although Marion claims she was always left out, and other "little kids," if they weren't away in summer camps, hung around the edges).

Our excursions and productions resembled those of our predecessors. We swam at Sulphur Springs and paddled down The Cut. We explored haunted houses and visited the ghost town of Pere Cheney. We walked to Roscommon on one occasion and visited a Tent Revival on another, sending Howie forward to be saved. We played "Sardines" after dinner in the woods until the summer a bunch of us discovered we'd hidden in a patch of poison ivy, and we went on Snipe Hunts and Scavenger Hunts and had Hare and Hound races. We occasionally took over one of the tables at the dining hall so we could play "Pass the Word" and "Pass the Spoon" which, after each of us had placed a choice edible—pinch of salt, macaroni curl, green bean, crust of bread, eye of newt, dab of ice cream—on the single spoon, made a nice mess for the waitresses. We put on plays in the garage, presenting performances outside and closing the garage doors on our audiences during scene changes, which effectively locked them up. We became experts at round-robin Ping-Pong.

Warm, windless days we devoted to the raft, our small flotilla of canoes, rowboats, and Sailfish strung out one after the other like a kite's tail. We developed innovative swimming strokes—the Egyptian crawl, the Australian wrench, and the lighthouse churn—and water sports—"Statue," "Tag," "Leap Frog," and "Treading Air," which involved doing handstands on the bottom of the lake and waggling your legs in the air. We learned to leap straddle-legged off the diving board onto roller pontoons floating below in the water as well as to mount five or six of us onto a single pontoon. We built sand castles on the end of the diving board, only to watch them wash gradually away by gathering together on one end of the raft so that the board dipped slowly into the lake, and we did chorus lines off the board.

Despite an open-door policy, the BOAs also defined themselves through identifying an opposition. We, too, practiced skullduggery and engaged in warfare. As most of our parents sailed and as some of us had our own Sailfishes, we came to think of ourselves as belonging to a sailing elite. We were yacht snobs. We disdained motorboats, calling them stinkboats. Our boats and our methods for traversing the lake demanded more intelligence, were intrinsically more elegant. We spurned the speed of motorboats: they went fast to go nowhere while we tacked. They leaked oil: the rainbow colors seeping from the sterns of Chryslers and Chris-Crafts seemed perversely lovely. They sputtered and farted, ripped and roared, and we believed that their noises and their disruption of the waves' regular rhythm disturbed the natural order of the lake itself. Crisscrossing the lake at random, they got in the way of sailors trying to keep a calculated course. The troughs they gouged through the water as they zoomed in front of our bows caused our boats to come whacking down on the waves as if to shatter their hulls and their delicate arrangement of lines and stays. The fact that the motorboat could force the sailboat to make such a racket added insult to injury. The only thing these boats had going for them was their independence from the wind—the very element that gave the sailboats their grace. In writing this, I feel the old BOA animosity rising up in me. And only begrudgingly do I acknowledge that in times of crisis—when the sailboat had capsized and could not be righted, when the sailboat was becalmed and could not budge—we yearned for the sight of a friendly powerboat.

We didn't sabotage any gas tanks, but on one occasion we took shameless pleasure in pouring sticky BOA venom over the seat upholstery of an especially sporty Chris-Craft. We were never pursued, and no one ever took retribution. We always came home to bed on time and made it to the dining hall for all three meals, preserving our respectability every bit as much as Tom Sawyer, and perhaps because our parents had had their own gang-related rumbles, we were never scolded.

Humans do gang up—as gun clubs or conservation groups, churches or cults. Within the gang, the individual finds ambiguities resolved and anxieties eased. A gang provides protective coloration. In giving an individual the security of the collective, it allows the cowardly to become mean-spirited or courageous, the shy to become pretentious or brilliant. The difference in outcome depends on the stakes set by the gang. In the Pinewoods gangs, competition and comparison have been mild-mannered, and consequently the primary prize for participation in them has always been wild delight in discovering a diversity of connections with other people and with nature. Thus, my mother's gang encouraged her to discover audacity and exuberance, and as the BOAs did for me, it gave her a web of friendships. Pinewoods, a model for the best of gangs, provides the means for our growing toward others.

PLAY

I've heard Mother's description of Pinewoods as the place "where there's no time to do anything and not enough time to do it in" since I was a child. Commercial images of "Vacation at the Lake," "Going Up North," "Endless Summer" perpetuate our longings for a time and place of leisure, interrupted only by bouts of play. From the camp's beginning well into the 1950s, the dining hall and its staff, laundry ladies and cleaning ladies, the camp caretaker and rounds of nannies guaranteed that this longing would become a probability. Today, the dining hall staff, the caretaker, and multiple service people in Roscommon County, as well as vacuum cleaners and washing machines in every cottage, ensure that play is a part of Pinewoods life.

Sports and games organize some people's lives during the summers. Sports at Pinewoods are those activities that require setting time, spending money, extending the community to include strangers. Games, however, can begin at the drop of a hat, may take a slight initial investment, and may involve friends' interests. Sports usually are played by the light of day, but games can go on into the night. Both necessitate the coordination and exercise of mind and body and some finely tuned competitive sense. They elicit sweat and occasionally that adrenaline thrill that prickles along the spine and may be associated with good sex and great beauty.

Under the category of sports at Pinewoods, I place the friendly rivalry of the century-long summer baseball competitions between Lakeside and Cottage Grove. Cottage Grove and Lakeside have diamonds behind their camps, and their teams meet every Sunday morning. Although Pinewoods never had its own team, boys from our camp were welcomed to join the Lakeside and Cottage Grove teams and often played with distinction. In the same category with baseball, I also place our participation in the Higgins Lake Boat Club Lightning races and national regattas on the lake every Saturday afternoon during the 1950s and into the 1960s. Sailing competitively demands alertness—to wind shifts, adjustments in lines, balance of weight, the proximity of other boats. It demands subtle anticipations, quick decisions, and physical alacrity in response. Whether we were in a gale or "a dead clam," you couldn't relax in a race: it was stress and strain. But it was also acting in perfect harmony with the two other crew members. Remembering how we could bring *Flicker,* our Lightning, on a tight tack to the mark and how at the precise moment we rounded, the spinnaker opened up in front of us like a cloud for the downwind beat, still lifts the heart. The rush produced by the tri-camp baseball games seemed an inferior sport by comparison. Of course, no girls were allowed in those games, and thus our role in them was only as spectators and groupies. In sailing, however, Mother was one of several women skippering sailboats, and girl crew members, like myself, were as plentiful as gulls.

Golf and tennis fall somewhere between sports and games at Pinewoods. Dates have to be made for golf at Ye Olde Golf Club and for tennis on the camp court in the woods alongside the dining hall. At mealtime, there's a certain scurrying about from table to table as people line up their golf and tennis dates. One of the principal uses of the telephone at Pinewoods nowadays is for arranging these games if plans aren't solidified at the dining hall. Some people are booked every day of their summer holiday; their sailing spot for the summer is Ye Olde, a nine-hole course halfway between Pinewoods and Roscommon. As a kid, I yearned for invitations to the swimming pool at the Flint Country Club in June before we made the trek to the lake. Later, however, when Mother and Daddy actually became members so they could play golf, I spurned the country club for its discriminatory racial policies. Transferring this hostility to Ye Olde, I sensed what a snob I'd become, visiting it only once—when Daddy took me to see the blue bird boxes he'd helped put up on the edges of its fairways.

I simply ignored the tennis court. Considerable camp resources have gone into upgrading and maintaining the surfaces, nets, and backboards of the courts, for they're used by young and old, by members of all cottages. Walking on the trails behind camp, you hear the rhythmic thud of a ball bouncing from court to backboard. You hear the calls of the specialized language of this game—"Love two. Deuce. Game." And laughter. Annually, during their brief two-week stay at the lake, Harman and Joy Foster arrange a "Rat Race" on the tennis courts. Although their three boys are grown, Harman and Joy continue the tradition they created of organizing all willing members of camp into tennis teams of four, putting two teams and eight players on the court. In a whirlwind, day-long competition, the teams swing it out against each other until only two are left. Each year the teams, assigned specific colors and themes, are expected to dress for play appropriately. Winners are announced at dinner, with Harman awarding mouse traps, cheddar cheese, and chartreuse Higgins Lake ball caps to the Orange Melons or the Silver Sharks.

Seeking reasons for my disinterest in tennis and its variants, activities that seem so silly to me and so exhilarating to everyone else, I rationalize it as antipathy for competition, general uppityness, and contrariness. I cherish the square dances on the tennis court with people playing a motley array of instruments and children doing do-si-dos with adults, and I look forward each summer to the tennis-court lunches following the camp's annual meetings. I recognize my desire for solitude—time away from the antic community; consequently for me the tennis courts provide a sun-filled opening in the woods, a meadow space where sweet, wild strawberries and milkweeds can grow and where an iron pump still stands, drawing up a trickle of icy blue water from secret springs.

Ping-Pong (no one calls it table tennis in Pinewoods) games take less organizing than golf and tennis. Several cottages have tables outside. Unused for decades, ours was hauled out of the boathouse and put up in back on a trio of sawhorses during the heyday of the BOA Club. When the Big Taggart Cottage was constructed, Ping-Pong was given special consideration. Space was allotted next to the cottage for a swing hung from the branch of a tall white pine and for a cement slab where the Ping-Pong table was set up. Benches are placed alongside it for the kibitzers and the next round of players. Paddles holding down balls wait at either end of the tables, making pickup games possible any time for anyone walking by an unused table. Unlike other games, Pinewoods Ping-Pong is impulsive. At times, the table is in use all day at the Big Taggart Cottage. Kids play in bare feet and bathing suits through the morning, teenagers after lunch, and adults get into a game just after dinner in the evening and before a walk to the end of Lakeside. When two of the camp masters used to play Ping-Pong, people left the path and the child on the swing let the old cat die to gather and watch. Both men, tanned dark, were dressed in impeccable whites—long-sleeved white shirts, cream-colored trousers, white bucks. As evening deepened the small white ball, leaping from one side of the table to the other, brightened, and the men, swooping in place with deliberation and elegance, became large moths in a ritual ceremony.

In BOA days, Ping-Pong was fiercely competitive. Each of us worked on developing a treacherous serve that would send the opponent's return careening off the table. We honed our skills collectively in round-robin competitions which tested our accuracy and endurance. When adults would join us, we could have as many as eighteen circling the table, leaving us all gasping and laughing at the end. Our Ping-Pong table is stored away in the garage, and fewer people play the game in camp now. The paddle tennis court down at the Wills, however, is in regular use, and an annual tournament draws crowds. Demanding arrangements of time like other sports, however, it lacks the zany spontaneity of Ping-Pong.

A natural athlete, neat and graceful in all her movements, Mother excels at both sports and games. They have surely contributed to her ninety years of active life. Her skills and enthusiasm for them keep her identified with America's youth culture. She calls me from Michigan to tell me how the Kansas Jayhawks are doing during the basketball season. In part it's the social aspect of sports and games she enjoys—the contract to play at a set time with set rules, the shared language and the subsequent discussion of the event—as much as the challenge to her body and mind. When she is without golf dates, she has told me she feels ostracized. Wondering why the group that plays regularly at

Ye Olde hadn't asked her for a game recently, she surprised me; it's the only time I've ever heard a note of self-pity. Sitting out these golf games, perhaps she remembered Daddy, who was a ready partner. He was a fair athlete, and the two of them teamed up for both golf and tennis, each playing as well as the other. In our big sailboats, the Seagull or the Lightnings, however, he never held his own. The boats were always hers, and she was always at the helm. She insisted on fast reactions, weather sensitivity, and perfect knots. He learned to keep out of her way during a sail, seating himself up on the bow, because he couldn't get it right for her. At some point he stopped sailing with Mother. On summer afternoons when we were racing, he was polishing Petoskey stones at the dock or back in the woods hauling pineknots out of stumps. Now she polishes stones when the golf game is in full swing.

Over the years, her involvement in the intensity of summer sports and games has decreased. In 1960 she sold the Lightning. In 1990 she gave up tennis. No one had Mother's tennis serve—an elaborate and intimidating swirl up over her head, like Victorian calligraphy in the air, which sent the ball spinning exactly into the opposite court. The pennants from our winning sailboat races still hang in the pumphouse, and a quartet of tennis rackets still hangs in the central hall of the cottage. When the wind and temperature is right, Mother still rigs her own Sunfish, and sails nonchalantly out of sight of Pinewoods for hours. She swims; she canoes; she walks; she encourages me to join up for the "Rat Race."

There is also bridge. Bridge is sport for nighttime and rainy days. For Mother, bridge dates for her evenings are as important as golf dates for her mornings. Although she never missed a Tigers game on the radio, bridge was the only game my grandmother played. Her legacy to the cottage includes maple card tables, satin card-table covers, stiff decks of cards, and stacks of old scoring tablets. You can't walk down the path at night without seeing a bridge game in process in some cottage living room. Through the window, these games have the look of political plotting: four people are suspended within a globe of thick yellow light, drawn up around a square table and concentrating intently.

I don't think kids play bridge at the lake now. But one of the first things Dave Robinson wanted his Thai wife, Pen, to learn was bridge. With Marilyn, my childhood chum, I played every kind of cards. We worked our way up from Old Maid and Fish to bridge, badgering her older sisters to teach us how to play and then to let us play with them. We hung around our parents' evening card games, peeking at their opponents' cards and sagaciously advising them on bidding until they got wise to us and shooed us away. We played cards all day and all night, on the low roof of the pavilion in front of her cottage, on our beds, on our porch swing. In between our games, we went from cottage to cottage, collecting cards from broken decks in shoe boxes. The favorite cards were oddly shaped—half the size of the standard card or twice as large, even round—or jokers with picturesque clowns, including caricatures of Hitler and Tojo. Occasionally now I'm drawn into a game of bridge, making a convenient fourth, a simpering dummy, but I appall everyone for knowing none of the conventions and for talking. I prefer Chinese checkers despite the fact that even with my classy opening maneuver, Tammy usually beats me; the drama of a journey through complex and colorful patterns is what matters.

Some card games as well as all of the word games I learned as a teenager in the Loomis cottage border on being play—Dictionary, Adverbs, Definitions, Categories. We play these games at least once a year now at our cottage, inviting people in from up and down camp. It is simple. We gather in a circle, pass out pencils, paper, and magazines to provide a writing surface. Begin. Unmarred by competition, this play does not stimulate the adrenaline; it does not generate strife. Simply silly, it encourages nonsense and engenders laughter. There are no winners, and no mistakes are possible. It is communal, collective, creative and, weak from laughing, you sleep better after such play.

Play—noun and verb—takes my time at Pinewoods. "Play," too often set in antithesis to "work," becomes regarded as not serious, not significant, not productive. It is "no sweat." Play, classified among those childish things we are taught to put away, is also associated with children. But we pity Pip, the poor and very anxious young narrator of Dickens's *Great Expectations,* who is commanded to "Play" by the imperious and aristocratic Estella, but who doesn't know how to begin. "Playing" is different from "playing at," which connotes a dilettantish dabbling, and from "playing with," which connotes manipulation. "Playing," in my mind, may connote a way of living. It allows us to luxuriate fully in being—like the lilies and like Emily Dickinson's grass: "The Grass so little has to do / I wish I were a Hay—."[70] We play games, and we play instruments and complicated musical compositions, but in playing by ear, we also allow for the unstructured, untimed, unpredictable. Growing up with play at Pinewoods, when it came time to work, we found that work could also be play.

Playing is a walk, a talk, a jog, a sail, a swim, a cleaning up, a sweeping out, a shaking down, a bike ride, a good read. It is a musing. It is a dawdling. It happens when we're not watching, but enjoying. It happens with someone else; it happens by and for myself alone. It happens when mind, imagination, senses, and body seem spun together of the same stuff. It happens when I've taken the Sunfish out in an easy wind. It dies, and I am drifting in the island's lee. Streamers of clouds reflected in ripples oiled with smoothness trail behind me. The triangular sail stretches gleaming across the water like a white manta ray. The heat becomes visible as it shimmers off the deck. The sheet is slack; there's no need to hold the tiller. I've forgotten my sunglasses, and my eyes burn like automobile cigarette lighters. My body, torpid, gradually decomposes. A curled feather floats past; the clouds become plumes. A song—Daddy's favorite, "Beautiful Dreamer"—surfaces; a breeze comes, and I find myself grabbing simultaneously for the sheet and tiller. Playing happens when you're writing an essay.

Pinewoods is my playground.

BOATS

Here is the dock. It projects perpendicularly straight out from the shore into the lake. Sections of wooden slats are raised up on sawhorses. Its uses are several: exhibition area for stones selected from the shore and shallow water, sunning space by day, stargazing space at night, meditation space, gathering space, departure point for swimming, weather post, shade for swarms of glittering minnows and schools of striped perch, safety for the increasingly elusive crayfish, in recent years a resting place for four or five black ducks. Above all, the dock serves boats and boaters.

Radiating out from it are the lines to which we tie the small boats in our fleet: canoe, putt-putt, Sunfish. But located in relationship to it are the larger boats: the hoist for *Stray Cat,* a sixteen-foot Hobie catamaran; the buoy for the *Lemon Drop,* a fifteen-foot sloop. In the past when we had gaff-rigged catboats and large sloops, Seagulls and Lightnings, these were anchored about 300 yards off the dock in deeper water, and we would have to take one of the small boats out to reach them. At other docks, hoists hold braces of jet skis or racks of speedboats, while power launches or float boats sit anchored out in front, like dogs pulling on their chains. In preparing for any boat journey on the lake, we use the dock as the launching point. Paddles, cushions, gas tank, life preservers, snorkeling apparatus, sails, daggerboard, bucket, sponges, anchors, lines, dog, beer are all heaped together on the dock and loaded one by one into the boat before setting out onto the lake.

If docks give us access to boats, boats give us access to water. On the shoreline Ishmael and "thousands upon thousands of mortal men are fixed in ocean reveries." Not only "every robust healthy boy with a robust healthy soul in him," as Melville has it, but every robust healthy girl as well is "at some time or other crazy to go to sea." A boat takes us farther out than we might go by wading or swimming into a medium so different from land: fluid, flowing, shifty, supple, transparent and, as Ishmael learns, "ungraspable."[71] A boat, whether powered by oar, sail, or motor, also invariably engages us with the medium of air, blown up into wind: we row with it or against it; we tack up into it or go wing on wing with it; we open the engine and let our hair and words fly. The shamans of indigenous peoples living on the shores of Costa Rica and Alaska admired the marvelous ease of amphibian and avian creatures such as lizards, crocodiles, and loons that move between several media. Through boats we explore multiple media; through boats our land-animal self becomes fused to fish and bird.

I learned early on that a boat transports us beyond planet Earth. It is a spaceship circling Jupiter; it is Wynken and Blynken and Nod's wooden shoe in which I sailed into sleep—"Sailed on a river of crystal light / Into a sea of dew"—as Daddy read me Eugene Field's poem until I had it by heart.[72] Through boats, I sail into the space of cosmos and dreams. In wholehearted agreement with the water-rat's matter-of-fact assertion to the mole in *The Wind in the Willows,* "Believe me, my young friend, there is *nothing*—absolutely *nothing*—half so much worth doing as simply messing about in boats,"[73] I also know that boats place us in this physical world of water and wind, wood and metal, scraped knees and broken fingers.

Boats tell the particular history of Pinewoods. Inscribed with the names of founders in Pinewoods memories and memoirs, they record our changes. In Pinewoods the first boats were canvas canoes, wooden catboats, rowboats, and sputtering gasoline launches with generous seating for a dozen; during the late 1930s sloops—particularly Lightnings, designed for racing with spinnaker rigging for the downwind course—replaced catboats, sleek powerboats built like cars with seats for two couples replaced the launches, and outboard motors replaced oars. From the 1960s, with the number of large sloops declining, big catamarans and flashy Hobie Cats began to appear. Plastic, aluminum, and fiberglass displaced canvas and wood; white sails are now dyed rainbow colors. Boats for individuals—Sunfish, Lazars, windsurfers, jet skis—supplement slow-moving party boats. The thrill of speed seems increasingly significant. Plato honored sailing as a noble activity because it encouraged "a surging motion,"[74] a commitment to progress and positivism. In recounting the history of his family's powerboats in 1987, Nick Dewey focuses, with pleasure and pride, on their increasing speed:

> Boats and the speed with which they traveled have changed dramatically. For example, my grandfather had a 16-foot 300-pound oak fishing boat, powered by a 1.1-horsepower Alto engine. Top speed must have been three miles per hour. I know it took well over an hour to get over to the sunken island to go fishing. In 1940 my father bought a modern streamlined 5-horsepower Johnson, which when placed on the back of an 80-pound Penn Yan car-top boat, produced a speed of about 17 miles per hour. Except for the DeCamp's [sic] Chris-Craft, purchased about 1939, it was clearly the fastest boat in camp until Mike Taggart got an Evinrude 9.8-horsepower engine on his boat, which was just a little bit faster than my boat. In 1949 I got a small racing boat with a Mercury engine, which packed 16 horsepower. At 30-plus miles per hour, it truly was one of the fastest boats on the lake. How times have changed![75]

Although Howie keeps oars in his new aluminum motorboat for an emergency, I've never seen them used, and nowadays one of Pinewoods's newest members is the only person at Higgins who regularly rows. But canoes, supplemented recently by kayaks, continue. Right after breakfast, the first morning after arriving at Higgins, I'm out in the canoe with Mother, paddling with purpose among the boats anchored in front of Cottage Grove to reach the shore of No Man's Land. Here we dawdle, aware of water frothing against sand, stones protruding, kingfisher streaking, bank eroding, flowers multitudinous. After lunch, I paddle out with Aunt Mary in the bow and my grandniece Hillary in the middle, learning how to dip and pull. After supper, I watch a man, seated low in the center of his canoe, switching his paddle quickly from one side to the other, making fast tracks somewhere while a Cottage Grove family paddles straight into the sunset.

Powerboats at Pinewoods appear anonymous in contrast to other boats in camp which are particularized, named, and remembered. They have genealogies. I grew up hearing about the *Mist,* one of the legendary catboats from the early years at Pinewoods. Easily winning pennants and cups in the first organized sailboat races on Higgins, the *Mist* was her owner's delight. In the 1920s when she was declared unsafe, she was brought on shore and with mourners from every cottage surrounding the pyre, given a memorable funeral. Preserving her centerboard, boom, and gaff, the owner's son, Bill Taggart, honors her memory. To replace her, he acquired *Mist II*—a Cape Hope sloop and the first keeled sailboat in camp—from the Herreshoff boat yard in Bristol, Rhode Island, in 1931. She rode high and elegant, unapproachable at her anchorage in deep water, her name, spelled out on her stern in clear letters, epitomizing the allure of sailing. Taken out of the water at last, she was escorted back to Rhode Island to become part of the Herreshoff Museum collection of champion yachts. In the 1950s, the sight of the *Mystree,* the third generation of beautiful Taggart sailboats, slicing the waves and heeling in a hard wind, could also cause me to swoon with longing. Bill Taggart keeps Pinewoods's memory of a century of catboats and of his family's nautical past alive with his spiffy wooden Cape Cod cat, *Sandpiper.* Unapologetically, he proclaims, "I love catboats."

In the early years, boats were named for places and individuals, some imaginary. The names of several Pinewoods women were bestowed on boats, which were beloved by the entire camp: among them were the launch, *Edith,* and the broad-beamed catboat, *Laura. Edith* arrived in Pinewoods in 1892. Originally a steamboat and later fitted out with a gasoline engine which, according to one account, "increased her efficiency and life,"[76] she was the first powerboat on Higgins, apart from the lumbermen's tugs. She was put to good use in fishing expeditions and in rescue missions, going regularly to the aid of sailboats in distress. With an extended tow-line of small boats, each filled with women, children, and picnic hampers, while others were seated inside along her port and starboard benches, the *Edith* could transport the entire camp to the island or Sunset Beach. The capacious *Laura*, remembered for having an iron tiller which took two to guide, could hold as many as fifteen passengers; *Laura* allowed women in their long skirts, corsets, and high-buttoned shoes the thrill of wind and water without disturbing either their composure or their coiffures. Only one woman in camp actually sailed the old catboats, however. Other women may have gone along for the breeze, but Floss Plum took the helm and managed the tiller. She is also known to have taken the precaution of always carrying a knife in case the boat capsized and she'd have to cut down the sails.

That Pinewoods's boats exist primarily for pleasure is reflected in the prevalence of humorous names, with puns predominant. One Sunfish, made by Alcort, Inc., is *Louisa May Alcort;* another, made by Phip Will from a kit, was *Ivory* ("It floats!"), but when it was bequeathed to the Higgins Lake Boat Club, the name was changed to *Free Will;* the two Sailfish which Howie and I received for Christmas one year and with which we began our sailing careers were *Miss* and *Chief.* One Rebel-class boat, jointly owned by three families, was called *Treble,* while a P-class sloop, jointly owned by four families, was called *Fourtuitous.* Lee Cochran's Rebel was the *Robilee,* and a car-top sloop was *Autopsy.* The names for the camp's float boats, those easygoing, lugubrious pontoon rafts, have come in for particular ribbing: one that takes crowds out to the edge of black water for an after-supper liqueur and sunset viewing is *The Destroyer;* another has two names, one on either hull, *Geriatica* and *Watercrate.* On a summer day our neighbors issue invitations to young and old to grab a towel and join them on their float boat, affectionately known as the *Ponta,* to go over for a swim at the drop-off between the two points.

The association of our boats with the possibilities of wind and water is suggested through other names: my grandfather's *Spray* and my mother's two Lightnings, *Flicker* and *Spindrift* (a later Lightning owned by three families was *Spendthrift*); the sloop, *Sweet Water,* the first Pinewoods sailboat with a covered cabin and sleeping quarters; the Alex Taggarts's dignified white launch, *Rainbow,* and its descendant, another Taggart sloop, the little *Raindrop;* Hank Taggart's new keel boat, *Spray II,* an unconscious tribute to my grandfather's boat. Mother and Bill Taggart, who remember all the boats of the past, recall favorite names as they might dear friends—Bill claims *Spray* and *Whitecap,* Mother, *Whim.* The *Rainbow,* named in 1919 for the bread the Taggart family gave to America, replaced the *Edith* in toting Pinewoods picnickers and swimmers about the lake, in towing as many as seven canoes over to The Cut, in carrying the distinguished Wright wedding party, in assisting with rescues. Consistently mentioned in Pinewoods memoirs with communal pride and fondness, the *Rainbow* has become known as the "Queen of Higgins Lake" and has appeared, decked in balloons, leading a parade of boats around the lake on behalf of the Higgins Lake Foundation. Although for decades she rode out all weather at anchor in front of the Big Taggart Cottage, she is now placed in a hoist by the dock. Occasionally, however, she is taken out at sunset on a slow cruise. Long and low, she moves with leisured majesty. We stand at attention at the ends of our dock when she moves by.

Boats generate stories. Because of an adventure on a boat, an entire summer becomes inscribed in memory. Ted Plum's summers were shaped by the lessons learned sailing the *Mist,* by a near disaster in the *Laura,* as well as by the tragedy of the *Pickle.* He also remembers sailing *Laura* in the evenings. "On moonlight nights, it was just beautiful." One summer, however, he and three of his gang, having sailed into the little bay and mesmerized by the moon, discovered they were becalmed. "For some little time we took turns diving off the stern to push the boat forward until we got around the point and got a little breeze."[77] And, we assume, got home again. Another summer was distinguished for George Harman by another moonlight sail. Out in the *Don Lee* with his sister and her friends, they "were about half a mile west of the island [when] the moon disappeared, and white caps came in from the Northwest. We came about and thought to head for home when a pin in the rudder jammed. We dropped our sail and were washed toward the island. . . . We came ashore on the rocky west side, jumped out, and pulled the boat around to the lea [*sic*] of the island."[78] George flashed SOS with his flashlight, and eventually his father and two other Pinewoods men arrived in the camp's fastest outboard. To George's disgrace, he was sent back to camp with the girls.

Recently, Bill Taggart came to call on Mother just to share his memory of the day of the line squall with her. She remembered it, too. She was out with her father in *The Little Green Boat,* the family's first sailboat and the boat in which she had been taught to sail. Down by Cold Springs, at the west end of the lake, they saw the squall approaching fast, rendering sky and water opaque. Called "Hawk" Shaw because of his quick eye and mind, my grandfather knew what to do: he assigned Mother the tiller while he hauled down all sails, securing them tight about the boom. With the wind roaring behind them, they then sailed "barepole," as Bill heard my grandfather later describe the experience, past all three camps and straight down to Sulphur Springs, well beyond Pinewoods. On the way, they rushed past Bill, standing at his dock with his own motorboat turned turtle. He laughed to see them as they sped by. Both Mother and Bill remember 1930 as the summer the *Spray* was condemned with dry rot. Towed out to the edge of black water one evening and filled with rocks, she was set ablaze. She burned through the night. As the Taggarts keep relics from the *Mist*, the *Spray*'s traveler continues to serve as a towel rack in our pumphouse, and the bold brass letters of her name, which once arched across her stern, remain tacked up in Howie and Tammy's bedroom.

Boats shape my mother's life. She not only knows them by name and remembers their stories, she also muses over them and ministers to them. She describes the boats that the Shaw family acquired with the purchase of the Stanley cottage in 1914 as "the most thrilling accessory."[79] There were three: the *Spray*, a three-horsepower Evinrude, and an eighteen-foot green canvas canoe, with overlapping brass hearts on stern and bow, which could transport a dozen little girls in white dresses. In time, Mother mastered the sailboat and the canoe, but not the outboard. The first in camp, it could be started only by her father, and then only after a few carefully chosen cuss words. Mother learned the special language of ships and sailing—a language designed not to mystify landsmen but to safeguard sailors (and their cargo), who in dangerous seas must be able to give specific directions. She insists on the differences between rope and line, standing and running rigging, halyard, sheet, and painter; she takes pleasure in recognizing the differences, but she also knows that life and death may lie in that recognition. Mother learned not only a diversity of knots but also taught herself splicing. On windless afternoons, she sat in the sun in front of the pumphouse using her father's awl and sailor's palm. Over and over, she meticulously intertwined the strands of rope together to create the eye-splice, the short splice, the long splice to turn lines into loops and to make old lines last longer. Not perfect, she pulled the strands apart and started again. She keeps the ends of clothesline from fraying by whipping them neatly and sends me packages in Kansas tied in twine with precision square knots and sheep-shanks.

Mother keeps things shipshape, a habit reinforced at nursing school, where she learned the expression, "A place for everything, and everything in its place." She loves the wildness of the woods, but delights in the order of boats, houses, and lives. Home from sailing, the boat is put to bed, with everything in place: halyards snug, jib sheets coiled, sails stashed, centerboard raised, bilge bailed, anchor line secure. In need of a pair of scissors, a stamp, a serrated knife, I can always find them in my mother's house. A boat neglected—rigging slack and slapping, sails bedraggled and mildewed, oars not shipped, but left dangling in the oarlocks—is a shame and a sin. Above all, Mother learned to skipper, to guide, to control, to direct. She feels less comfortable as crew. She sets her courses straight and clear, with the well-being of her ship and crew a central concern. As her balky crew and daughter, I have only now perceived this to be her course.

Boats demand Periclean morality: doing the right thing at the right time. Even now Mother wonders if she made the right decision one afternoon when heeling along on her Sunfish in the green water in front of No Man's Land, she caught a glimpse between boom and lee of Sue Bennett capsizing. Repeatedly Sue tried and failed to right her small boat. Each time the sail sprang dripping up out of the water, the wind caught it up and threw the boat back down. Sailing over to her, Mother shouted encouragement and advice: "Hold on to the bow and swim it up into the wind." And most important: "Don't leave the boat! Hang on!" Could Sue hear her through the wind and her panic? Then she watched as Sue's boat turned upside down, the mast and sail underneath the hull. Mother came about and debated if she should leave her own boat to help Sue. Would she be able to swim to her? If she went under, no one would be helped. Even if she got to Sue, she couldn't right the upside-down boat. And in the meantime, her own Sunfish would have careened over the horizon and with it all means for getting help. She called again, "Stay on the boat! I'll get help. Sing!" The best option, she decided, was to sail directly for Cottage Grove motorboat aid. Sue was rescued, but Mother still worries about the pale girl, shivering and sprawled over the upside-down hull of her drifting boat.

From boats come the moral principle that invigorates my mother's life: freedom follows care. In all matters, she balances an appreciation of liberation with a knowledge of limitations. If the wind is right, she is on the dock. For several years she has suffered from bouts of skin cancer, especially on her hands and face, those areas exposed to the brilliantly piercing sun of Higgins for eighty years. Now she slathers sunblock on nose, cheeks, and forehead, and smears zinc ointment on her lips. She dons sunglasses, one of Howie's cast-off, long-sleeved shirts, a pair of Bermuda shorts, a sweater with darned elbows, her life preserver, a Budweiser cap, fished from the lake and taken from a row of caps hanging in the pumphouse. She carries mast, sail, booms in one trip to the end of the dock; daggerboard, sheet, cushion in another. She lowers herself down into the water to rig the Sunfish. Doing it methodically, stepping the mast, hoisting the sail, cleating down the halyard, inserting the daggerboard, dropping the rudder, clipping the sheet to the rudder, stringing it next through the blocks on the boom and into the chock on the aft deck. She stands holding the bow, gauging the wind. In a moment, she disengages the painter, places the cushion on the windward edge. She is off, then, to the far horizon. She is past ninety. She sails alone this afternoon. Had you happened by when she was rigging the boat, though, she would have invited you along. Alone or shared, sailing's the thing for orchestrating water, wind, and self.

"READING"

Thoreau writes, "Books, the oldest and best, stand naturally and rightfully on the shelves of every cottage," [80] and so they do in Pinewoods. Bookcases are built into the living rooms of most Pinewoods cottages. Along with the fireplace, which dominates cottage living rooms, they are the only fixed features. Often flanking the fireplace, these bookcases indicate that our forefathers and foremothers placed the heat and light generated by books as well as by fire at the center of their lives.

The books placed there, however, are not necessarily "the oldest and best" by Thoreauvian standards, which set Greek and Asian classics at the pinnacle. I suspect that instead Shakespeare's complete plays are in most cottages, remnants from earlier summers when a particular drama was chosen for the season's communal entertainment, when it was possible to count on the full *dramatis personae* remaining in camp for the time necessary to complete the reading of the given drama in its entirety. Our cottage also comes with complete sets of Balzac (in translation), Dickens, and Irving. One might suppose with these volumes connoting an international sophistication, in their fine leather bindings and marbled paper endpieces, that they were all for living-room show. But taking the volumes in my hands now, I don't think so. The pages have all been cut, and some jaggedly as if they were page-turners, and the eager reader ripped the pages open with the handiest screwdriver. The spines have pretty much all been broken, and any number of pages are imprinted with vestiges of the reader—a marginal check, an underlined phrase, a brown smear which a forensics analysis could distinguish as coffee or blood from intense engagement with a mosquito. A bit of the bug itself also appears like unraveling print. Certain of the Dickens volumes, those that Daddy took every summer to the pavilion swing after lunch, have sprung out of their boards despite his attempt to hold them together, as the addition of masking tape to their bindings testifies. Only during the summer was there time to read *Bleak House* or *History of the Life and Voyages of Christopher Columbus* nonstop, let alone consider going on to *Our Mutual Friend* or *The Alhambra*.

Then the shelves are filled with assorted novels, for which Thoreau had as much contempt as he had for newspapers. Here are novels by Elizabeth Stuart Phelps and Helen Hunt Jackson, whom feminist literary critics have recently resurrected; by Gertrude Atherton, a popular novelist early in the twentieth century whom the contemporary critics have yet to review; by Edith Wharton, Willa Cather, and Edna Ferber. Was all this women's fiction considered light summer reading? On the flyleaf of each book is the signature of either my grandmother or my grandfather, in fading ink, but in both instances still bold and clear. Their signatures as much as the texts of these books they imported to the lake challenge interpretation. Beneath the "Howard L. Shaw," swooping in the confidence of his ownership of the book and the culture it bestowed, is usually the date when he finished reading it and a commentary. Of Cather's *One of Ours*, which he read in the summer of 1922, the year it won the Pulitzer Prize, he wrote, "What a waste!" Was he commenting on the book itself, or was he referring to the loss of the young, idealistic protagonist's life, or could he have been exclaiming about the Great War itself, the central event in Cather's novel and in the lives of my grandfather's contemporaries? Reading the books they read, I grow better acquainted with the aspirations and wisdom of Kirty Eddy and Howard Shaw, who formed the core collection in the cottage library.

Diverse interests have contributed to the cottage library. There's a reference section which started with a Webster's and an Atlas, their etymologies and typographies still current despite the changing boundaries of language and nations. The library also reflects our panic in the face of diminishing natural species. With an awareness of the loss of birds and wildflowers at Higgins, we started accumulating field guides in the 1930s. Our yearning to know these species grew as we studied words and pictures; it was almost as if we hoped that through such symbols we might prevent the fringed gentian and the black-billed cuckoo from vanishing, and consequently we've continued to incorporate titles into the cottage library, recently adding volumes on snakes, mushrooms, and animal tracks and spoors. Daddy's books from his Yale forestry program and his mystery writers—Eric Ambler and Ellery Queen—are alongside Mother's on small-craft sailing and her nature writers—Edwin Teale and Rachel Carson. I've contributed contemporary women writers—Marge Piercy's *Gone to Soldiers* and Amy Tan's *The Kitchen God's Wife*—to the shelves. The shelves are open, and we borrow from the cottages to the left and right of us, and they from us.

I think I learned to read in summers at Pinewoods. Although I remember certain reading experiences in Flint, school often got in the way of reading. The good things about being sick in Flint were the radio and reading; lying in bed, you had enough time to populate an alternative landscape. But at the lake I didn't have to be sick to read. My reading picked up speed with the discovery of romance novels on the shelves by the fireplace with Mother's girlish signature on their flyleaves—*The Prisoner of Zenda* and *The Scarlet Pimpernel*. The dining hall bell and Mother's calls—"Come out into the sunshine! Come play tennis! Do something useful! Sweep the porch!"—were the only disturbances to my obsessive immersion. If I heard Mother at all, I retreated further into the swirling, dark worlds of romance.

At Pinewoods in the summer, time and space are reconfigured by the illusion that both are endless. As an apparently alternative world itself, therefore, it's not surprising that it nourishes the alternative worlds you discover in books. You take a book and stake out a place: your own local habitation. On overcast and rainy days and at night, you are inside the cottage in one of the nearly sprung chairs around the fireplace, prone on the living room couch, or in bed propped up on pillows. But on warm days, after morning chores and into the afternoon, you have your choice of the pavilion, the lower deck, the concrete breakwater in front of the pumphouse, or the dock. When I found an anthology of *The World's Great Ghost Stories* on the cottage shelves when I was somewhere between eight and nine, I went up to Aunt Betty's room, closed the door, and lay on my stomach across her bed with the big book out in front of me. Isolating myself from the hubbub of the cottage, I was consciously conjuring up an appropriately scary atmosphere, in addition to communing with my elegant and mysterious aunt. Long before I read *The Divine Comedy,* I appreciated having a guide, and I knew that with her as company, I could enter these alien realms. I don't think I knew what I was getting in for. But I read compulsively on and on, mesmerized by "The Pit and the Pendulum" and "The Tell-Tale Heart," my body atrophied, my imagination palpitating. That long-ago session also introduced me to "The Yellow Wallpaper." I had never forgotten the horror of the animated wallpaper, the creeping women who came to life behind it, and the narrator's confinement, but in 1973 when I again read Charlotte Perkins Gilman's story, reissued by the Feminist Press, I was astonished to realize the full depths of its horror: the Gothic ghost story was also a powerful analysis of the effects of patriarchal oppression.

For the reading of *The Diary of Anne Frank* and *Three Came Home* when I was eleven or twelve, I chose the canvas swing on the lower deck. Midway between the upper pavilion at the top of the bank and the pumphouse on the beach, the lower deck, off the steps on the way down to the lake, has the advantage of being both private and public. With no roof, the deck is open to passing gulls and dropping pinecones, but a canvas cover over the small swing in the corner provided the necessary seclusion. I must have felt that these books, related to the war just over, would be even more terrifying than the ghost stories and that I needed company coming to sit on the deck to assure me of the reality of Pinewoods. At thirteen or fourteen *Gone With the Wind* kept me occupied for days, mostly stretched out on a towel on the dock so that I could simultaneously be working on a tan. The only problem with this strategy, however, was that while the backside would become inflamed, the front side, to my disgust, remained white as the driven snow. But it didn't trouble me enough to change my position. The waves pounded beneath the dock as Richmond burned, and the rest of the family walked over me as Rhett attempted to seduce Scarlett. The chosen place of late is the pumphouse on the shore where it's possible to keep an ear cocked to the sound of water and words simultaneously, to look out to the sun polishing the water and in to the shaded words.

Up and down the camp many people read; I wade over from our dock to a friend sitting in a deck chair on her dock to ask her if she's finished A. S. Byatt's *Possession*, drop in on another cottage to discuss Ivan Doig's works and William Least-Heat Moon's *PrairyErth*. Pinewoods is where busy people bring the books they've been saving to read through the year. During graduate school, newly conscious of myself as doing literature and anxious in the doing, Pinewoods people helped me read better. At a pavilion cocktail party, one elder barked with derision when I gave him the latest literary theory on Hemingway. Stunned to silence by his response then, I've realized since the value of simply saying what I like in a book, rather than translating its meaning or leaning on a theory. If some questioned, others listened. Arriving at Pinewoods immediately after my dissertation defense, Aunt Adelaide asked me to visit her to talk Henry James in the "Grumpus Room." "Isn't James just the most insightful writer? Does anyone else see the need for a moral imagination quite so well, quite so clearly?" Her interest identified for me a community of readers beyond the university and beyond Pinewoods, and her caring questions gave me membership.

I keep on reading at Pinewoods, even when most of my family members walk around me. Mother reads, and it's a deep and quiet pleasure when the two of us share the same lamp light in the cottage living room of an evening, she with *Time* or one of her environmental magazines in the black rocker and I in the blue chair with a novel brought from Kansas which I must get read in time for fall classes. In contrast to my younger days, now when I'm reading in the living room alone or out on the pavilion and someone comes by, I'm glad to put the book aside. I confess that in doing so, I am hoping for someone to ask me what I'm reading and tell me, in turn, what she's been reading. Pinewoods nurtured my eagerness for books and for book talk, for opportunities to go on finding connections to other worlds. Nesting in this place, I discovered that books gave me sumptuous wings with which to fly to other places.

"A Perfect Day at Higgins Lake"
By Beth Schultz
Eighth Grade, Third Hour
Whittier Junior High School, Flint, Michigan

The sun has reached its Zeneth [*sic*] over Higgins. Dust seems to cover the ground and the air is stifling and almost suffocating. The stately pines even look as though they might falter under the heat and the birds' merrymaking is subdued. All is still, no ripple breaks the sky's looking glass.

A seagull screams, ripping the silence apart and with all the fury of a witches [*sic*] wrath, the storm crashes through. Giant drops of water hit with tremendous force, shattering the calm of Higgins Lake. Then with the same abruptness, the wild rampage ceases and a dazzling rainbow peeps out from behind a cloud to brighten the day.

Once again peace is the supreme master of Higgins Lake. A lone sail is seen drifting with the soothing and wafting breeze. The contented buzz of misquitos [*sic*] mingles with the lapping of gentle waves upon a shore of golden sand. A rustle is heard high in the treetops, as a mother squirrel settles her wee ones for a long night's rest. Just as a solitary star begins to twinkle in the gathering dusk, the sun sinks behind a gilded curtain, ending another perfect day at Higgins Lake.

Right at the beginning of *Walden,* Thoreau spells out his expectations of other writers, thereby implicitly laying on himself identical expectations: "I, on my side, require of every writer, first or last, a simple and sincere account of his own life, . . . some such account as he would send to his kindred from a distant land."[81] My eighth-grade account of "a perfect day at Higgins Lake" seems simple enough, but its clichés, demonstrating the curse of early literary self-consciousness, challenge sincerity. I wonder, Henry David, my kindred now in a distant land, how you would judge the simplicity and sincerity of this present account. I wonder to what degree that "Little Bit of Heaven" alluded to on the long-ago Christmas card and tacked up in our living room, Grandma Bruske's paradisial vision of ties "sweet and enduring," my childhood conception of "a perfect day," and perhaps this account are all projections of nostalgia and dreams of the idealized summer and the happy community—too simple, more sentimental than sincere. Having struggled to describe Pinewoods perfectly since the eighth grade, I appreciate Thoreau's standards. Yet I find Pinewoods inhibits final definition. The most familiar perspective of the lake from the pavilion continues to change, and only change is familiar. As with writing, I say simply and sincerely that seeing the lake, the trees, and the community has become all process and discovery.

During those few days, weeks, months when we are at the lake, some of us also write to kindred and friends, and given the differences between the paths and bells at Pinewoods and those in our workaday lives, we write as if from a distant land and a distant time. Part of the summertime convention is the "Having-Wonderful-Time-Wish-You-Were-Here" postcard, which may be simple, but rarely sincere. When The Store was part of the dining hall, a rack held postcards with black-and-white photos of each cottage and of generic camp scenes—the busy beach, pines silhouetted against a setting sun, a Lightning under full sail—which could be purchased for a nickel apiece. At Au Sable Drugs in Roscommon as at Evergreen Stop 'n' Shop, it's possible to choose from a variety of postals. As a kid, I was especially intrigued by those cards in the drugstore with headings such as "Weather," "Scenery," "Company," "Food," and evaluative characteristics listed beneath them, ranging from "super" to "lousy," which the writer could check to describe in an instant the quality of the vacation. The possibility of actually sorting out my responses to the summer and then the possibility of manipulating them to evoke admiration or sympathy in my correspondent clued me in to the power of the chosen word.

Phones in every cottage—and increasingly computers—make it fast and easy to maintain connections with the world during the summer. People outside of Pinewoods—at the Grayling Hospital Emergency Room, the Traverse City Airport, the Roscommon Cinema, the Interlochen Symphony, the Stratford Shakespeare Festival, and all our relatives who are carrying on with their lives beyond Higgins Lake or who may be trying to get to the lake for their annual visit—are a call away. Those who stay at the lake for any period of time, however, write letters. In the late twentieth century when phone calls, greeting cards, and e-mail have supplanted written correspondence as the means for maintaining connections, at Pinewoods, these speedier methods of communication are either unavailable or inconvenient. Instead, the habit of writing letters continues here, as does, I think, the desire to report to others from the distant land of Pinewoods. To outsiders, our natural and communal state may seem exotic, but to kindred, news from the lake arrives as tonic. In the hot soup of a Kansas summer, I breathe deeper reading in Mother's letter that the dining hall is full and that Jeff Harman's family has come from Hawaii; that "Hat Night" was zanier than ever and that negotiations with Cottage Grove regarding our land purchase continue; that Howie's Hobie Cat survived a storm and that the lake's water quality has not further deteriorated; that we have an abundance of acorns and a corresponding abundance of black squirrels.

At Pinewoods, there is still leisure for letters. In the southwest corner of the living room close to both fireplace and bookshelves is Mother's desk where she keeps her stationery, printed with our Pinewoods address, and the small red suitcase I traveled to the lake with as a child, now recycled as her briefcase. Unvarnished pine, with no drawers and only a few cubby holes for postcards, bills, pens, and pencils, this desk is not much more than a small table, but as much as the helm of her Lightning ever was, it is Mother's place. Daddy, who sent long letters from the lake, did his writing out on the pavilion, and I retreat to my desk upstairs when the cottage is in full swing or use the dining table in the nook off the living room when no one's about. I see Mother sitting at her desk early in the morning, first thing after breakfast, or sometimes late at night, the little wall light above the desk a dim glow. I see only her back, bent to her task. She may be making lists, the most obvious means by which she orders her life, or paying bills, for she has always assumed the costs of maintaining the cottage, but most likely she is writing a letter—to Shirley in Flint, Lucy in Chicago, Blanche in Tennessee, the Department of Natural Resources in Lansing, the directors of the Higgins Lake Foundation. She writes with simplicity and sincerity.

Finished, she stacks the letters near the back door in the kitchen. They will then be taken by anyone heading into town or out to the mailboxes. Usually, it's the latter. Because the letters we write and the letters we receive—not to mention the magazines, newspapers, and junk mail—are a lifeline, a link, to the lives we left behind when we arrived for our summer sojourn, mail going out and coming in is handled with respect. The delivery of the mail, as much as the dining hall bells, structures our days. No matter what kind of news it may bring, we await it for reassurance that we are not in a land too far distant. In the camp's early days, mail was delivered sporadically, by drivers of the horse-drawn rigs that campers hired to bring them from Roscommon out to the lake. But I also remember when each cottage had a path out to the Stage Road behind the camp with a mailbox on a post at the end. Frank, assigned the rural route around Higgins, delivered the mail then, giving several blasts on his Chevy's horn as he came through camp. When I had sent out several letters with SWAK ("Sealed With A Kiss") written across the envelope flaps with a sense of delicious conspiracy and raised the red flag on our mailbox as a sign of faith that letters similarly sealed would be returned, I used to wait with longing for the sound of his horn.

In those days Daddy was also a mail courier, arriving at the cottage late Friday after a full day's work in Flint with the week's accumulated mail. I see now how little I appreciated his long week at the office and his long trip through the night on narrow two-lane highways, crowded with holiday-seekers going north, for as soon as the obligatory hugs were out of the way, I demanded the mail. Plundering his suitcase, mad for the new issues of *The Saturday Evening Post* and *Life,* I spread them out on the living room floor while Mother went to get him a beer, and he lay back on the couch, his eyes closed, his legs straight out. Later, when I had scanned all of the *Post*'s cartoons and was engrossed in reading *Life*'s version of a Hollywood scandal, which I had to know about, I would be vaguely conscious of Mother saying that they were going down to the dock to look at the stars.

Now Howie brings Mother's Flint mail up to her, and because the county has designated the Stage Road as private, the camp mailboxes are set up collectively at the entrance to Pinewoods in two rows, like coconuts in a carnival shooting gallery. Today's mail is picked up and delivered silently and anonymously. But for those who stay in camp longer than a weekend, it continues to structure the day. Whether or not the mail has come by lunchtime is usually a subject of discussion in the dining hall. Given that the paper from the city is bound to be one day late in reaching Roscommon, it is imperative to have the mail before supper. Never mind that, as Thoreau suggests, "the first news that will leak through into the broad, flapping American ear will be that the Princess Adelaide has the whooping cough."[82] Being at the opposite end of camp from the entrance, we often collect the mail for our neighbors on either side as they do for us; someone goes, unasked, undesignated, and returns to distribute the mail to others. Of all the paths in the woods, the one leading to the stand of new mailboxes is most worn.

Taking up residency in grandmother's bedroom, I installed the small leaf-drop desk from her Bay City house in a corner of the room. At the desk, all morning or all afternoon, no one knows I'm in the cottage. Invisible, yet here in this chair with paper before me on the desk, I can feel suspended in the very center of the cottage. In Japanese the ideograph for writing, drawing, painting is the same; once all done with a brush, the process of putting marks on paper still involves the transformation of interior vision to outer signs. Putting pen to paper in my place here, I realize I can re-create the path, the pavilion, the shoreline—all those places of perception. At this desk I've pursued a diversity of writing projects, none associated with Pinewoods. I've corrected graduate students' dissertation chapters, reviewed scholarly articles, translated Shiga Naoya's "Bugs and Bees," revised my own manuscripts, and written poems.

Before I had the desk, I did other kinds of writing at the lake. As children, Marilyn and I drew up secret plans and devised hilarious messages, which we sent over our cottage roofs and through the trees to each other in a matchbox. My teenage friend, Esther Greenleaf, and I started *Pine Smoke,* a camp newspaper. Typing it ourselves in two columns with multiple carbon copies, we reported on "the Glorious Fourth" ("the best Higgins fireworks we can remember"), "the road situation" ("Could we continue to receive federal mail on a private road?"), slumber parties and canoe trips down The Cut, musical and sporting events, camp characters and quaint quips. Over three summers we must have written and produced a dozen issues, with the big news always being our own delight in all Pinewoods events. Of course, in featuring our siblings, parents, neighbors, and rivals, we made ourselves the heroines of our own narratives. Esther also wrote dramas, which she and I directed and in which the whole BOA gang starred, staging them in the garage in back of our cottage. We tickled ourselves silly before the Pinewoods public. It was as if we couldn't get enough of ourselves and our discovery of words. The current Pinewoods newsletter, *Pinewords,* connects us through the winter and has a rotating editorship.

The summer after my senior year in college, where the only praise I'd received was for using words well, I came to the lake to try to write. I sat at Mother's desk in the living room and on the pavilion swing, but no words worked. I wrote sentence and phrase, sentence and phrase, and crossed them out again and again, leaving indentations in Mother's blotter. I had heard of "writer's block" and of Flaubert spending a day seeking the perfect word. I set about looking. I took my pad and pencil down to the seclusion of the pumphouse in early morning before anyone started fussing with boats. Here the lap-lap-lapping of the lake against the shore was like the drip-drip-dripping of the water off the roof. I went out to the clearing by the tennis court in late afternoon when all players had become swimmers and sailors. Here with gnats and no-see-'ems swirling around me, the pad became a swatter. After supper, I paddled out to the raft. I tied up the canoe, washed off the gull gunk with the old broom that was always kept under the diving board, and tried to write. A calm evening with the raft pounding gently on the waves, water sloshing and gurgling underneath. Although the gulls stayed away, their residual smell was overwhelming. But just as I realized I'd never be Flaubert and should head back to the dock, I found a word: "wafer." It described the white quarter moon coming into being in the pale blue eastern sky. I would take it and pocket it. This word stays with me, part of the process and discovery, simple and sincere.

ROMANCE

The Evergreen Park Stop 'n' Shop is on the blacktop just beyond Lakeside. It was the frequent destination of my nieces before they could drive, in mid-afternoon when they'd had enough of lying out on the dock. Reading wasn't under consideration. They would set out walking, wearing their bathing suits, with loose shirts flapping about their thighs concealing and revealing their emerging young curves. A bag of chips or ice-cream on a stick, unavailable at the dining hall, was the stated goal, but given Evergreen's halfway position between the seclusion of the camps and the traffic of the great world, there was always the possibility that a guy from the nearby

B&B Boatyard or from a far more outlandish place might be dropping into the store. Limited to two aisles, several display racks, and an enormous freezer, Evergreen manages to sell necessities and amenities for the road as well as all the stuff the resorter might have forgotten at home or realized a sudden craving for. It also perpetuates the dream vacation and does its bit for tourism on the north side of Higgins by selling postcards with photographs of the cute raccoon or the noble buck, an Ozark outhouse captioned, "There's no place like home," or a buxom bathing beauty proclaiming, "C'mon in! The water's fine!" There is a table laden with T-shirts in vibrant colors depicting tilting sailboats or the moon shining down on cattails at the shoreline (though there are none yet on Higgins's shores). I can imagine Evergreen also selling bumper stickers making the case that "Higgins is for Lovers."

Summer warms hormones. On a windless, hot Sunday afternoon in August, the lake is littered with pulsating young bodies—sunning on towels at the end of every dock, sprawled on the back of powerboats, drifting about in inner tubes. With a Chris-Craft's great roar and rush, one of these bodies rises up suddenly from the lake's placid water, like the shining sword Excalibur, to career about miraculously on a single ski. The flesh is greased to tan or to resist tanning. The redolence of coconut oil suggests Maui rather than Michigan. Bathing trunks bulge; bikini bras overflow. Water runs in rivulets among the hairs of male chests and arms and legs; it runs in glistening beads off hairless female arms and legs. In close encounters out of water, bodies stick together; in close encounters underwater, they slide together. Sounds of elastic being snapped, of backs being slapped, of erratic splashing jostle the heat.

The cool of an August evening at Higgins does not diminish the body heat that has been mounting through the day. Despite the attempt to look cool, to wear the most "in" blouse, the most outre shirt, the contrast between the cloth and the supple flesh at shoulder, neck, knee only accentuates the glowing flesh. Unseen sweat forms in the creases beneath scrotum and breast. The whites of teeth and eyes flash. At the Pinewoods dining hall, under the eyes of parents and neighbors, it's possible for young lovers to prattle glibly, to move place mats about in order to sit at the same table. After dinner, the gang gathers in a cottage living room, on a pavilion, on a float boat, at the movies in Roscommon. But as night deepens and flirtation is transformed into urgency, couples drift away into their own dark spaces.

We simmer through our teenage summers. Cooling off on those hot, still nights, we go out to the end of the dock to sit separately, pondering shadows black on the gleaming black surface of the lake, lights from the opposite shore, stars above. Cooling off on those nights, we wade into the lake or paddle out to a raft to skinny-dip. To take off your suit and flip it up on an anchored boat is to feel the weight of former definitions lifted. To have shamanistic powers to convert from human to fish, to leave earth and air for water. Swimming naked in the night with your lover, you both become silvery trouts; you glide over and under one another, turning, spiraling, liquefying. You return to the cottage to continue this conversion into dreams.

Pinewoods—place of cathedral pines, place of intimate family and friends, place of romantic memory—has been the site of several weddings. Aunt Louise is allotted an entire section in the 1928–29 Pinewoods history to describe "Betty Wright's Wedding, Aug. 24, 1921," "the prettiest and most unusual event in the history of Pinewoods":

> On that perfect August morning . . . the guests assembled in one of "God's First Temples," the wooded ground . . . where a broad path led up from the lake to a natural altar among the pines. Down the lake from [a] dock at the west end of camp came the bridal launch, our old friend the "Rainbow" draped in glistening white and garlanded in green, bearing its cargo of beauty. . . . All waited breathlessly until the first strains of the bridal chorus were wafted up from the shore below, and up the path came the sweetly impressive procession.
>
> First were the ushers, our ten big boys . . . who made way for the [twelve] girls. . . . [who] came singing the bridal song written for the occasion, accompanied by the flute . . . and by the forest birds; and carrying the cedar garlands to form the aisle for the bridal party. . . . as the singing ceased, and the little Bruske organ . . . pealed forth the Mendelssohn wedding march, . . . the lovely bride [appeared] in her summery dress of white georgette and simple white hat, bearing a sheaf of rare summer flowers.

Years later, some of the "singing girls" still remembered the bridal chorus, sung to a tune from *Carmen:*

Stately pines in majesty

Pointing upward to the sky,

Swaying, softly whisper in the breezes gently blowing,

While the waves and ripples bright

Sparkle in the morning light,

While the sun's warm rays unite our hearts with love o'erflowing.

Surely naught but love and joy the future may betide;

Earth and heaven shower blessings upon our charming bride.[83]

The fabled marriage of Betty Wright did not endure, and others, believing in the promises of her bridal chorus and choosing Higgins as the site for their marriage, also failed. Yet the lake's pure waters, the pines eternal green, Pinewoods's sense of continuing community go on prompting matrimony in pavilions, on the shore, on cottage porches, in Cottage Grove's Dell—a rolling green sward cleared in the woods and equipped with electronic sound.

When I returned to Pinewoods after Japan, I brought my lovers to the lake just as both my mother and my brother brought their newly wedded spouses to Higgins for their honeymoons, as my nieces have subjected their future husbands to the cottage during their courtships. To share the lake, the woods, the path, the pines, the cottage or, most seductive and treacherous of all, Pinewoods itself—the camp in full swing in mid-summer—is to share what seems most special in our lives. It is also a risk and a test for romance, for it exposes the claustrophobia of this dearly beloved place to outsiders even as it demands that they endorse it wholeheartedly. It did not enhance my own romances.

For honeymooners the test is perilous, for the marriage has already occurred when the newcomer is introduced to the lake. In bringing Daddy to the cottage out-of-season in October, however, perhaps Mother faced a lower risk. Or perhaps she knew that alone in camp, without pressure from the primal heat of summer, he could better learn to love her and Pinewoods. I see them in a canoe, he at the stern, she at the bow, their paddles dipping in unison; they glide over the lake's sateen surface, the V of their emerging wake reflected overhead by the V of Canada geese flying. Howie and Tammy come up to Higgins in all seasons, often with friends or grandchildren, and always with a menagerie of dogs and cats. They've ritualized their days in Pinewoods comfortably and companionably—they rise often at dawn and, with the new outboard, motor across the lake to the quiet of the island harbor for the sunrise; Howie swims when they return, and Tammy makes coffee in the kitchen; they walk the dog together after breakfast and again after lunch; they tend to separate for diverse tasks and pleasures through the morning and afternoon; in their downstairs bedroom they keep a radio or CD player turned on low to Willie Nelson or Elton John; in the evening friends arrive for beer and long conversations in the living room or out on the pavilion; at night they pile into their double bed with an assortment of pets.

I mention to Howie over the phone that "romance" is the subject of the Pinewoods essay I'm currently writing. His instant response is, "Don't forget about the suckers!" He describes them for me: visible in the shallow water by shore in the late spring, pale green and tan, with a dark stripe going their length; if they would lie still, they'd blend with the rippled lake bottom. But they can't. Their writhing and gyrating so agitates the lake surface they just about stir up a geyser. Several smaller males cluster around a larger female, and all together they dance like whirling water dervishes. The faster they dance, the more likely this annual ritual of romance—of swirling a depression in the sand where the female may deposit her eggs and the male may fertilize them—will reach its frenzied culmination. With blessings from us all, who go on remembering and endorsing romance.

ADULTS

The gangs of children at Pinewoods all implicitly hang out signs saying, "No Adults Allowed," whether they have clubhouses or not. I think this was so for my mother's HC Club, even though they had to have chaperons for their 'round-the-lake canoeing ventures. I know it was so for the BOA Club. After recognizing that adults held absolute authority in certain regards—

they granted permission, they set rules, they had money, they had some kinds of information and knew how to do some kinds of things—we could ignore them. They were the "groanups." We kids lived in communal solipsism. We acknowledged adults, but went right ahead and planned our days according to our own designs and desires, defined by impulse, a shift in the weather, the chance discovery of a photograph album. We listened only to ourselves and found ourselves endlessly entertaining. Watching Pinewoods gangs now, I see all of us: sequestered together on a cottage porch, flocking together into the dining hall, racing pell-mell together down the path. Gangs of Pinewoods children move within a bright intensity beyond which adults lead their own irrelevant lives.

The language and the laughter of that bright enclosed space was quite enough for me for several years. Yet even then, conscious of being able to discriminate among adults, I sensed other possibilities on the periphery. My parents, of course, existed in a specific category unto themselves, but then so did the parents of the other kids in the gang. In addition, there were families with extended networks of aunts and uncles and cousins—so unlike my own small family—not to mention the whole Taggart tribe with their collection of six cottages. Beyond the complacency of the gang's collective ego, in a category different from that of my parents, were my grandmother and my aunt.

Their arrival at the cottage was an event, their coming an annual miracle. It was prepared for with the opening of the two front bedrooms upstairs and all the windows across the front of the cottage on the second story, a making of the beds and a shaking of the rugs off the porch outside grandma's bedroom. Knowing they would drive up from Bay City in Aunt Betty's Pontiac after lunch and arrive in mid-afternoon, all morning I had the faith of a true believer and kept close to the cottage waiting for their arrival. About the time I'd given up, put on my suit, and gone down to the dock to get ready to go out to the raft, they came. Mother, waiting in the pavilion, heard the neighbor dogs barking when the car pulled in behind the cottage and called down to me, and forgetting how pine needles stabbed wet feet and how back woods shadows chilled wet suits, I ran to meet them. My lady grandmother with her white-laced shoes and her white hair knotted and piled high, all smiles; my stylish aunt with her elegantly tailored slacks and sunglasses casually pushed on top of her head, frowning slightly. All four doors of the big car and the door of the trunk stood open with suitcases, garment bags, baskets, and boxes piled up to be carried into the cottage. Their coming—predicted, expected, anticipated—was both necessary and surprising: necessary because they gave our small family the resonance of ritual, surprising to me because they extended my personal sense of the possible. They never stayed for long, but during our time together the air in the cottage quickened.

From year to year I'd forget how much I needed my grandmother to fill the blue bowl in the cottage with red cherries and place it on the long front windowsill in the living room, but in my own house now every summer I wait for cherries in the Kansas supermarket to place in a blue bowl on my coffee table. At the cottage my grandmother always appeared girdled in, wearing a dress, with a lovely brooch at the collar, and the palest of nylon stockings. She claimed the front porch, set back from the lake, the path, and the pavilion, deeply shadowed by the cottage and the oaks around it. Although she may have taken a parasol to sit on the lower pavilion, I don't remember her ever wading, swimming, canoeing, sailing. I remember her sitting: sitting in the tall rocking chair in the living room, sitting in the swing on the front porch, sitting on the bench in front of the cottage. Often she was sitting and sewing, the big cookie tin with its wooden darning eggs, silver thimbles, and spools of silk threads in a rainbow of colors beside her for company. She mended the curtains, the dish towels, her slips, my shorts with stitches as invisible as spider tracks. Mother continues with the cottage's mending, the familiar cookie tin by her side.

In the kitchen my grandmother kept an elaborate silver tea strainer, picks for sliced lemon, and an English bone china teapot and cups, which were flared at the lip and printed in a pattern of her beloved blue. Around four, tea was served on the porch. Although she herself might have been her only guest, she gave meaning to Henry James's assertion that a summer afternoon tea could seem "a little eternity."[84] At the lake, however, she missed listening to the Tigers games on the radio, and while she was with us, we subscribed to the *Detroit Free Press*, which she read after lunch on the porch swing. I remember that my grandmother was unfailingly kind—did she ever scold me?—but I can't remember asking her even once a question about herself or ever offering to pour her a cup of tea.

I had endless questions for Aunt Betty: How were Katie and Jane (the two beloved mutts, left behind in the Bay City kennel)? Can I put on some of this perfume? Can I try on this fuzzy sweater? When are you going to New York again? What was it like being an actress? I must have driven her nuts, for as soon as she arrived, I hardly left her alone. After we got all the suitcases out of the car and upstairs, I hung around in the doorway to her bedroom. With feminine elegance suddenly personified in my aunt, I was eager to help her unpack the cases of matched luggage, hoping that I might be included in its aura. Layer after layer of slacks, blouses, dresses; each carefully separated for the two-hour trip with tissue, each a texture, a color, a flair *Life* magazine only hinted at. This was sophistication made tangible, sensual. She opened the makeup case, setting out the vials, jars, creams, lotions, and powders before the three-way mirror on her dressing table where, reflected in triplicate, they dazzled like nothing else in the cottage. Last to appear was the jewelry case, a treasure box from which I knew she would produce for dinner, one by one, her star ruby ring, her mosaic pin of an Egyptian mummy, her perfect marquisette bracelet.

When the clothes had been unfolded, hung up, and adequately admired by her audience, Aunt Betty announced she had to get in the water; it was what she lived for, she said. I watched her strip. Even as she aged, and she let her hair turn silver, her body remained lithe and lean, her breasts flat and her pelvic bones jaunty. Although she bought a new Janzen every year, for her first swim she took down one of the old wool tank suits hanging in the closet. We went down to swim together. Soon, however, she had stroked far out from me and the shore, the regular rising and falling of her arms and head so smooth she seemed a wave blown by a single stray blast of wind. She headed for Mother's anchored Lightning where she took off the suit, tossed it up over the transom, and swam dolphin-like until the first bell rang. She was the only person I knew who had the nerve to skinny-dip in the daytime.

After the swim, in preparation for dinner, Aunt Betty did her eyes. I got dressed fast so I could watch. I was fascinated by the instruments of artifice: the tweezers, the eyebrow pencil, the eye shadow, the tiniest of brushes for the eyelashes. (Powder, a dab of rouge, lipstick were my mother's limit.) She stood in her sleek white undies wearing no bra, leaning in toward the mirrors so that she could see to rim her lids. I knew that Aunt Betty still had *beaux,* but it didn't occur to me then that this precise process of dressing and designing could be for anyone's pleasure other than her own (unless it was for mine). Only later did I realize that she may have loved her image better than she loved herself. She seldom joined Mother and Daddy in the pavilion for cocktails and arrived at the dining hall by herself after we'd all gone over, her high straw wedgies giving her added stature.

At the beginning of the war Aunt Betty left New York to return to Bay City where she lived with my grandmother in the great old house on Center Avenue. She drove for the Red Cross, acted in community theater, and continued to have a steady stream of *beaux*. She used a cigarette holder and with her eyes closed leaned in toward the person who would light it for her. I wonder when she started drinking. For seven years she was married to a man with a movie star's name, Ford Carter IV, and set up housekeeping at Wing Lake, a Detroit suburb. He was a fortune-teller's ideal of "tall, dark, and handsome," and I was entranced. Arriving at the cottage, he greeted me by lifting me high above his head and spinning me about so that I felt I flew in an iridescent circle among the pines. Aunt Betty was his fourth wife and she raised his son "Little Ford" who, new to Pinewoods, was shy about gangs. For Aunt Betty and Uncle Ford's sake, I took days out building sand castles on the beach with this new cousin.

Uncle Ford had invented a better flyswatter, and what I heard when the divorce came was that he had taken back the only thing he'd ever given Aunt Betty—the engagement ring—and taken her investments for marketing the flyswatter. Divorced, Aunt Betty was a "grass widow," a term which I think has completely fallen from usage by now. Both her divorce and this cryptic designation stirred my imagination of the exotic. No one in my family had ever been divorced, and almost no one in the 1940s and 1950s was divorced at Pinewoods. Understanding nothing of adult anguish—indeed nothing of anguish other than my own—my childhood perspective on divorce was dual: on the one hand, my deepest dread was that my parents might be divorced; on the other hand, divorce as an event in someone else's life was a subject that shimmered with sexual implications, a subject that shone with possibilities for gossip. With the divorce, Uncle Ford and Little Ford vanished forever into the remote tropics of Florida. When Howie and I were dismantling the Bay City house following Aunt Betty's death, I found boxes in the basement from her life with Ford Carter. They contained Mexican silver candlesticks, colorful Fiesta ware, and California tiles with elaborate arabesques, suggesting she had tried for beauty in her marriage.

After her divorce, she again returned to Bay City. This time to stay. To care for my grandmother until her death. To become increasingly reclusive. Although there were rumors of old *beaux* still showing up, her principal contacts were a few friends from primary school, all of whom kept connections with one of the three Higgins camps, and the now very elderly women who had always done housecleaning for my grandmother. She never forgot my birthday. Her cards came with doodled blithe spirits dancing in the margins and news about her pets, but never any news about herself. It caused her considerable anxiety to crate the cat up for the kennel and lock the house up for two weeks—anxiety that I know now whenever I leave Kansas for Michigan—but she never missed a summer at Higgins. What brought her back—communal routines and rituals, a fix of forgiving family and friends, a claim on a past, a good swim—continue to bring us all back.

Aiming for some earlier notion of gaiety, Aunt Betty feigned a British accent and took to calling me, "Old Pot. Old Bean." (Her Pirate friends went on calling her "Bed-Bug" and "Bed-Day.") But when I was fifteen or so, and she told me during a conversation at the lunch table that I was the only one in the family ever "to have run to fat," it made me want to run all the faster. I could have retorted that her famous thinness was making her look "cadaverous," the word I'd heard someone whisper at cocktails, but I found I had increasingly little to say to her. In those teenage years when the gang was thick as thieves, all adults were so thin we saw right through them. I would plunge in the back door of the cottage and out the front, in between picking up the bathing suit, the book, and the handful of peanuts, and saying "Hi" to Aunt Betty standing by the window in the living room.

On days of endless rain when candles in the clubhouse couldn't dispel dankness or tedium, and we chose to assemble ourselves in the cottage, Aunt Betty retreated to her bedroom. As I do now. Downstairs we began marathon games of Monopoly, Category, or One Word, hooting or howling with consensual delight or disgust. Upstairs she read. As I do now. She brought a stack of books— new hardback bestsellers, some old-timers—with her to the cottage. As I do now. One summer she took on *War and Peace*, and she would leave it on the coffee table in the living room when she came up from reading on the lower pavilion. Each time we found the book, we set her bookmark back a hundred pages. Hiccupping our pleasure, we believed that our prank bestowed amazing cleverness on us, and believed Aunt Betty would be reading *War and Peace* forever and a day. So we relegated adults to alien status and reveled in our youth, and without thinking about it, believed we would be living it forever and a day.

With the exception of those seven years of life married to Ford Carter, my Aunt Betty was a single woman. By first looking on her as exotic and then treating her condescendingly, I failed to appreciate that she was all along showing me a path—how not to live, how to live. Her wit and elegance belong to her alone, but she showed me how to walk on the edge of eccentricity with grace. Other single women at Pinewoods showed me variations on the theme.

On occasion Marilyn and I spent all day sitting on the hot flat roof of the Schirmer pavilion playing cards. In addition to Fish, I Doubt It, Spit, Concentration, Crazy Eights, Seven-Up, Hearts, Russian Bank, and Rummy, we also played Old Maid, first removing all the Queens but the Black Mariah. No one wanted to eat the last cookie on the plate for fear of being an Old Maid; no one wanted to be left holding the Black Mariah in her hand for fear of being an Old Maid. The Black Mariah also spelled out bad luck in Hearts, but to be left with her in Old Maid was more seriously ominous. The Old Maid was the outcast, the drudge, the dreadful, the ugliest of the ugly, associated with witches and warts. I had old-maid schoolteachers—for first-grade Miss Limon, known as Miss Lemon, and for third Miss Payne, known as Miss Pain-in-the-Blankety-Blank—and when I moved out of their classes, I wanted no more to do with them. Certainly my gay aunt, divorced and still with several *beaux* on the string, did not fall into the category of old maid. Nor did the three Taggart sisters—Aunt Lillian, Aunt Mona, Aunt Gertrude—who had a large cottage and a pavilion to themselves and their own table in the dining hall. In their loveliness and graciousness, they seemed like the other queens in the deck.

The Taggart sisters were my grandmother's contemporaries and, like her, wore white tie shoes and kept their white hair heaped upon their heads with only an occasional stray wisp escaping like milkweed fluff. In between shoes and hair, they were corseted smooth; their summer dresses, buttoned to the throat and belted, gave them the coolness of good china. How their temperaments and desires differed from one another, no one ever said: they were the Aunts, the Taggart Sisters, and their own best friends. Their three brothers had all married and had their own cottages in Pinewoods, and with no children of their own, the sisters opened their cottage to the nieces and nephews, grandnieces, grandnephews.

In late afternoon on the porch that wrapped three sides of their cottage, they served lemonade to any youngster who came down the path. Squeezed by hand, the lemons had been purchased on a lengthy trip into town with gasoline rationed. The ice, brought from the icehouse behind the dining hall where it had lain packed in sawdust since the winter, had to be cleaned and chipped, and the batiste napkins with their delicate crocheted lace trim starched and ironed. If they had the leisure to be gracious, they also took the care. Paper napkins were not imaginable, not even at picnics. When the nights were hot and still, they hung Chinese lanterns in their pavilion. Testing myself to trace the path home in the dark without my flashlight, I was glad for these globes of soft peach-colored light. In separate rocking chairs they were silhouetted against the lake, which stretched out before them like the tarnished silver of an old mirror. There was no conversation as I passed, only the easy movement of their pleated fans and of desperate moths flinging themselves against the lanterns.

It's hard to come by heroes now; sociologists have assigned us role models, and occasionally, in academic settings, we have mentors. If in retrospect I now see my mother fulfilling these various positions, when I was growing up, I thought that Sally Loomis took the cake. Unmarried and childless, she was adored by eight nieces and nephews (she once remarked that she had longed for triplets to name "Shirley," "Goodness," and "Mercy"), and all of the BOA gang. She was the only adult who ever entered into our play. If the game was "Pirates of Pestilence," she indulged us by being the captive maid, and we tied her to a lone pine with cruel knots; if it was "Dr. Freud and His Fiendish Friends," she instructed us in psycho-babble. As agile at climbing trees as at inventing limericks, she joined us outside and in, with the sparks of her quick wit, her inquiring mind, her generous spirit kindling ours. At five feet, she came close to being our size. But none of us had her stiff fox-colored hair, her wild cackle of a laugh, and the deep dimples that startlingly appeared like extra eyes in her face when she let loose her laugh.

I adored her, not because I had her nieces' and nephews' advantage of proximity—of having her sing parodies of campfire ditties after supper or read stories at bedtime—but because of distance.

Distance allowed me to make her magical. Because we didn't share a table at the dining hall, she could become my Baba Yaga. Although it had neither the legs of a chicken nor responded to her command to stoop down, she did have her own cabin in the woods—"Aunt Sally's cabin." A small brown house beneath cedar and birch, just off the path going down to the dock from the Loomis Big Cottage, close enough to the lake to hear water rustling against the sand on calm nights. The cherished room of her own. The cousins, off and on, were given the privilege of staying overnight with Aunt Sally and even, on occasion, of using her typewriter. The door, like all Pinewoods doors, was never locked, but I hesitated to enter on my own business. I must have peered through the cabin's screen door more than once, however, for I remember the spare order of its interior: a round braided rug in the center of the floor; a narrow bed covered with a hand-woven white coverlet on the west wall; the tall typewriter and a goose-neck lamp on the smooth pine desk by the door; an area curtained off to closet her clothes and a stand for the enamel wash basin and pitcher in the back; a small wooden horse, red, and a bottle, blue, on a window sill. Books by authors I wouldn't know until much later on a single shelf going all around the room. Aunt Sally didn't fly through the night in a mortar, steering her way by pestle; her special magic was in the form of words. Through her words—in the games she devised for us, the stories she told, the poems she shared—we all flew.

But the flight, so exhilarating for us, I see now was more arduous for her. Although the nieces and the nephews joined the jays in congregating about it, the cabin in the woods was modeled on Thoreau's. She may never have missed a meal at the dining hall or failed to participate in the after-dinner musicals and games in the Loomis Big Cottage, but the cabin was necessary for solitude, for retreat. She wrote continuously—essays, poetry, letters. Her writings were political, theological, epistemological in their intellectual orientation; wry, skeptical, ecstatic in their search. Pinewoods knew that in the 1930s Sally was a fellow traveler, and I, first hearing the term, conjured up magic carpets, mysterious journeys to faraway places. More disturbing for Pinewoods's social conservatives was the rumor that she had had an abortion, a word which, despite its aura of sexual allure, I, as a child, could regard only as a nasty abstraction, and could not factor into my myth of her.

Much later the outlines of the legend were clarified for me: a Ph.D. student in English at the University of Chicago, she left the academy believing that literary criticism would not improve social conditions and turned to teaching in Appalachian one-room schools and in Brooklyn factory-schools.

There she met and loved a young rabbi, and their love, which could not be consummated socially, flourished for forty years through letters. Now, years after her death, her cabin is occupied by grandnieces and grandnephews. They know her story; they know she was no fairy book sprite, witch, or crone, but an inspired teacher, a persevering seeker, a passionate and vulnerable human being.

I think of the single women now at Pinewoods—those who only a few years ago would have been categorized as Old Maids—Marion Foster, Martha Hansen, and myself. We belong to our families, but we are not their spinsters, for I would like to believe we each belong to ourselves and possibly to each other.

With college, work, marriage, and children, our gang dissolved imperceptibly. There was no formal rite of passage. Mother simply cleaned out the clubhouse when I was at college, tossing out everything but one of the chairs we had found at the Cottage Grove dump. The BOA Club emblems have been shoved to the back of my bedroom closet shelf, copies of *Pine Smoke* pasted into a scrapbook, and the play scripts rolled up in desk drawers. I am seldom in close touch with that old gang of mine. The Pinewoods community has survived the shifting of several generations of gangs, but it is friendships that sustains us. Neither Marion nor Martha belonged to the gang: Marion was simply my brother's best friend's little sister, a tagalong, and Martha didn't appear in camp until 1976 when her family bought the cottage next to ours. My friendships with Marion and Martha now transcend summer; we share our winter lives with each other and our lives as single women.

Our families have accommodated us as the Loomises accommodated Sally by allowing her time off in her private cabin. We each have our declared needs—Marion's to paint, Martha's to meditate, mine to read and write—and our eccentric habits which, while not necessarily appreciated or comprehended, are nonetheless absorbed into the family hubbub. We are sisters and aunts, but primarily we are daughters with our mothers still strong presences in our lives. In returning to Pinewoods, we return to our mothers' cottages and wings. The unseen cottage chores they did, we are just beginning to discover; the stories they knew, we are just beginning to understand. As I eat with, walk with, talk with, play with, pray with, stay with, work with, wait for, wait on, wait with my mother at Pinewoods, so did Martha and Marion while their mothers were living. Norma and Martha Hansen told their dreams to each other; Florie and Marion Foster set up their easels beneath the pines together; Lucy and Bethie Schultz still paddle a canoe together along the shore of No Man's Land, looking for Petoskey stones and collecting beer bottles.

That we talk about our mothers, however, distinguishes us from them even as it defines us. In recent summers, as soon as we meet, we make plans for a talk. Finding the private space, the quiet time, necessitates planning. We agree to walk the firebreak after breakfast. We conjure up a trip to Grayling. On a rainy afternoon, we seek shelter in Marion's back house or down by the shore in our pumphouse, sitting on the low beach chairs before the open door and watching the rain erase the dock, the boats, the lake. We talk of our mothers, our brothers and sisters, nieces and nephews, our concerns for them, our differences from them. We talk about our relationships with people at Pinewoods and with people at home. Perhaps because of the security of the pumphouse curtained off by rain, of Marion's back cottage, or of Pinewoods itself, perhaps because of the summer illusion of endless time, perhaps because of our shared status as single women wherever we are, in our conversations it seems so simple to spell out the complex narratives and problems from our faraway, workaday, winter lives. Having made clear choices regarding their lives, both Martha and Marion continue to search. They listen carefully; they question sensitively; their judgments are insights. I express anxieties about these Pinewoods essays. Martha advises assertion, Marion counsels patience when I explain that Mother has admonished me "to say nothing unkind"; they both encourage me "to tell the truth." Remembering Aunt Betty and Aunt Sally, I realize that although "the truth" can only be my story, my story connects with theirs. I realize that a story, untold and unshared, resembles a single hand clapping, but that a story, told and shared, is a hand held out.

*S*tudying American literature in the 1950s and 1960s, one became familiar with several versions of The Fall: as the loss of Eden, as the loss of the American Dream. The lovely land, the lofty ideals, the innocent individual were challenged, corrupted, or diminished. The culprit in Hawthorne's Salem was inevitable—a fatal human flaw; on Twain's Mississippi it was specifically hypocrisy, greed, and violence; in James's country estates, it might have been innocence itself. A lethal combination of these factors, translated into slavery and further polluted by technology, did the trick in Faulkner's Yoknapatawpha County. In the prelapsarian world of my Pinewoods childhood, suffering and death—the Old Testament consequences of the first couple's sin—didn't seem to figure. From my present Kansas perspective, however, I realize we were shadowed from the beginning. Consequently, when I met the Cottage Grove caretaker one morning on my way into the woods, I could hardly stammer a reply to his greeting, "Perfect day in Paradise, isn't it?"

The story has been told before. How it started with the displacement of the Chippewa and the desecration of the wilderness by lumber, railroad, real estate speculators. How this desecration continued with the influx of year-round pleasure-seekers. Ike McCaslin of *The Bear,* reading the family ledgers, pieced together a record of rape, incest, avarice, betrayal. In checking camp histories and minutes of Pinewoods, I haven't discovered such horrors as these. Memory brings back private hurts and prompts awareness of my own responsibility for bruises. But in between accounts of changes in the dining hall regulations, concern for the upkeep of the rafts, words about the necessity of controlling dogs, our communal records also reveal a sense of loss. At Pinewoods, if we are not, as Ahab says of himself, "damned in the midst of paradise,"[85] paradise can nonetheless be streaked with cruelty, anxiety, fear, anger, pain, and loss—all alien to the pastoral world. Accidents also happen. Poison ivy and swimmer's itch are merely reminders.

Certainly, children at Pinewoods go out of their way to scare themselves. Mother vaguely recalls the Swamp Angel, who lived on the margin of Lakeside and on the margin of Mother's blithe girlhood. Arthur Rosenau writes that "like the Hermit of the Island twenty years earlier she aroused the curiosity of young people by her solitary existence. They sneaked past her shack to catch a glimpse of her and in the evening experienced a small thrill stealing a few inedible apples from the tree adjacent to her hut."[86] Messy, single, and struggling to survive economically by herself, she must have epitomized "The Other" to these middle-class young people. Although she had a name, Lillian Morris, Mother remembers her only as the Swamp Angel and remembers nothing about her death—frozen upright in her chair by a cold, cold stove.

My BOA buddies, like our mothers before us, got our "small thrill" exploring abandoned farmhouses between Pinewoods and Roscommon. As did Huck Finn in the derelict house on the flooded river, we found in these houses evidence of quick departure—strewn playing cards, a thick scum of grease inside a frying pan still on the stove, empty whiskey bottles, torn letters, chairs tipped over, and dresser drawers pulled open and emptied. In our desire to shake our own innocence, we tried to invent those lives we had stumbled into, piecing together the scraps of letters. We considered writing to an address in Bad Axe, a town in the Michigan thumb, printed in an archaic hand on an envelope found amidst the debris. I think now that homeless folks, those we once called "tramps," must have preceded us into these homes and depleted them of order. Huck discovered a dead body in that floating house, but we discovered only snakes like thick twine magically untangling and unwinding over the sun-warmed pine boards of a porch. If my gang was thrilled and chilled by haunted houses, my nieces' gang got their kicks from ghost towns. We had made our own forays down the ruts of the old lumber roads to Pere Cheney, looking for china shards in the sand, but my nieces, as soon as they were able to, drove over at night to investigate the broken monuments in the Cheney cemetery.

Mike Taggart's 1987 account of the origins of his interest in the mysterious topography of the lake bottom and his present-day guided tours for camp children of these particular wonders suggest a continuing fascination with Higgins's "little lower layers."[87] As a boy, Mike became acquainted with the Kellers, a childless couple renting a Pinewoods cottage. They not only provided him with the occasional nickel to purchase candy at the dining hall store, but they also took him rowing across the lake to look down over the gunwale at underwater curiosities. From summer to summer one of these curiosities in particular lingered in his imagination: a small anchor with a bit of chain attached to it, "The Little Lost Anchor," Mr. Keller called it. No one knew if it had been abandoned by the large vessel to which it had been tied, or if it had failed to hold that vessel which then would have been dashed upon the shore. "The Little Lost Anchor" raised questions of bereavement, failure, separation, and loss, and each summer Mike went over the lake by himself looking for further evidence of unanswered questions on the bottom.

"The Big Square Anchor," which once moored my grandfather's large catboat, *Spray,* and remains in the water out in front of our cottage although the *Spray* was long ago set burning on the edge of black water and sunk, terrifies him inexplicably. He told a camp memoirist that "each year, the first day he arrived in camp, he went out on the lake to make peace with 'The Big Square Anchor.'"[88] The nieces, returning from a cruise of the lake bottom with Mike, reported that he believed the solid concrete slab connoted an "evil presence." To others' eyes its absolute geometry merely contrasted with the undulating patterns in the sand, its stationary state with the gliding fish and the flickering sunlight in the depths. If you ask him, Mike will take you in the *Rainbow* to muse over the sunken island and a wrecking ball dropped into a tractor tire off Gerrish Park; he'll guide you to a spot just beyond old Hotel Burdell on Flag Point where a car supposedly sank in 1945; and to another spot where, he reports, professional divers have seen clusters of great water-soaked logs, lost from the lumber rafts, standing on end and "swaying perpetually back and forth in unison with the rhythmic motion of the water like an aqueous forest, the ghostly mirror image of the pines on land."[89]

Stories about the island hermit were still in circulation when I was growing up. With the stone home belonging to the island's owner, the only habitation on the island, we were full of inquiries about where the hermit lived and why he was there. After all this was Treasure Island, and vaguely we associated the hermit with Stevenson's romance and dragons sitting on golden hoards. We went to the island to swim off its sandy point, however, and never seriously considered penetrating its poison-ivy thicket to search for either the remains of the hermit's hut or his treasure. Besides, we liked the little shiver created by unanswered questions. We didn't think then to ask ourselves how he lived or, as Thoreau would have put it, what he lived for. We didn't wonder if he had a bean field or even a boat to transport him between shore and island.

Rumors at the turn of the century conceptualized the hermit in a sensationalist mode: he had accidentally killed his wife and turned recluse; a Civil War bounty jumper, he was a fugitive from federal agents; he was mentally deranged as he claimed that he had invented and could operate "a heavier-than-air machine which would fly." But people at the turn of the century also knew the man: like the Swamp Angel, he had a name, Israel Porter Pritchard. Young Lloyd Harman sailed over to the island to visit him numerous times, recalling his meetings in the early *History of Pinewoods Camp:* "He was a tall, spare man with a full beard and long scraggly hair but he had a kindly manner and kindly eyes."[90] An 1896 *Roscommon County Centennial* photograph shows him posed before his hut, looking directly at the viewer with the jauntiness of a Whitman. In a vest and porkpie hat, he retains a sense of the sartorial, and with one arm cocked and his hand on his hip, he appears both dignified and dapper despite the overall dilapidation of his duds and digs. Meetings early in the century with Mr. Pritchard occurred at his one-room cabin built close to Pinewoods's picnicking grounds on the island, but one year Uncle Lloyd returned to find the cabin empty and Pritchard gone, perhaps, he speculated, to try city life, perhaps to elude the feds. In his absence, camp boys burned down the cabin.

In a few years, however, Pritchard returned, taking up residence in a dugout made by hunters. Soon after arriving at the lake in the summer of 1900, Uncle Lloyd sailed to the island to visit the old man, but found him ill. The next day he brought food and medicine from "the mothers of the camp . . . in an effort to bring him back to normal." The next summer, Uncle Lloyd explains that Pritchard "sent word to me asking that I again act in the capacity of his physician," but "upon seeing him I felt that he should have the attention of someone other than an amateur." Consequently, Uncle Lloyd reported Pritchard's situation to the Roscommon County physician, but in his account he reveals his doubts as to whether this worthy ever checked up on the man despite that fact that Pritchard had become "a county charge," and was thus his responsibility. Sailing the Bruske's *Alma* to the island a few days later with food, blankets, and a gang of girls, Uncle Lloyd sought out Pritchard, leaving the girls with the boat on the beach. "Why I took this precaution I do not know except that I wished to prepare Mr. Pritchard for callers. Not receiving any answer to my hail, I stooped and looked in the door of the dugout where I found Pritchard's body, death evidently having overtaken him several days before."[91]

Perhaps the passage of time and the use of rhetoric provided Uncle Lloyd with the means of distancing himself from death even as his nice Victorian scruples had kept the girls separate from the man. In his account, he sets out so precisely names, times, objects. But he cannot describe the shock of seeing the dead man, his "kindly manner and kindly eyes" gone, nor the impact upon his younger self of having a living being reduced to a mere "body," to "remains." He cannot describe the pastoral transformed, the summer idyll lost. Instead, he gives us further narrative details, concluding with an elaborate epic flair: "Pritchard's body was laid upon a piece of the dugout roof for a stretcher and placed in the rowboat to be taken to Roscommon for burial. It was a dark, windy day much in keeping with our mission and we landed the rowboat with some difficulty at the old Hill Road below the camp. Such was the bier and such the funeral of Israel Porter Pritchard." Yet the very simplicity of the opening sentence of Uncle Lloyd's reminiscences reveals that this man's life and death tinted his view of the lake: "My earliest recollection of Higgins Lake includes the Hermit."[92]

Ted Plum concludes his detailed and affectionate memoir of his Pinewoods summers, saying, "Those were the days, my friends, back in the early 20s."[93] His black hair parted clean a little left of center, a wide and gracious smile, Ted seemed to me, when he visited in later summers, like Clark Gable just dropped into Pinewoods from Sunset Boulevard. The organizer of camp sing-alongs, in which he played the ukulele and the slide whistle, and of parties to which people came dressed as their favorite songs, he was the epitome of conviviality. When he arrived in camp, things began to swing. Yet death marks his memoir. Ted remembers that in 1912 his uncle, George Augustus Harman, died of a heart attack in the cottage. A horse-drawn hearse pulled up on the path in front of the cottage to take the casket away.

He also remembers that during a Sunday church service outside the Big Taggart Cottage, he and his mates were called away to tend a swamped sailboat out by the Cottage Grove deepwater raft. They left immediately in the *Rainbow*, but cruising back and forth across the water in front of Cottage Grove, they saw no one. Not until they saw the bodies of two men, lying completely still, completely clothed, on the bottom of the lake. Mother, just back from her summer job as a camp counselor, went out with my grandfather in our putt-putt to assist, and she remembers the same event. The men, both members of the Yale swimming team, were visiting their teammate at Cottage Grove. Against all warning that Sunday morning, they'd borrowed the Loomis' catboat, *Pickle*, and had set sail in a high wind. When the *Pickle* capsized, the two visitors set out swimming for the safety of the Cottage Grove raft. Their Cottage Grove friend stayed with the boat and survived. To Mother, the moral was clear. Bill Taggart can still see their bodies laid out on the benches in his family's pavilion.

Ted also writes that he and about five other boys eagerly courted danger. Having taken out the Taggarts' *Mist* one afternoon, they thought it would be fun to swamp it. But an elder, watching from the shore, recognized what they were up to and later "gave us a beautiful lecture on the tradition of sailing or being in any boat on the lake without accident. It made a great impression on me, particularly the point he made on the pride they all had of sailing safely and not dangerously. It so happened that things can go wrong when you are not trying to have trouble." Such a happening occurred when the old catboat, *Laura*, tipped them all over one bright day off Sunset Beach. Ted describes it in detail: "We started to come about and didn't have enough headway and Pete had to pay off some to get headway again and as he did, the boom and corner of the sail got a wave in it and it just eased us right over." Determined to stay with the boat, they sat on the high gunwale, but "suddenly a wave lifted the mast up higher and a gust of wind got under the sail and lifted the mast and the sail up and the boat flipped completely over. We saw the boom swinging toward us. Pete yelled to dive into the cockpit. This we did and we were lucky. If that boom had hit us it could have killed us."[94] To prevent a reoccurrence of this terror, they cut the sail from the halyard. It sank out of sight, and the *Laura* with its crew soon drifted into the safety of a sandbar.

Capsizing the Sailfish when we were learning to sail was sport. We gibbed and were over in a flash; we got in irons and went over backwards; we surfed going downwind and nosedived under a wave; we broke masts beating upwind, and we turned turtle, but we came up for more. Even now Howie seems to take capsizing in his flashy catamaran, *Stray Cat*, with the same insouciance. I can't. Following the end of a summer of graduate school, one gray morning I was invited out in *Fourtuitous*, the Pacific catamaran, owned by four Pinewoods families and the fastest sail in camp. Despite a low-level depression—the miasmic sort which dims sensual responses and an interest in discovering meaning—a residue from studying Arnold and Milton, I was flattered by the invitation from Lee Cochran, Phil Will, and his son Phip, who were among Pinewoods's crack sailors. These men had a sense for the aesthetics of sailing, its very intricate and simple arrangements—a legacy they passed on to their sons. The wind was high this morning. On the dock, we donned slickers and decided against reefing. Under way, Lee and Phil were interested in clocking our speed—between twenty-five and thirty knots—and we all took a turn at the helm. With the sail tight in, and the boat slicing through the water, you have the illusion not simply of harmony with the elements but of prodigious and uncanny control over them.

Young Phip was at the helm when we went over. I slipped from the windward side down under the sail and slipped into drowning. The sail pressed from above, allowing light but obliterating both horizon and the multitudinous things of this world. I couldn't breathe. Weighed down by my slicker and my depression, I couldn't swim. I remember gasping, gagging, groping. This was a watery womb with no exit. I gave one final kick with my clumsy leaden legs, assuming it was for the bucket, and was astonished to discover myself standing on solid lake bottom. My feet secure, I could lift my head to create an air bubble between the sail and the water and breathe.

Over in an instant, this near-drowning seemed everlasting. I praise our astonishing survival instincts which keep us afloat. In his memoir Ted calls these sailing disasters "tragic" and "harrowing." Yet paragraph by paragraph, they alternate with descriptions of his tasks as a dining hall chore boy, of Shoppenagons's appearances at cottage fireplaces to perform "Indian dances," of the Lakeside dance pavilion, midnight sails, baseball games, musicals, and blueberry pie. They alternate with those kicks that keep us attached to foundations—earth and community.

It used to be that to go up to Grayling from Pinewoods, you couldn't avoid Dead Man's Curve. Even though you craned your neck out of the car window at this treacherous intersection on our two-lane county road to see what cars were coming up on the blacktop from Roscommon, you couldn't see them until they were upon you. Now the entire curve is sodded over, and Queen Ann's lace and blazing star dot the green. There's no shortcut now, only a simple four-way stop with a flashing overhead signal. It was August 1955, the summer after my freshman year in college, and I read the news in a letter from Mother on a train from Paris to Ostend: Ann Decker Kohring, the lovely girl I'd watched come of age next door, had been killed in an automobile accident on Dead Man's Curve. She was in a car with other teenagers from Lakeside on the way to a movie in Grayling. I turned toward the strange fields of France being harvested out the train windows. So far away from Pinewoods, these fields spread out beyond the window's apparition of the lake, misting over as I would see it from the pavilion, and I couldn't stop crying.

Mother told me later that Howie, who idolized Ann—his first crush, whose teenage stunts were devised as ways of attracting her attention as well as defying his parents—lay for a day on his bed with his face to the wall and long after her death carried her photograph in his wallet. At Pinewoods, no one speaks of Ann now. Writing about her death, I had to. In late August of 1996, one of Ann's younger sisters and I talked down in their beach grotto. The lake, like Whitman's "cradle endlessly rocking,"[95] lisped to us, whispered to us as we talked and as we wept. At camp in Vermont when Ann died, her younger sister told me, it was decided that she and her twin should not come home for Ann's funeral. She remembers that when they did return, they found hanging in their basement a large wreath of cedar boughs—made and sent by Pinewoods. It stayed in the basement of their Detroit home for years, as did the grief. Ann herself isn't clear in her sister's memory. She remembers the weight of sorrow. Ann's mother told me she was comforted by the fact that Ann, who would be in her fifties now, did not have to live with suffering and anguish. Neither of the two recent Pinewoods histories, both of which have genealogies, refers to Ann, but the name of her niece does appear: "Anne Decker Hoey b. 1967."

The first summer the Reverend Bruske and his wife spent at Higgins ended with an epidemic of typhoid fever. Contracted from contaminated food and drinking water, typhoid results in headaches, backaches, coughing, nosebleeds, diarrhea, exhaustion, and eruptions of rose-colored spots. In that summer of 1879 it affected the Bruskes' three-year-old son, Grandma Bruske's sister, as well as Edith Plum. When the disease broke out, young Paul was rushed by his father to Saginaw, his wife following two days later with her sister and Edith: "We arranged a double bed in the stage and took them out together. The afflicted members of our camp all recovered."[96] A gap of anxiety and pain exists between these two sentences, and at least one person from Cottage Grove died that summer. Now we send water samples from the dining hall and our individual cottage wells—one of Mother's constant worries is that the septic tank is too close to the well—to be tested for purity at the Michigan Department of Public Health's epidemiology laboratories in Lansing. No one has been stricken with giardia, but we have our lesser epidemics.

The hospital closest to camp is in Grayling, twelve miles away, and people from every Pinewoods cottage have spent long summer hours in the Mercy Hospital Emergency Room's waiting room, caught between their worrying over a child's sudden fever and their yearning to be back at the cottage. Every cottage has its memories of broken bones, sprained tendons, lacerations, diarrhea, pneumonia, poison ivy, sun poisoning, and swimmer's itch. A stumble on a protruding root in the path, a slip on the tennis court, a bang on the head from a swinging boom make summer's ease as treacherous as winter's ice. The summer of 1946, everyone, including Minnie the cat, got sick in our cottage. I spent days in my upstairs bedroom, tended by a kindly Roscommon doctor who drove daily out to the lake to make a cottage call, and then Mother got sick, a general strep infection developing into pneumonia. I was playing down at the Loomises when we caught sight between the trees of the large white ambulance lumbering along the Stage Road. I had left the cottage because Mother was lying down and needed quiet, but it didn't occur to me that this ominous vehicle was coming for her. Nonetheless, it was an adventure sleeping over in the Big Loomis Cottage while Mother recovered. But then Howie was taken to Grayling, where, given an overdose of the new miracle drug, penicillin, he vomited up any food. Making my first hospital visit, I was shocked to see my spunky young brother look small, pale, and surprisingly pitiful, tucked flat into a Mercy Hospital bed, and I began to write anxious postcards every day to Daddy in Flint.

After the summer of 1946, any sense of adventure drained out of illness at the lake. From the 1960s through the 1980s, periodic migraines alerted me to my limitations. Of my two weeks at the lake, one day invariably would have to be spent in darkness. It always began in the morning. I'd be blanketed by suffocating nausea while sweeping the pavilion or leaving the dining hall after breakfast. On one occasion, desperate for the cafergot which I'd found was the only cure for these obliterating pains but which I'd left behind in Kansas, I spent hours at the Mercy Hospital ER waiting for a prescription. Through the phosphorescent pain behind my eyes, the thousand natural vicissitudes of summer were apparent all around—a child's chest had been smashed by a boat propeller, a Camp Grayling Army Reserve soldier's hand had been mangled in an automatic rifle, a guy in a visor cap had twisted his foot sliding into third, an asthma sufferer wheezed. In recent years it has been no adventure to take Mother to the ER—once with pneumonia, another time with a shin gash that wouldn't heal, again with diarrhea which laid her out on the living room couch. She sits in her discomfort, straight up in the waiting room's plastic chair, stoically reading her *Time* or *Audubon*. She diagnoses her illness for the doctor. He listens and assigns a remedy, which she notes carefully. We return to the cottage, and she heals gradually and steadily, not missing a meal at the dining hall.

I definitely panicked, however, the quiet afternoon in the mid-1970s when Mother returned from sailing out of her mind. I was propped up on my bed upstairs, reading, remotely conscious of the fact that it was a beautiful day and that everyone else was out of the cottage. Tammy's steps were distinct on the cottage stairs, her voice shrill before she appeared at the bedroom door, "Your mother's had a heart attack. She's down on the dock." I bolted. Running ahead of Tammy, lickety brindle down the cottage steps, past the pavilion, down the stairs to the lake. Mother lay on her side in front of the open door of the pumphouse. Her arms and legs seemed akimbo, as if she were a puppet dropped, not my upright mother. As I knelt down to try to gather her in my arms, she said again and again, "Quick, I've got to hurry. I've got to hurry. They're coming. They're coming for dinner." Her Sunfish bobbed obliviously out on its line, and I could see that she had dismantled mast, sail, and sheet, stashing them away in orderly fashion in the pumphouse. A missing daggerboard. Her glasses were still on, but she herself seemed dismantled and out of order.

She refused to be taken to Grayling. Vehemently and adamantly. We got her upstairs, out of her soggy sailing clothes, and into bed, and then I called the Mercy Hospital ER. All I could do was try to explain the inexplicable: my mother so suddenly and strangely not herself. The authoritative and anonymous voice, however, interpreted and identified her symptoms as probably a "Transient Ischemic Attack" or TIA which, translated into my language, was "a minor stroke." "Keep her well covered. Keep her quiet. Keep us informed." Back upstairs, she was further back in time, talking about Auntie Helen: "She wrote me that I wasn't to have a yellow kitchen. Red or white but not yellow. Red or white but not yellow." I rubbed her feet. "What we need is a cat," I said. "They've always been the best nurses in our family." I repeated, "They've always been the best nurses in our family" and, remembering the comfort of cats, she repeated after me. By the time a neighbor returned with hot soup, she was beginning to recall the events of the afternoon: the sailing was lovely; a gust of wind over by Flag Point, and the Sunfish gibbed; it turned turtle, and the daggerboard floated away; she saw advantage in the situation, however, and spent her drifting hours sitting on the upside-down boat, scrubbing away at the algae on its bottom. Eventually, two men in a powerboat found her and towed her back to camp. To this day, she cannot recall how she brought the boat in or how she put it up.

The next morning she was up early, out in the pavilion, looking at the water. She said she was fine. She said her legs seemed a little shaky, but she was fine. And the day was fine. I proposed that she might like to stay in bed through the day. She proposed that she was going sailing. I protested. The water glittered maliciously. The horizon stirred ominously. Yesterday's scare was seismic; Mother was the sun we circled around. With my sense of security altogether rattled, I proclaimed myself parent and pronounced there was no way she was going sailing. I couldn't let her. She insisted. I described her symptoms; I cited the authoritative voice from Grayling; I told her we had been frightened. As she went down to the dock to pull in her Sunfish, I shouted after her in a warning, more petulant perhaps than those we'd all heard growing up, "Alright, but don't you go into black water." She sailed that morning, and I walked up the path through No Man's Land to Lakeside, watching her through the trees all the way. She stayed within green water and arrived back at the dock in time for lunch as usual.

Back in Flint that fall, Mother had a checkup with her doctor, who sent her to a neurologist. This doctor insulted her by asking her to perform balance and vision tests, which proved only an aggravation, and she made an appointment with another doctor. Sensibly, this man realized that wet clothes and cold temperatures could cause hypothermia. We were relieved, then, quite after the fact, that there had been no TIA. The family's invitations to her 90th birthday party in 1995 consequently printed out the imperative, "Keep on Sailing, Lucy!"

My friend, Esther Greenleaf Murer, remembers another day from a summer in the early 1960s—"indelibly," she says. Returning to their cottage from lunch at the dining hall, she saw a visitor stretched out pallid beneath a dark pine. Others appeared on the path, including his wife, who pleaded, "Honey, speak to me, speak to me." Someone asked helplessly, "Is there a doctor? Is there a doctor here?" The only responses were two clicks—the sound of seeds in the dried gourd. Quickly the dying man's daughter was kneeling by her father's side, giving him CPR, trying to replace his breath with her own. Instead, she brought his blood into her own mouth. To this day, Esther wonders if she could have performed this deed of life-saving love, could have put her mouth on her father's to take his breath and blood back into herself. She focuses her memory on a cluster of alabaster Indian pipes, tinged pink, springing leafless from the dark earth near the dark pine.

Thoreau plants a dead horse at Walden in his chapter, "Spring," to remind him of the "inviolable health of Nature." He allows himself here to revel in "Nature so rife with life that myriads can be afforded to be sacrificed and suffered to prey on one another."[97] Such ecstasy over rampant life in the face of loss does not address human tragedy, however. Nor does the concept of *felix culpa*, translated so blithely as "happy sin," satisfactorily explain the sorrow that results from human mistakes. Only in novels does there seem a single "fortunate fall," a single episode of despair and disaster. In our spring and summer lives, as well as in our fall and winter lives, these episodes multiply; their effects persist. We may become more sympathetic, more forgiving, more committed to understanding each other's vulnerabilities as a result of suffering, but we are nowhere protected and never inured and never finished groping for understanding. We have heard the story of the Cottage Grove woman who walked into the lake after dinner one evening and kept on walking. We do not know her sorrow; we guess the sorrow of those who knew her; we go on telling her story.

The Woods

Cottage Fireplace

Mother's Desk

The Pumphouse

Boats at Moorings

Roscommon County Meadow

Jane Kohring

Into the Woods

Wintergreen and Reindeer Moss

Blueberries

Aminita

Indian Pipes

Fringed Gentian

Jane Kohring

Harebell

Chipmunk

Black Squirrel

Red Pine, Pileated Woodpecker Holes

Fallen White Pine

Sunset, Pavilion

Sunset, Pinewoods Docks

Moon over Higgins

ho can tell the forest from the trees? There, right there, are the pines, and there are also the oaks, poplars, maples, the ferns, bracken, moss, the blue jays, spider webs, gypsy moths, and they are all one forest, more than the sum of their parts. The woods are all around us; they are our frontyards and backyards. They have grown up about us, and we are not afraid of them.

Robert Pogue Harrison correlates the decline of forests among Mediterranean and European peoples with the rise of their civilizations: "For the abomination of forests in Western history derives above all from the fact that, since Greek and Roman times at least, we have been a civilization of sky-worshippers, children of a celestial father. *Where divinity has been identified with the sky, or with the eternal geometry of the stars, or with cosmic infinity, or with 'heaven,' the forests become monstrous, for they hide the prospect of god*. . . . In short, for the family to establish itself as a divine institution under the open sky, it had to clear a space for itself in the forest's midst. Only within the clearing could the family maintain its cohesion and guard its genealogy against the 'infamous promiscuity' of the wilderness."[98] And so the lumbermen, followed by railroaders and merchants, by farmers and their families, came into the north of Michigan and cleared the monstrous abomination away. (Finding, too, a monstrous profit.)

When the campers began arriving at Higgins, the forest primeval had been cut, and what wasn't cut had burned, leaving the great pines on our northern shore as a saving remnant. In early photographs some cottages seem almost suburban, as if situated on a grassy knoll with scattered trees and the lake gleaming in the background, as if planned to be part of a new real estate development. (Nineteenth-century American landscape gardening theorists such as Andrew Jackson Downing had to plead with developers to recognize the glory of native trees. Destroying them made deserts for new settlements; sparing them, he believed, made stately parks.) But the rusticators who built the cottages in Pinewoods did not, like suburbanites, tend to the grass, and if they paid attention to the trees, it was in admiration; otherwise they let them be. Consequently, quite without design, the woods returned to Pinewoods, and beneath its canopy have Pinewoods families found cohesion. The open sky above the lake provided a view of heaven, and individual white pines on the shore and in the woods have pointed straight to it. Especially if you allowed your search for it to begin with the wintergreen flower, small and bell-like, at the foot of the tree.

One Pinewoods memoirist explains that their father simply let "trees and shrubs [grow up about our cottage] willy-nilly, unnoticed and uncared for." Following his death, these were pruned so that "light came to the living room again . . . [and] we can see the beautiful lake from the front of the cottage."[99] Other Pinewoods people have pruned and trimmed the forest's growth in the immediate vicinity of their cottages, also seeking light and views: "sky worshippers" indeed. But with the exception of one cottage where cement dwarfs and Edwardian babies are exhibited in the frontyard, and luxurious begonias and lobelias in pots hang from the porch, no one gardens. In the rear of the cottages, trees, bushes, ferns, and grasses do grow willy-nilly, and our back buildings—woodsheds, garages, boathouses, guest cottages, laundry facilities—surrounded and shaded by them, seem almost incidental to the encroaching forest. Only the poison ivy has been deliberately eliminated.

The memoir written in 1948 by Uncle Paul, however, suggests that Pinewoods once had a management plan—of sorts—for the woods immediately surrounding the cottages. He writes that "Some of us believe in firmly managing our little personal forest[, while] others choose to let the trees boss their own job. So we have orderly little groves, primeval thickets, and many degrees of compromise. But we all believe in planting trees, and with us, trees means pines." His memoir proceeds, then, to provide detailed information for the most successful ways of planting both red and white pines, for guaranteeing their growth into "fine, symmetrical trees." He attributes the laissez-faire attitude of Pinewoods people toward lawns as part of the policy for growing superior trees: "Unlike other neighboring camps, Pinewoods long ago inaugurated the far-seeing policy of raking only around our cottages. Elsewhere we leave all needles and leaves to serve as needed plant food for our trees. Our pines, large and small, show the benefits of this policy." Zealous Uncle Paul recommended hardening hearts and sharpening axes in order to cut those trees—"wolf trees" he called them—which inhibited the growth of young pines into the monarchs he worshipped. These he designated as his legacy to future generations, querying at the conclusion of his memoir, "What better monument than a great pine can any of us ever leave behind?"[100]

Growing up with the pines of Pinewoods, assuming them simply to have sprung from seeds and to have been nurtured by changing weathers and seasons in the course of time, I never took them for monuments, part of a managed plan. Evidence of management, however, proliferates. For example, in the early 1990s Cottage Grove inaugurated a plan that led to selected cutting in the forest behind its camp over a five-year period. Pinewoods, seeking to preserve 110 acres from this devastation, proposed a purchase and was denied. Then, in 1995, the "clean-up crew" Pinewoods itself hired in the wake of the tornado schemed to take out trees only slightly damaged. Confronted with this evidence, I realize how long I have rejoiced in the illusion that our cottages would border in perpetuity on wilderness; I must now work at reconciliation with the loss of this wilderness by both natural accident and human design.

In 1933 two Pinewoods families determined to move the Stage Road behind the camp back away from their cottages. Their plan demanded the creation of a forest grove. Planting several hundred pine and spruce seedlings, they called on everyone in camp, young and old, to assist them through that long hot summer by carrying daily buckets of water up from the lake out to the young trees. Until the 1995 tornado, these spruces grew deep and dark along a section of the Stage Road, with the road providing a permeable demarcation between the surveyed cottage lots stretching toward the lake on the south and the seemingly indivisible woods on the north. Driving into Pinewoods along the Stage Road, we had to be initiated by passing through this dark grove before we were allowed to approach the glory of the lake's shining. The tornado, however, transforming this grove of tall spruces into matchsticks, transformed our entrance to the lake. Now sunlight splatters across the road. It will nurture the new trees that have been planted among the spruce stumps.

You can enter the woods on one of several trails off the Stage Road. After the Chippewa, the lumbermen and the farmers, the telephone and electrical linemen came into the woods to break through the density and complexity of foliage. They left their trails as well as medicine bottles and hand-blown light bulbs, which we occasionally discover when we stray off our beaten paths. Spending so many of his afternoons out in the woods chopping fallen trees and digging pineknots out of stumps rather than going sailing, Daddy added to these paths in the 1960s. He linked his paths with a firebreak which runs along the north edge of Pinewoods property and with mossy roads named for the long-time Cottage Grove caretaker, Art Williams, and for the unknown Mr. Wiseman, named as if for a character in a transcendental pilgrim's progress. For many winters Mother and Daddy went cross-country skiing along this network of paths and roads, which crosses over into Cottage Grove's large area of several hundred acres, once densely covered with diverse second-growth trees.

Despite their acres of woods, you don't see many walkers in the woods from Cottage Grove itself, although Pinewoods walkers are regulars. Julia McPherson, however, not only walked the woods but also protested the Cottage Grove management plan. Edging trails with logs and fallen saplings, she laid out a complex network through the Cottage Grove lands, connecting to the paths Daddy made. But Julia is gone from the Cottage Grove Association now. Griefstricken by her perception of her camp's betrayal of the woods, she did the unimaginable: she sold the family cottage and spends her summers in Maine. Her trails are now barely now discernible. Ferns overrun them, brambles cross them, rot erases the markers, but every summer I set out to decipher them anew.

Johnny Bennett also extended Daddy's paths, using axe and saw to develop them through Pinewoods's ten acres of red and white pines. His are professional trails, blazed with the woodsman's traditional diamond marks in several colors and mapped so anyone can trace them and return home before dark. The system of trails became further diversified when Howie and Tammy got dogs. It was easier to walk them in the woods than in front of the cottages where strangers' ankles might be nipped and where poop had to be scooped. So they worked weekends out of season shoving through tangles of bracken and brush, clearing the confusion of branches and young trees, many broken by the weight of winter snows, others bent and bowed by the weight of larger trees struck down by age, disease, or lightning. They routed their way around all living trees and laid leaf humus down behind them.

A trail might be an intervention in the wilderness, its purposefulness disturbing the very randomness of the forest, prying open the secrets of the forest's essential shade and shadow. It may eliminate the traffic of infinitesimal unseen life forms and lay the groundwork for turnpikes. So far our meandering Pinewoods trails go nowhere. Their destination is the pale wintergreen flower, the summer's first Indian pipe, the elusive black-throated green warbler, or a certain slant of light. They allow us to enter the forest and to return; they allow us to be embraced by the woods. So far the woods remain larger than our network of trails. A set of short boards are nailed one after the other halfway up the trunk of an oak along one of Howie and Tammy's trails. Who put them there and when and why no one knows, but they've come to be called "The Ladder to Heaven," for their destination is only upward. Passing the Ladder when I'm walking this trail, I think I just might get to heaven that way, although the steps are all askew and weather-darkened now, and my feet have no itching to leave the earth.

To domesticate the strangeness of the woods, we render them architecturally, referring to the forest floor below, the canopy of trees above. They are many storied with levels of leaf mold, moss, fungi; of grass, fern, bush; of young trees and of old. Shafts of light stream down through arched cathedral windows formed by the tallest trees, through the clerestory of their lower branches to reach the lowest cloisters. We make the woods "home" to bird, bug, and animal life. But the woods are not to be confined by human metaphors. The verticality of the pines and mature oaks and poplars is intersected by the horizontality of their branches, this linearity by the diversity of leaf and twig, by the mesh of shrub and bush, by connecting and encircling filament. To be in the woods is to feel surrounded by the stuff of life in the making. Spinning, shifting, spitting, shimmying, spiraling, crashing, carousing, the woods are always restless.

Even when it seems you sit or stand in the center of stillness and solitude, you catch the quick flash and glimmer of a single pine needle suspended and turning in a web, of beads of sap oozing along a limb, of an ant train running on a fast track. If you feel at ease standing among the steady trunks of great trees, observing each shining leaf in its place, a twig's sudden snapping will cause you to look up to see branches lashing out against the sky in the throes of wind. A tree falling generates sylvan geometry: a sudden diagonal across vertical and horizontal, linear and circular. It slashes at its fellows; uprooted itself, it uproots others, breaks and bends them. It tears through darkness, and stopping, hung up on those it has ruined, it opens the forest to sun and sky. Civilization does not spring up in the clearing, but the chemistry of light and time collaborates to quicken death and life—the rotting of the old tree and the sprouting of the saplings it once shrouded.

Entering the woods this time, you feel you're becoming acquainted with the trails; you can decide to take a path north of the firebreak, to pick up one of Julia's trails beyond the Cottage Grove dump, or head for the spot where five roads intersect, known as the Pentangle. You enter the woods expectant. Familiar, they are never the same. Of course, you realize timing is everything: the woods after rain have a drip, a scent, a glisten not present on sunny days; the woods at dusk thicken, darken, soften, and even as patterns of leaf, feather, and distance are obliterated, there are other revelations—the doe asleep through the day, roused by the dimming light, becomes a sudden silhouette; the woods in winter, written not in green and gold, but black and white, present not a diminished text but simply another text.

Perhaps the woods' intricacies demand most of your eyes, but to enter the woods is to have your ears, nose, fingers, and tongue fully and sometimes simultaneously engaged. Wintergreen huddles amongst ferns beneath small white pines, its leaves smooth, dark, green discs contrasting with crinkled fern fronds and feathery green pine needle clusters. You pick one leaf and lay it wafer-like on your tongue. Its fresh wild taste initiates you into the woods. Looking for mushrooms, you find instead a great horned owl's feather on the way home along Mr. Wiseman's Road. Lying upon the mound of dark needles at the base of the great white pine, it does seem dropped like one of God's handkerchiefs, an emissary neither seen nor heard. In your hand it is as weightless as a page. You return home with your eyes on the woods. If you watch only the path, you may find the feather but miss the bird.

*A*n the wild woods, arrangements are more vertical than in tame gardens. Although gardens do have their vertical dimension, horizontal patterns dominate. Harmony there—or controlled tension as the case may be—is dependent upon the proximity of green grass to clusters of flowers or, in the Japanese garden, of raked sand to sleeping stones. In a garden, the near and far seem the most important aspects whereas in the woods it's the top and bottom. A garden reveals itself as you amble along its paths, turning onto this alley, coming upon that prospect. Entering the woods behind the cottage, you're aware it's multi-valenced: at the top, up against the sky, is the upper story of living leaves; at the bottom, thick upon the earth, is the loam of dead leaves. Feasting on this loam, transforming it into earth, are the mosses, lichens, mushrooms, fungi, and ferns.

At the bottom of the heap that is the woods—and small in comparison to trees—this low life can go unnoticed; it can be casually stepped on or be pushed aside. So small, the mosses and lichens cast no shadows themselves although flowers and ferns may cast shadows over them. Without being anthropomorphic, we can say that mushrooms and fungus have flesh, flesh that can be bruised, can turn purple and a sick yellow if kicked or pulled up unkindly from the forest floor. I've seen ferns broken where deer have settled in amongst them for a snooze and patches of moss badly roughed up by dogs in search of a smell. But the wind never rustles moss: it is soundless, and its hold on the earth is tenacious. John Ruskin calls lichens and mosses "meek creatures, the first mercy of the earth, . . . creatures full of pity, covering with strange and tender honor the scarred disgrace of time, laying fingers on the trembling stones to teach them rest."[101]

What is the shape of moss? Bryologists give precise descriptions of individual plants, based on microscopic examination and accompanied by hairline drawings of exquisitely feathered and antlered parts. In his book, *The Mosses of Michigan*, for example, Henry T. Darlington writes of a certain sphagnum moss found in Roscommon County: "Plants generally delicate, in green or more often reddish, compact tufts. Cortical cells of stems large, thin-walled. Stem leaves large . . . ovate, quite concave, involute at the apex, with the border usually continuing across the apex. Branch leaves narrowly ovate, involute at the toothed apex."[102] Although Darlington's descriptions may assign the moss familiar arboreal and architectural characteristics, the living plant I hardly see at all here.

What I see in the Michigan woods is moss in the collective: Darlington's tufts, or hummocks, clumps, cushions, colonies. In the woods, where it patterns the bark of living trees, clings to stumps and fallen limbs, and seems to serve as place mats for wet leaves, I identify moss en masse by color and texture first. Checking on the cedar posts supporting the pavilion or looking down on the front porch roof from my bedroom window, I note that it is brittle or bright, gray or green. To see the flickering thread-like projectiles, the graceful necks, the stiff horns, or the bushy tops of individual plants you have to stoop down. Moss, like Whitman's grass, seems shapelessly democratic. Collections of an infinite number of individuals, it may be individuated by names such as British soldiers, hairy caps, humpbacked elves, forks, brooms, or maiden hairs, but often it is simply assigned a collective attribute such as shaggy, silvery, or green hair.

Moss is the earth's swaddling clothes, draped tenderly over stones and tucking certain trees in. It is the woods' hair—as shaggy gray beard on trunks, as gleaming merkin in the crotch of roots, as the earth's soft green thigh. In Kyoto, at Kokedera—the Moss Temple—beneath low pines and between dark rocks, moss reveals the complacent contours of the earth's body, showing the subtleties of its musculature—its shoulders, back, and buttocks. In the woods, when I've come across green hair moss, growing dense and thick as carpet in a Victorian library, I can't resist lying down and going cheek to cheek against it. Not to embrace it but simply to rejoice in connection as I do when I put my face against my sleeping cat. The moss is moist and cool and does not palpitate like a cat, and when I stand up, crumbs of bark and pine needle bits stick to my face.

Mushrooms and fungi are a different matter at Pinewoods. Although they may appear in families or communities, they often are loners: a definitive shape and color rising above the dark humus of leaves, casting a shadow over the bright moss, jutting out from the tree trunks. Depending on the year's rainfall, the numbers of mushroom and fungus rise and fall. In the summer following a winter with good snow and a spring with plenty of rain, mushrooms and fungi of unknown and never suspected shapes, sizes, species proliferate throughout the woods behind the cottages. Our forest, with its mixture of hardwoods and conifers, of shade and intermittent sunshine, of humus and sandy soil, is the best of all possible habitats for a diversified mushroom population, each species having different ideas about the good life.

In the summer of 1993, I decided I was going to learn mushrooms. It started with Mother's discovery of an enormous yellow excrescence midway up on a rather slender oak out by the woodshed. We identified it right away as a sulphur shelf from Charles McIlvaine and Robert Macadain's *One Thousand American Fungi*, published in 1900 and prized by one Pinewoods family because of their grandfather's notes inscribed in the margins. Peterson's field guide on mushrooms gave a confirming identification: "large, soft, stalkless brackets in overlapping rosettes; yellow to orange." The brackets are "fleshy and moist to firm with upper surface smooth to wrinkled; margin thick, often lobed or wavy."[103] Since the sulphur shelf is so aptly named and its characteristics so exactly articulated, I felt that here was a particular, individual fungus I could know and embrace. With Peterson's guide and the National Audubon Society's *Pocket Guide to Familiar Mushrooms* from the cottage library in hand, I headed for the woods.

When the Cochrans first began coming to Pinewoods, Lee went up and down camp photographing everyone's mushrooms. I remember walking the path and seeing him hunched down below on the bank in front of a cottage with his camera cases set out in the ferns and his long lens pointed at a cluster of small red dots. For many years whenever there was an evening of slides after dinner in a cottage, Lee would insert a series of his mushrooms. His close-ups were taken from various angles so at times these mushrooms became alien species or abstract sculptures; we were amazed and amused by their shapes and colors, and we hooted when he was dubbed a "photo-phungo-phile." But few others in Pinewoods have ever seriously—or even casually—taken up mycology. Carrying books into the woods, I felt encumbered and self-conscious: foolish. The jays cackled, and the black squirrels gossiped. It occurred to me that much of my knowledge about the lake, the woods, and the camp had come orally, through Daddy's recitations and Mother's narratives. They had taught by talking and doing; I'd learned by listening and trying. But when it came to mushrooms, I had no mentors. Books would have to do.

Peterson's guide provided me with fine schematic drawings, many in color, while the Audubon book had color photos. What could be simpler? Scanning through the pages, I delighted not only in the names of particular plants, but in the names of species: for example, earthtongues, grainy clubs, mushroom pimples; cup fungi; coral fungi and chanterelles; tooth fungi; woodcrusts, groundwarts, and polypores; stink horns, false truffles, and birds' nests; puffballs, earthballs, and earthstars. By far the largest species appeared to be the gill mushrooms and amongst them, I shortly realized, were astonishing varieties. The cap shapes could be convex, conic, humped, flat, depressed, bell- or funnel-shaped; their margins, as seen from above, could be round, crenated, scalloped, indented, lobed, streaked, pleated, grooved, or ribbed or, as seen from the side, upturned, straight, recurved, or incurved. Depending on their age, their colors also differ. Some are shaggy, others smooth; some have bulbous bases, others dainty skirts halfway up their stems; some, marked in the guidebooks with the old skull and crossbones, are poisonous, while the sign of a simmering pot designates those rated delectable. They are all strange fruit, their roots and branches spread out imperceptibly underground.

Spotting a fleshy, lavender-hued mushroom lounging in a lopsided fashion among the pine needles by the path just at the entrance to the woods, I began my study. The fine print describing the several thousand North American mushrooms and fungi in Peterson's guide blurred together, and I zoomed in on the colored pictures in the center of the book. But with more than 450 of them, I had to determine whether I had a hardwood waxy cup, a variegated brittlegill, or a fleecy milk cap before me. To identify my specimen exactly, however, I had to read, and in the reading, I realized that to know this mushroom I must pluck it up from its bed of ease, take a spoor print, decapitate it to see if it bled milk, taste it, smell it. Not an exotic, this mushroom which I'd never distinguished with a name and previously accepted as a commonplace about our cottage was an enigma. For the sake of science or curiosity, however, I was not about to gather it, slice it, subject it to various tests. I imagined stiffened mushrooms nailed in rows on the back porch wall where the umbrellas hang. Not only was I opposed to such mycologizing, reluctant to focus on the fungus and miss the woods, but in taking the exaggerated environmentalist's stance, I also wondered if decapitating mushrooms might not be analogous to chainsawing trees.

I closed the books and continued into the woods, looking still for mushrooms and relying on metaphors to help me carry my information home. Here were two large red-roofed ones with white soffits and stems, a group of small golden parasols, a single white porcelain saucer balanced on a slender stalk, a creamy clump of woodland coral, a bird's fan-shaped tail attached to an oak trunk. Back at the cottage, I seriously considered gills and stems, pondering my books and the relationship between the word and the object. To have the name would be to have the mushroom. As I went out day after day that summer tracking mushrooms in the woods behind the cottage, along the firebreaks, and along Julia's overgrown trails, I was gleeful to realize how many names are metaphors in the fungus world even though the caps and parasols and corals quickly become redundant. That initial enigma's name is blewit (blue cap), and the others I remember from that first day out I came to know as sickener, yellow waxy cap, deathcap, cauliflower coral, turkey tail.

After working on his beans for two years, Thoreau gave up. He tells us he couldn't know beans. Bryologists and mycologists also know they cannot know mosses and mushrooms. Darlington writes, "While this manual provides a record of the known moss flora of the state [of Michigan] and its distribution, the author realizes that it can never be complete."[104] Kent and Vera McKnight, in their introduction to Peterson's guide, acknowledge, "To date no comprehensive inventory of North American fungi has been undertaken, so mycologists . . . do not even know how many mushroom species occur within our borders."[105] An argument being made about the necessity for preserving the rain forests concerns the multitudes of species still undiscovered, uncatalogued, the multitudes of species with the potential either to cause cancer or to cure AIDS. The meek and mild, the low life of the woods humbles me.

FLOWERS

Off and on at supper during the winter Daddy would anticipate spring. He couldn't wait to see the trailing arbutus in the woods at Higgins. He wondered, too, how many pink and yellow lady slipper orchids would be in bloom in April. We used to make at least one trip a spring to Pinewoods to check that the cottage had weathered the winter. That was Mother's spoken reason, but Daddy's unspoken desire was to ascertain that these fragile, exquisite flowers continued to appear among the snow-damp leaves and emerging fern fiddles. He used to find the same arbutus and the same lady slipper in the woods he'd explored in Connecticut as a boy. The flowers connected him to all that was lovely and lost in his boyhood; when he talked of them winter evenings, he was filled with *nostos* (homecoming) and *algia* (pain). As a child, I was greedy in snatching at flowers, and having once brought home a dozen or so red tulips in a clutch from a neighbor's garden, I was taken in hand by Daddy into her dining room to make a formal apology. But in the quickening woods of early spring at Pinewoods, when we first came upon the arbutus's secretive flowers—palest pink against the dark remnants of winter—or the lady slipper—its intricate blossom balanced on a plain thread-like stalk—I turned shy. Since my father yearned for them throughout the winter, I reacted as if in the presence of the sacred. We did not see these flowers every spring, and in the summer woods, without their distinguishing blooms, their foliage fused into the crowd of greenery.

Greenery owns the summer woods. At the bottom of the scroll, a fleck of fungus or spot of mushroom may punctuate it with contrasting color. Not enough sun sifts through the complexity of branches in the woods' upper stories for many flowers in midsummer. Only a few—waxy white wintergreen blossoms and Solomon seal's speckled yellow berries, dangling under the plants' arched stems—manage among the woods' shifting shadows in July and August. Northern Michigan's summer flowers revel elsewhere, however: along the paths and roads, by the shore, across the meadows.

On the long ride by car from the Traverse City airport to Pinewoods, the flowers in the fields are the first sign that you're getting there. With Queen Anne's lace edging them, the fields stretch away to the dark woods, streaked pink with blazing star and clotted lavender with asters. Down the road and closer to Higgins, orange and yellow hawkweeds and white daisies have stitched themselves into the grasses. An intimacy about these Michigan meadows differentiates them from the expansive prairies of Kansas; it's not only that the forests close them comfortably round, but it's also their glad profusion of flowers. They seem to have nothing to struggle against in Michigan's meadows. Caroline Kirkland, in her 1839 autobiographical novel, *A New Home, Who'll Follow?* details the trials of creating a settlement in Michigan and writes that during her first days in the territory she "picked upwards of twenty varieties of wildflowers—some of them of rare and delicate beauty." She declared that "The wild flowers of Michigan deserve a poet of their own."[106]

In Pinewoods and the other camps, women have always tended to flowers. If flowers are not cultivated outside around the cottages, inside the cottages and at the dining halls, vases filled with flowers, ferns, or sprigs of cedar command the centers of tables, window ledges, and mantle pieces. Women friends from all three camps have always enjoyed floral forays together. In the past these women returned with their bouquets from roadside, field, and forest; now they often go forth to identify and photograph new or rare species and to leave the bouquets growing. They canoe down the Au Sable River to see the cardinal flowers flaming along its bank; they seek out the increasingly rare and endangered fringed gentian on The Cut. Their photographs and memories of their slides go home with us at summer's end. Through these women, their bouquets and images, we embrace Gary Snyder's poetic imperatives:

> stay together
> learn the flowers
> go light[107]

From the canoe, you can look Higgins's flowers in the eye. I paddle out around the Cottage Grove docks down to No Man's Land's deserted stretch of shore for a look. I let the canoe drift, just pushing with the paddle to keep it from scraping the rocks or from beaching. Like the woods, this amphibious, marginal shore challenges vision. It will make you dizzy if you try looking everywhere—in the water, on the sand, up the bank, in the air, or if you keep on looking at and for everything—the perfect puddingstone, recyclable debris, a belted kingfisher, dead fish, the missing gentian. The gentian begins blooming in mid-August, the time I've been able to come to Pinewoods in recent years, and it takes on a grail-like quality in my annual search. I realize each year in searching the bank that to try to see it all is to see nothing. I've got to drift with the canoe, and as I let myself drift, I find myself, like Wordsworth wandering among the daffodils on the hills and in his memories, claimed by flowers, then and now.

It's a high sandy bank in No Man's Land, and near the shore only a few trees have been able to stake a claim and then only with difficulty. Here a cedar leans out over the water, and down the shore a bit a clump of birch holds tightly together, leaving space and sun for sumac, witch hazel, horsetail, poison ivy, sweet fern, and a panorama of flowers. Yet in this gorgeous general display, each particular flower is so precisely designed, each of its parts so well organized for the task of living beautifully. Although yellow dominates—cinquefoil, salsify, bread and butter, false foxglove, goldenrod, jewel weed, black-eyed Susan, common St. John's wort, hawkweed, stately mullein—whites and pinks intrude. Here are the familiar fleabane and bladder campion. Baby pink petals surround the yellow disks of three wild roses; beach pea works its way through the tangle; clusters of dusky pink florets dangle from the top of several milkweed stalks; beebalm, with its pinkish mauve tufts, appears casually in and out of the bank's display. Pursuing beebalm back in Kansas, where it tosses its head alongside many roads, I learn from Clinton Owensby's *Kansas Prairie Wildflowers* that it truly is a balm: "The aroma from dried leaves of this plant can be used to freshen closets, trunks, and other areas. A tea from the dried leaves has a delightful aroma and a pleasing taste. Oil from this plant has also been used as a fixative in perfumes. Thymol, an antiseptic drug, can be extracted from the plant. Dried leaves are said to be good for nausea and for vomiting in bilious fever. The Choctaw Indians gave it as a cathartic, for colds, and to promote perspiration."[108]

There's no red on the bank, and blue is a rarity. I put the paddle blade down between two stones to bring the canoe in closer to the shore. Now I can see the delicate azure harebells in amongst the grasses. A solitary harebell grows up from the edge of the coarse cement in front of our pumphouse. Its stem, its narrow leaves, its bell-shaped bloom all so frail it's a wonder how it manages to return every summer; it just goes on nodding at us serenely as we rush in and out from the pumphouse to the dock, preparing to swim or paddle or sail. I push the canoe along, and as a pileated woodpecker can appear in the woods when you're not looking, suddenly the deep cobalt of the fringed gentian appears on the bank. "More and more rare," writes Kathryn Loomis in her 1966 "Pinewoods Nature Notes," and "on no account to be picked or transplanted."[109] Once plentiful on the shores by our cottages, the gentian now grows only on the banks of The Cut and No Man's Land. Several gentians hover in the background behind milkweed and goldenrod. Inconspicuous until you see them and then, like the word you've just looked up in the dictionary, you can concentrate on no other. Corseted in a tight bud, it opens into a fussy flower, its petals frilled like a flapper's skirt. Yet its color, deepening toward the heart's core, conveys an unsettling darkness. Paddling home, I clutch in memory a bouquet of profuse colors with deepening blue unfolding in the center.

Another flower that I seek every August proliferates along paths and back roads and through the woods: the Indian pipe. As the pink lady slipper shows itself only in the early spring, Indian pipes are a late-summer phenomenon. Their annual appearance is so reassuring that as children, each of us wanted to be the first to discover them, to be the one to lead the grownups over to the spot where, unexpectedly, there they were again, just starting to push their white knuckles through the dark ground. You don't see flowers like this every day. Although we expect them in our midst year after year, their arrival is always startling. Translucent succulents, Indian pipes have neither chlorophyll nor leaves. Along their stems are scales, and their flowers form the pipe's bowl. Revealing themselves first as knobs, they soon stretch and stand and shake off pine needles, upright figures with nodding heads. As newborns, Indian pipes seem roseate alabaster. But even then, they're filled with a ghostly light, and as they stiffen with whiteness and eventually darken, they bear more prolonged greetings of mortality than do other flowers whose gaiety fades overnight. As my friend Esther learned encountering death on the path. Seldom do you find a pipe alone. Grouped together, they share a common awareness of light and dark, a common elegant and elegiac demeanor. To anthropomorphize is to degrade and diminish; it may also be to connect. Greeting the Indian pipes each summer elicits the same feelings—reassurance, delight, concern—that I have when greeting a dear Pinewoods friend on the path for the first time in a summer.

If Pinewoods collectively worships its pines, we collectively demonize poison ivy. We live with them both and take neither for granted. Poison ivy has no problem in Michigan's sandy soil and grows with green abandon throughout Pinewoods. If some of us learn the bank where the rare fringed gentian grows, all of us know the banks where common PI grows. PI's three shiny green leaflets, the Norway pine's cluster of two needles, and the single Indian pipe are your first numerals at Pinewoods. Among your first lessons is to beware of those bright green leaflets. The taboo remains as powerful as skull and crossbones, and to this day I watch out for PI whenever I get off the beaten track. Despite communal consciousness and attempts by all families to eradicate PI in the public spaces about their cottages, everyone at camp sooner or later is touched by it. Mother has had swaths of it on her face and neck. I've had it between my fingers and up to my elbows. Playing Sardines—that game that reverses Hide-and-Seek by having everyone hide together rather than separately—at twilight one summer, a dozen of us kids crouched down into a patch of PI and woke the next morning with it. The pale translucent blisters spread across a body into a rash causing an itch which reams beneath the skin's surface to sit carousing on raw nerves. Ordinary scratching causes the blisters to suppurate, but won't reach the prickling itch. It rages hottest at night, like larger pains, a rotten apple that taints your barrel of dreams, destroying concern for anything but itself.

You don't have to touch PI to be made miserable by it, which is part of its fiendish mystique. Its meanness can be invisible, airborne like viruses; it arrives when you pat Minnie the cat or Ginger the dog. You slather on Calamine lotion, the common balm, for a momentary calm and coolness. But it resumes, demanding your full attention. In the dining hall, the Calamine lotion's white patches establish you as an initiate into communal commiseration. We all remember our own bad patches. In time your own particular itching does abate, but poison ivy as a species persists. It will not be exterminated—not by pulling down its vines and pulling up its roots, not by powerful chemicals, not by burning. Its signature green leaves return, below our pavilion, along the path to the mailbox, by Marion's back cottage. I greet them, familiar demons.

On the way home from the mailbox after lunch, Mother and I walk up the road to the cottage. Mother passes the wrapped *Flint Journal* and the advertising flyers she was carrying over to me. Her hands free, she begins pulling up the broad green-leafed plants and their jangling yellow berries along the road and loading up her arms with them. Never mind the dirt and sand on her shirt sleeves. "I can't stand these things," she mutters, "they don't belong here, and they're going to take over the woods." This is an old song and dance, which she performs against nonindigenous plant species every time she comes up this road. I grieve that she sings and dances it mostly alone, but her anger and distress leave me clutching the mail. All I can do is keep pace with her while she stoops to pluck up more of these noxious lilies-of-the-valley. She moves over to the neighbors' garage and attacks the snow-on-the-mountain, another stranger to Pinewoods.

Years ago previous owners of our neighbors' cottages, violated the unspoken camp regulation against gardening. They planted gladioli and Asiatic lilies, veronica and, to Mother's present frustration, the lilies-of-the-valley and snow-on-the-mountain, both of which are creeping into the woods back of the cottages and which she is presently determined to root out. By the summer of 1996, she had uprooted the lilies-of-the-valley from the woods behind our cottage, while behind the neighbors the aberrant green patch has spread. No one outside of our family seems to know about her campaign, and only Howie has assisted her, spraying Round-Up, a withering nontoxic chemical, on the lilies' bright life. I am cowardly and uneasy about pulling up the lovely plants I've cultivated in my Kansas garden. I note that a bushy hydrangea, also a vestige from the days of gardening, flourishes in solitary peace between our cottage and the cottage next door.

I weed my Kansas garden vigorously, refusing all chemical assistance. In April I'm after dandelions in the lawn with a vengeance, and throughout the summer every morning after breakfast I'm out in my nightgown looking for broadleaf, bind weed, crab grass, lamb's quarters, and sticktights. I keep my murderous tool—the weeder—by the back door and have learned to use it with exactitude. In midsummer, those parts of the garden given over to indigenous Kansas flowers—fleabane, butterfly weed, columbine, coneflowers—run riot with color and pushy plants. So aggressive, they overshadow plants closer to the ground such as the verbena and coreopsis; they grow stalky and gawky and are walking over into the peony beds. I remind myself of Vita Sackville-West's advice—"You must . . . be ruthless about it. That is the only way to garden."[110]—and seriously consider the necessity of a massive uprooting.

The bank of wildflowers in No Man's Land with its wondrous diversity of ordinary and extraordinary, my own Kansas garden, and the spreading patches of the lilies-of-the-valley and snow-on-the-mountain prompt me to engage in the familiar debate regarding the difference between weed and flower. When is a plant a weed? And when a flower? When do we want to unearth it, exterminate it? trash it? And when do we want to cultivate it, provide the best in nutrients for it, treasure it? Who arbitrates for the beauty of beebalm or hawkweed? What is the place of poison ivy? And so even the gentle language of flowers turns philosophical, psychological, political, invoking questions which turn the primrose path toward hell. Despite evolutionary processes, despite a century or more of human pollutants, despite our anxious questions, the woods and fields and banks surrounding Higgins are so generous, so tolerant of a wild diversity that any distinction between weeds and flowers must be irrelevant.

I know that I want to have my wild woods and to cultivate it, too, like Caroline Kirkland, who planted hyacinth bulbs as soon as she settled into her Michigan home. Pinewoods is a garden in the midst of forest. Here is health and beauty, for beauty in the eye of this beholder is health. Health is beauty; beauty is health, and as arbiter of my eye, that is all I know, and perhaps all I need to know. Hyacinths are no substitute for fringed gentians, I know. When the lovely lily-of-the-valley or the sprightly gray-headed coneflower becomes an invader and destroys the health of other living plants, it becomes a noxious weed, diminishing health and beauty. Our task, then, is to seek from becoming noxious weeds ourselves and in our deeds be true to health and beauty.

BUGS

There are no chiggers at Higgins Lake. The scourge of summer walkers and picnickers, chiggers keep me on Kansas's beaten paths and away from the waving fields of grasses from May through September. When I tell people that Higgins has no black flies, those pestiferous mites that destroy the Edenic possibilities for campers in other northern states, they stand incredulous: "No chiggers!?" "No black flies, either!?" "This place can't be real!"

Other bugs swarm at Pinewoods, although concepts of "God's country," "Paradise on Earth," or Eden never include insects. Even if the Utopian community was set in south Florida, the inhabitants quickly learned to rub fish oil over themselves to ward off mosquitoes, banishing them forever from the text. Yet bugs, like our dogs and cats, exist wherever we do, the world over, except perhaps at the poles. We carry them.

The adults used to complain constantly about carpenter ants in the cottage, and because I don't see them around now as I did in childhood, I assume that a successful chemical campaign was waged against them in the days before we became conscious of the dangers of applying chemicals at random, or perhaps with the advent of a furnace in the cottage, making it less damp, they've simply all moved out. I believe I also contributed my bit to the general demise of carpenter ants in the cottage. I pursued each shiny black body I saw as it raced across the floor or up a wall, heading for the security of a wainscoting or a windowsill, until I could squash it dead. A slight crunch under the foot or the fist, and I had done a noble deed. The truth of the matter, though, was that my feelings about carpenter ants became conflicted when I learned to connect them with the labyrinthine patterns engraving the cedar posts of the porch and pavilion and the supports of the porch and pavilion swings. Secretly, wondering whether my action was aiding and abetting the insect enemy, I peeled back the bark on the swing to detect the ants' mazes. They wended their vermicular ways without beginning or end, purposeless it seemed. Sometimes these paths were stuffed with sawdust, and I scraped them clean with a fingernail to discover the sheen of the small wooden channel. Little did I know how functional the ants' elaborate labyrinths were, excavated as nurseries for their young.

Spiders claim occupancy of the cottage and the woods year-round. Without them, bugs would control Pinewoods and the world. Their webs between window frames and windowsills, discovered when we arrive at the cottage after the long winter, reveal a diversity of unseen insect life in the cottage. Husks of small flies, beetles, moths, and gnats interrupt the webs' symmetry. Below these discombobulated webs, the sills are peppered and salted with the remains of their gorging. Such detritus suggests an intensity of activity which proceeds beyond our knowing. Despite a frenzy of dusting throughout the summers, webs appear again at the windows from nowhere, the spiders themselves the cottage's invisible but constant occupants. Daddy longlegs, however, are jauntily apparent at all hours, in all places. The world presents no obstacles to them as they high-step their merry way across pumphouse workbench, along pavilion railings, or down the path with the rest of us.

Throughout the woods is evidence of diverse spider artistry—filmy domes, doilies, lattices, bowls, hammocks, traps, and orbs. Early in the morning, the spiders' shining threads become spun sunlight. Before anything moves, these threads link twig and twig, tree and tree, cross from porch to porch, wrapping us all in a gauzy shimmering. Joggers speeding down the path to get their running in before breakfast, and Howie dashing down the steps to take an early morning plunge into the lake, all unwittingly snap a thousand spider bands. Mother, always the first one up and to the dining hall when she was growing up, used to carry a large stick before her to break the spider webs across the back path. A good deed to begin the day. Yet every summer the cobwebs with their droppings appear in the corner of the window frames, and every morning they are renewed across the path, and I think of Yeats's commentary on human civilizations: "All things fall and are built again, and those that build them again are gay."[111] Occasionally, out sailing, I've been surprised by a spider drifting gaily in from the air onto the boat. Its thread dangles from a cloud. Its trajectory spins from an island pine. Ballooning, students of arachnids call such traveling; "venturing, throwing, seeking," Whitman calls it—or possibly faith.[112] Its legs clutching and unclutching air, this wisp climbs up air to reach the forestay, adding its invisible lines to the rigging.

Near the shore, burnished blue dragonflies embroider the air, often stitching themselves together, and just before a storm, water striders and whirligig beetles begin to skate and dart furiously over the surface of shallow waters. At the dock, just as you decide not to go out for a sail but to settle down into a beach chair and a novel, you can be buzzed and bitten by a horsefly, whose one bite may be the nasty equivalent of a dozen black flies. Nothing sluggish about these creatures. Occasionally, horseflies and other insects leave the land for the high seas. The butterfly or bee, discovered wandering over the middle of the lake, is always greeted as a fellow traveler. Aunt Betty, swimming far out in front of the cottage, finding a ladybug or grasshopper gasping for air in the water, always brought it into shore. I've seen her walk the whole way back with her hands cupped prayerfully before her. Not stopping at the dock, she stepped out on the shore near grasses and opened her fingers.

Between the roof rafter and the center post in the pavilion, a marbled spider constructs a hypotenuse. With her triangular space defined, she weaves of fine silk a geometrical wonder, a circular web of multiple, connected radii within it. She takes up residence in the center, where she can survey her glistening estate, where she can sway with winds coming up from the lake, where she can respond to the slightest vibration in the radii. Evening after evening, sipping our wine, counting ducks on the dock, watching dusk come in across the lake, we look up and admire her from our seats in the pavilion. Her fragile architecture supports us. I show her to my grandniece, Hillary, "See the spider in her pretty home." Hillary has doubts. We sing "The Spider Song": "The eensy-weensy spider went up the water spout. . . ." She joins me, imitating the song's gestures with glee. I suggest, "Let's stand up on the seat to see the spider in her pretty home." Hillary screams, wraps her arms around herself, runs out of the pavilion, "No! No! Bad! Poison!" We retrieve her and comfort her. "Everything is OK. You don't have to see the spider. The spider doesn't want to hurt you." The web billows; the spider holds tight. I wonder how we failed both this dear child and the marbled spider.

Instead of chiggers and black flies, no-see-'ems attack on the land, and invisible flatworms attack in the water. Unseen themselves, they can produce large red welts, very visible on the skin of white folks, tender tots, and tough old salts alike. These sneaks are responsible for changing the carefree summer into the seven-day itch for some. After waiting several days for that perfect Higgins afternoon, I waded out from the dock into deep water with my niece Lucy for a long-anticipated swim. We lollygagged along, giggling as the cold water crept up our bodies. When it reached our temperature-sensitive breasts, Lucy expressed my sense precisely, "I wish I could unscrew my teats." We kept our arms raised above the water, only occasionally lowering them to rest on the lake surface, and we walked on tiptoe until suddenly the cold was in our armpits. With a splash, both of us were swimming and snorting in the water. We frisked about all the way back to the shore, switching from side-stroke to crawl to easy float. That night I started itching, and itching; I couldn't stop, and I couldn't sleep. On the edge of sleep, my "imagination of disaster"[113] stirred, and I was awake with the dread that I'd contracted Lyme disease from the increase of ticks and deer back in the woods. Surely it wasn't chiggers. Then I knew it had to be the notorious swimmer's itch, rumored as a threat at Higgins for several summers, but never before revealing itself in its true colors in our cottage.

The parasitic flatworm, the culprit behind the itch, has aroused the ire of vacationers, the interest of resort owners, and the concern of the Higgins Lake Foundation. The eggs of this flatworm find an initial host in the lake's snails, but with their transformation into larvae, a second host is needed, which is usually a merganser, but a human being who spends a long time wading out into deep water and swimming back will also do. One attack has resulted in another, however, and consequently Higgins's merganser community is now at risk. Given that copper-sulfate compounds, which can effectively destroy the flatworm eggs and larvae, are also damaging to benign zooplankters, fish eggs, and minnows, local volunteer harassment patrols were created to "capture, inoculate, and remove" mergansers from the lake, intending thereby to disrupt the snail-duck cycle. The Higgins Lake Foundation newsletter for fall, 1995, thus reported: "In their second year of service, the volunteer patrols, using their own boats . . . , performed many hours of service during the merganser mating and nesting period. Their effective use of shotguns to fire scare shells reduced the total hatch to only one brood of birds which was removed."[114]

Mother, who spends hours messing about in the water, insists that the welts on her legs are caused by the woods' no-see-'ems. Appalled by the treatment of the mergansers, the possibility for error in identifying the waterfowl on the part of the volunteers, the diminishing number of water birds on the lake, she writes long and passionate letters to local organizations: "Have the sufferers from so-called swimmer's itch been to a dermatologist for a clear diagnosis? Are they certain they are not bothered by a lack of immunity to 'no-see-ems' [sic] which attack in the woods, in yards, and on beaches? This discomfort can be healed with a prescription salve or antihistamine pill." I am with her in the opening salvo of her first letter, "Our family continues to be extremely dissatisfied with any harassment of ducks at Higgins Lake,"[115] but nevertheless, the next morning I'm on my way to Roscommon for Ken-Tox, the magic medicine for swimmer's itch. Worrying that she'll fear the lake as well as spiders, we wonder what kind of medicine to apply to little Hillary's tender skin and psyche before she sets out to test her water wings.

Worse, perhaps, than the horsefly or no-see-'em or even the parasitic flatworm was the plague of gypsy moths that began to infest the woods in 1988. Initially, the gypsy moths were baffling. Named without sensitivity to the Romany people, the moths are vagabonds; at Pinewoods they seemed to come from nowhere and to settle in to stay. Entomologists claim they spread by hitching rides on whatever's going—trains or planes or motorcycles. There is no romanticizing their behavior. During that first year we noticed only a nondescript moth, small and dull brown. It kept low, flickering in and out of sunlight. Innocent in its soundlessness, in the delicacy of its motions. Even then, however, you sensed something ominous in its ceaseless movement, in its daytime appearance in the woods. What was the moth's business with our woods? The next year, connecting a handsome hairy larva to the moth and identifying the moth as the male of the species, we began to understand the business at hand.

People arriving at Pinewoods for the opening of camp were startled by a bizarre sound that seemed to surround them. They heard it everywhere—sitting out on the pavilion at dusk, trying to fall asleep at night, taking a walk to Lakeside. They described the sound in different ways—as the ripping of taffeta, the sloshing of bilge, the slashing of long grass, but always they described it as incessant. It was the munch of the larvae eating oak leaves. With the camp's young oaks losing all their leaves to this devouring in a mere two or three years and with the older oaks subsequently threatened by their voracity, people started discussing the moth's life cycle at the cocktail hour. We observed that under cottage eaves, on tree trunks, and off porch swings, the larvae were forming countless squirming and squirting nut-brown pupae. By then people had also noticed another moth, the more secretive female, all white, with prettily patterned wings, so soft and sedentary: a lovely Victorian maid, who in pressing herself against her rough tree trunk sofa, dies after giving birth to a mass of tiny eggs.

The gypsy moth, unlike the clothes moth with which individual cottages have to make their peace, involved all of Pinewoods, the other camps, and finally the whole of Roscommon County. It very obviously demanded more than mothballs in the closet. In Pinewoods it led to the organization of an Ecology Committee; information was ordered from diverse sources and distributed to all cottages; an entomology expert arrived from the Department of Natural Resources to lecture at the dining hall. We moved beyond knowledge of the gypsy moth's life cycle to information on its extermination. If we feared for the oak trees, we feared even more for the pines, which the experts declared would become prey once the oaks were gone. Envisioning disaster far worse than clear-cutting, many of us went to work. Mother was maniacal about it. At our cottage, we got under way just after breakfast, and everybody had a task: ladders up to the window ledges and to the eaves to get the pupae; knives to scrape the egg masses off the trees and into buckets of soapy water; burlap to tie around the waists of as many trees as possible to provide dark caves for the larvae which could then be found and easily squished.

During the summers of 1990 and 1991, although the lake sparkled in front of our cottage, my thoughts were of doom and gloom in the woods. The moths were killing the trees, but there were moments when I felt that we, embarked on killing the moths, were ensnared in an oppressive Death Squadron, characterized by a railing rhetoric, self-righteousness, and obsession. We kept score on the numbers of larvae, pupae, moths, and egg masses destroyed around the cottage, undaunted by the countless numbers in the back woods, down in No Man's Land, even next door where we could not wage our murderous knives and suds. We shook our heads in dismay over members of camp who were not responding to the plague with equivalent zeal.

A crisis evolved over the issue of aerial spraying in the camp. On one side were the "realists" who spoke of the futility of our piecework destruction, and on the other side were the "environmentalists" who realized that the chemical *Bacillus Thuringiensis*, commonly called BT, would not only exterminate all lepidoptera but also reduce the population of song birds that would feed on poisoned insects. Roscommon County was all for spraying, with those individual cottages desiring not to have their air contaminated requested to fly white balloons from their rooftops on the day designated for the planes to let loose the BT. We flew our balloons, and the woods were sprayed, and by the summer of 1992 the gypsies had decamped. The ominous flittings in the forest ceased, and in 1993 the oaks were dressed to the nines in frilly light green. Here and there a smear of hardened pus, an ancient egg mass, appeared on a tree trunk, evidence that the woods had endured the worst.

One morning during my days in the Death Squadron, I checked the dark burlap folds for larvae and discovered no worm, but a bug of quite a different order. A beetle, about an inch and a half long, with audacious eyes, fierce mandibles, and a carapace of dazzling, iridescent malachite. Mother kept her eye on him while I raced into the cottage for the *Guide to Familiar American Insects*. Here was the intrepid caterpillar hunter beetle known, according to the guide's description, to attack and feed on gypsy moth larvae. Thus all along we had had a knight in shining armor in our midst. In the summer of 1996, entomologists reported a parasitic fungus living on and dealing death to gypsy moths. Perhaps there'd been no need for spraying or burlap wrappings or the plastic Chinese lanterns radiating the female moths' pheromone we later hung throughout the woods to seduce and destroy the male moths. It is we, of course, who desire to be saved and yearn for knights, who need to be saved from ourselves. Caterpillar hunter beetles and parasitic fungus, like gypsy moths, simply go about their lives.

The light outside the front door of the cottage stays on until everybody's in. Teenagers are always the last ones. Sometimes now Howie and Tammy talk late on the pavilion with friends, and sometimes I go down to the dock to catch the stars or to watch the moon track across the lake. There's always a halo of small insects that not one of us has ever taken the care to identify—the same anonymous variety that end up in spider webs—spinning an ecstatic Sufi dance in miniature round the front-door light when I return. Surely they would find stars to worship if our light was not here.

"*T*his country offers unusual attractions: game of various kinds being said to be plenty, such as bear, deer, wolves, elk, lynx, wildcat, badger, foxes, beaver, otter, martin, fisher, mink, wild duck, partridge, grouse, and other species, the best hunting season being in October and November."[116] So wrote A. Button in the summer of 1873 in an attempt to attract Civil War veterans to homestead in the cutover areas around Higgins Lake.

In all the years I've walked the forests behind Pinewoods, of all these animals, I've seen only deer and the occasional fox, in addition to raccoon, skunk, porcupine. And there are always rumors circulating about Pinewoods of an elusive wolverine, the Michigan state animal, now officially extinct in the state. The names of these animals, common North American mammals known to most school-children from alphabet books, Thornton Burgess's Mother West Wind stories, and zoos, read now like a litany for lost souls. I repeat their names, for after all we retain the names, and each name reminds us of a definitive shape, a certain color, a peculiar glint of eye. But only a few of the creatures themselves continue to run in our woods. Roads, houses, subdivisions, shopping malls press in, sending no eviction notices.

Following the lumber barons, the pleasure-seekers of Pinewoods and the other camps prepared the way for the animals' silent departure. Uncle Paul, describing his boyhood at the end of the nineteenth century at Pinewoods, recalls that he and his companions "shot partridges in the low ground along the lake. . . . Our chief diversion was to chase fish ducks and shoot at them with Sam's 22-calibre rifle. This process is not as murderous as it sounds. We occasionally got one." He remembers that Roscommon at this time was a town without restriction on either drinking or hunting: "There was a saloon on every corner. Men in Mackinaws paraded the streets and made merry. There were no game laws. Hunters went into the woods year round."[117]

Uncle Paul's father, the Reverend Bruske, was both a hunter and a fisherman but one who, in his wife's words, "loved the woods and waters" and who "for years had ceased to shoot game for the mere purpose of achievement." Grandma Bruske recalls in detail, however, his thrill one day at seeing "a large fish hawk majestically soaring over the lake" and his subsequent resolve "with all of a hunter's enthusiasm to be up with the sun next morning to secure the prize." Off the next day, she narrates, he was distracted from his quest for the fish hawk by the appearance of a large deer, and "true to his hunter's instinct," killed it with a single shot. He did not realize that in 1881, following on the agitation of the Michigan Sportsmen's Association which recognized that market hunters were diminishing Michigan's game supply, a state law limiting the killing of deer except for household food or scientific purposes had been passed. The Reverend Bruske, consequently, was soon visited in Pinewoods by the state game warden. As the deer had already been dissected, with its meat distributed to the cottages throughout camp and its head prepared for mounting and display at Alma College, he successfully argued that household needs and scientific purposes were served. The Reverend Bruske was exonerated, as his wife notes in concluding her account: "The jury was unanimous in acquittal and the game warden heartily approved their decision. The incident furnished a bit of pleasant gossip for the newspapers of the state especially in exploiting a joke on a minister . . . However, the campers . . . were jubilant over the achievement and outcome, and the college appreciated the fine specimen which still adorns its museum."[118]

In the nineteenth century, it was the concerned action of hunters which resulted in restrictions on the slaughter of wild animals. Henry Roony, assigned in 1877 by the Michigan Sportsmen's Association the difficult task of working with northern woodsmen to compile statistics on this slaughter, reported back in 1881 that more than 70,000 deer had been killed the previous year and sold out of state for venison and hides. Consulting station master receipts, Roony learned that the weight of their carcasses necessitated adding extra freight cars onto the trains passing through Roscommon. Although enforcement of hunting laws proved problematic in the nineteenth century, Roony's statistics were compelling to both the gentlemen hunters and the legislature, and from 1881 on Michigan developed laws restricting and defining hunting, limiting the length of the season and the number of deer to be killed, determining the counties to be open and permissible weapons.

I can't ever be jubilant over the death of a deer. During the time when Howie and I were in elementary and junior high school, we always went north over the long teachers' convention weekend in the fall, a weekend that fell in the middle of hunting season. Although "No Hunting" signs were posted in our woods, the echoes of shots seemed to ricochet around the lake through the entire week-end. On our way home, when a car with a deer strapped over a fender passed us, Howie and I rushed ritualistically to roll down a back window and to shout out as loudly as we could, "BOO HUNTER!" When one car after another passed with its trophies callously displayed, we became hoarse with shouting. We had been well conditioned by *Bambi*. Often three or four deer would be tied on one car, and once a bear was stretched out on a car roof, each leg pegged down to a bumper corner. Thinking back, I'm surprised no one shot back at us. Yet with the moral certainty of anyone with a quaking identity, I was vehement in my disgust with hunters. After all, at age seven or eight, I knew definitively what I wanted to be when I grew up: a veterinarian living in the woods whose sole pur-pose was to care for animals wounded by careless hunters. Since I had entertained myself during a week sick in bed drawing blueprints for the Hansel-and-Gretel cottage where I would do my work, I had even committed myself to such a future on paper.

A major sport for us then, once or twice a summer, was to pile into a car just after dusk to go look for deer. Adults and kids, we wanted them alive; we came back from these excursions exuber-antly reporting to those who had stayed home the number we had seen. (Someone had tacked small round reflectors on trees at the entrance into camp to fool us upon our return into thinking deer had been lurking all along back at Pinewoods.) In those earlier days the deer appeared at the edge of a meadow which once had been a farmer's field. Or occasionally alongside a road. Sometimes alone. Sometimes in family groups. The car crunched to a halt, and in the presence of the living deer, the bunch of us were stunned into silence. Here was the mysterious other, but like us—ears alert, eyes staring. We passed the binoculars silently, and even though the light was thickening, we could study the fine hairs on a tail or a moist nostril. What did they see in us? The tail twitched, the nostril wrin-kled, and in an instant the deer had flickered back into the forest. Or we left first, the silence broken with the charged ignition, the deer still standing in a freeze.

During my childhood we seldom saw deer close to the cottage out of season, although occasion-ally we would discover the quotation marks of their hooves bracketing stones along the Stage Road. It is commonplace now, to see their tracks out back, and in the winter, it's apparent they're every-where in camp. Several winters running, they've generated a browse line in camp, chewing the low cedars in front of some cottages down to their trunks. I imagine them in the winter standing in the pavilion gazing out at the frozen lake with their clear eyes. The Department of Natural Resources points to an increase in Michigan's deer population. Residential subdivisions all around the lake have likewise increased, including one subdivision just east of Pinewoods with a street named "Rising Fawn Trail." There are accounts of deer wandering into Roscommon's main street, startled by traffic, by street lights, leaping over cars only to stumble and break their legs on the sidewalk, crashing into holiday storefront windows only to sever arteries and bleed to death at Santa's feet.

Lately, when out walking the trails behind the cottage by myself after breakfast or dinner, I have frequently been surprised by deer, and they by me. I am hearing only scattered birdsong in the upper reaches of the trees and attempting to be attentive to the diversity of fungus at my feet. Thus, the snapping of twigs in the middle distance comes unexpectedly, and I look to see the deer rise. Fleet, it is already vanishing like smoke through the scrim of trees. So much that we live through we forget as dreams, but this ascendant deer, passing in an instant, rises repeatedly in memory.

About ten years ago, on the trail out to the mailboxes after lunch, I bumped into a mother raccoon with her toddlers strung out behind her. I was perambulating and so were they, and we might have continued along the same path together. I must have smelled all wrong or they had business in another direction, for quickly they took to the underbrush. Yet they visit camp nocturnally, surprising a neighbor who's sleeping in a hammock, investigating vulnerable garbage bags, and leaving their antic handprints on the shore. Perhaps it was twenty years ago when Mother had me look up into the top of a slender young pine in back of the dining hall. With the sun behind it, the tree appeared to have developed a deformative burl: a large, bristling porcupine. Its spines, however, shone, which gave the creature a Byzantine saint's halo, showing the whole spectrum's prismatic colors. A dark face was concentrated in the center of the halo: small bright eyes and two long teeth like orange rinds. I stared; it stared. No saint. A splatter of pee, and that was the last live porcupine I've seen. (They lie dead, unhaloed clods along I-75 going north. Their quills nothing up against a machine.) By checking middens of sawdust pellets at the base of pines, Mother has always been able to keep track of the porcupine population in the woods during the summer, naming the group of trees with the largest heaps "The Porcupine Condominium." But tramping the woods in the summer following the tornado, I located no inn at all. There was only an abandoned foxes' den, with the debris of feasts—squirrel skull, rabbit bones, and turkey feathers—marking its several exits and entrances.

In the early days of the camp, wire fences were set up to keep cows from nearby farms from wandering in along the path in front of the cottages. Those farms had largely disappeared by the time of my childhood, and Ed Sisco kept no cows in his pasture—only his two large work horses, Fanny and Maud. They served us well, hauling the clumsy wooden cradles, which held our boats, out of the boathouses behind the cottages at the beginning of every summer. Turning easily in their heavy steel harness to the commands of "gee" and "haw," they pulled the boats down the ravine separating Cottage Grove and Pinewoods and out into the lake until they could float free from their cradles, and then they pulled them out again at the end of the season. As much as the opening and closing of the dining hall, this event ritualistically began and ended the summer season at Pinewoods, and many people were on hand for the excitement when a big boat like the *Rainbow* went in—the men there to assist Mr. Sisco, and the children to watch his wonderful horses. Marilyn and I, eager to change our status from spectator to participant, got the idea that we could help with the operation by wading out to collect the horses' floating turds in coffee cans. There is no record of the last time Fanny and Maud brought the boats up the ravine, as there is no record of their deaths. Each Pinewoods family now cares for its boats independently, putting them in by car or simply taking them up the lake to B&B, the closest boatyard, where all the maneuvering is done with machinery and cranes. The corrugated boathouses behind our cottages are gone, as is the Sisco barn, although the Lakeview Riding Stable on the blacktop continues to manage a few horses.

Our pets have always been with us at Pinewoods. For many years dogs have been leashed by camp regulation to keep them from straying into cottages where they aren't welcome or into the dumpsters behind the dining hall. Like its boats, Pinewoods's pets are remembered by names and stories and are integral to a family's identity and history. Boats and pets bring forth our tenderness and sense of whimsy. Nobody in our cottage opens the linen closet upstairs without remembering that this is where Minnie, the tiger cat, chose to have her first litter of kittens. A second litter, born in the woodshed, was murdered by a weasel. Howie and Tammy made their trails through the back woods to accommodate their dogs, and some summers ago Howie showed me the peculiar "Key-Hole" tree beneath which they placed the ashes of their German shepherd, Bandit. The ashes of their first dog,

Betsy, are in deep grass down by the shore. Some pets swim, some sail, some go canoeing, some disappear beneath their cottages and are not seen for days, others wait patiently at the end of a dock until their particular person returns from the water.

At Pinewoods, inside and out, day and night, you can always count on the scurry and flurry of small mammalian life. Mice live with us in the cottage. You seldom see them in July and August, but at night you can hear them between the walls scurrying on about their business. On arrival at the cottage for the summer, you can determine what their business has been during the winter, for in a couple of dressers in upstairs bedrooms we find drawer linings, dresser scarves, and whatever duds had been forgotten from the previous summer shredded and wadded into nests. Mice, moths, and changing fashions meant the end of long-legged woolen bathing suits. Squirrels—black, red, and gray—risk life and limb in their leaping from trees to dash across roofs, to rush around porches, to chase each other in rings, to return to the trees to begin the mad scramble again. Chipmunks are everywhere underfoot. Our paths cross countless times on a daily basis. Their attendance at pavilion cocktail parties is *de rigueur,* whether they know it or not. They sit among us on their haunches, so very bright-eyed and expectant. *They* are satisfied with small peanuts. But they aren't conversationalists and don't stay long; in a flash, they take their peanuts and go home. Scattering like leaves in a gust. They'll be back, though, to check the pavilion for crumbs after we've gone to dinner.

One summer Emily Morgan, age three, got to pet a snake. Her mom had found the garter snake lounging on the warm concrete steps going down to their waterfront just as Mother and I were coming by their cottage on the way back from picking up the mail. Letting the snake wrap its lovely limber body around her left wrist, Emily's mom showed it to her: "Look at its little red tongue. Look at its pretty yellow stripes." She traced these pretty stripes with her right index finger, and Emily followed with her index finger. Watching Emily and her first snake with her mother, I remembered Mother sitting in her bathing suit on the ice-age boulder by our dock, her bare arm entwined with a milk snake. "It doesn't hurt," she had said. "See, it's soft and dry. It tickles almost like a feather." Ever instructive, she added, "Michigan has only one poisonous snake—the Massasauga rattler—and no one's ever died from its bite." Because of that summer I got to pet a snake, I can look a snake in the eye, and it will look me back, smell me with the flicker of its tongue, and be off. In Kansas, where Rattlesnake Round-Ups occur every spring, snakes are demonized and then cooked up and sold in hot-dog buns.

I didn't grow up to be the veterinarian of the forests. Cleaning cages and preparing special diets as a volunteer for the injured creatures brought to a Kansas wildlife rehabilitation center is as close as I've come to fulfilling that childhood vision. Here we're trained regarding the dangers of imprinting. If we must have wild animals in our lives, let them stalk and slither and romp through our dreams. There's wildness still in the cast of jungle green in my cat's stare at certain instances and in the sudden flex of her muscles and flashing leap for an invisible sun mote. As much as I might yearn to meet a wolverine on the mail path, I cherish more the illusion that its disappearance signifies safety—not absence. The DNR set loose pairs of wild turkeys in Roscommon County several years ago, and they have proliferated now into flocks. Going down a back road, you'll see them just inside the edge of the woods, standing stiff like bowling pins in their awkward dignity, only their heads turning as you pass by. Recently Howie had to slam on his brakes when a mother turkey, followed by her gang of gawky adolescent offspring, stepped out from the grass to cross the road. On their heels came another mother with smaller youths, followed by a third with an entire brood of toddlers.

BIRDS

At the turn of the century, while ornithologists were in the process of establishing precise nomenclature for North American birds, state legislatures began imposing the first laws governing the hunting of game birds. Cultural historian Peter J. Schmitt notes that at this time popular writers, moralists, and manufacturers were acknowledging that birds had come to have diverse significations for Americans.[119] The subject of numerous books and sermons, certain birds were classified as virtuous—for their cheerful daytime songs, their industry, and their domesticity—others as vicious—for their aggression and their sloth. Bird books—both sentimental and scientific—sold by the millions, and bird motifs accompanied commercial products: birds meant business. In the cottage, bird books abound—from several decades and for several regions, for children and for experts; for the generalist there is Roger Tory Peterson's *Field Guide to the Birds of Eastern and Central North America,* "the birder's Bible." And birds abound as well: cardinals fly across bedroom curtains, nightingales sing among the plum blossoms on dresser-scarves, pelicans perch on coffee mugs, cormorants dive on a wall-hanging, a gull soars on a couch pillow, and a cast-iron loon holds the living room door open.

Birds are like certain books I've known: barometers of changing perceptions. My first birds were in a book, the 1901 edition of Neltje Blanchan's *Bird Neighbors,* which Daddy had received from his grandmother for his ninth birthday. With fifty-two colored plates, it was subtitled "An Introductory Acquaintance with One-Hundred and Fifty Birds Commonly Found in the Gardens, Meadows, and Woods About Our Home."[120] After taking it down from our library shelf in Flint, we'd sit together on the couch beneath the multicolored afghan knitted by his mother and once again go through the book, the plates arranged by the birds' most conspicuous color, until I could identify almost every one. Accurate identification of common birds is as reassuring and pleasing as slipping a saucer under a cup, as recalling a name to accompany the face of a person who appears, after years, in the grocery-store aisle. As a child, birds meant the pleasure not simply of my father's approval but also of participation in his sphere. He told me about the wrens in the wisteria arbor in his Connecticut boyhood home, and the penguins parading along the Patagonian coast he'd seen on a voyage to Buenos Aires in the 1920s.

Around the second grade, I acquired a pack of small cards, identified as "Useful Birds of America" and made available by Arm & Hammer and Cow Brand Baking Soda. Each card had a picture of a bird on one side, information about the bird on the other, with an early environmental commandment—"For the good of all, do not destroy the birds"—printed in capital letters beneath. Shuffling them over and over in bed before turning off the light at night, I became acquainted with particular colors, shapes, and names: the Baltimore oriole, the rose-breasted grosbeak, the yellow-billed cuckoo, the belted kingfisher, the indigo bunting. From my bird cards, the process of learning to celebrate and cherish difference began: here was my introduction to diversity, to multiculturalism, to infinite variety. Though I'm far from adept at differentiating among the species birders know as the LBJs—"the little brown jobs"—this sense of diversity became intensified when I realized that I had to start paying attention to differences in mature and immature birds, in sexual coloration, nest shapes, eggs, flight patterns, songs.

Walking through the Flint Junior College Natural History Museum on the way home from elementary school, I discovered much of this diversity had been immaculately labeled, ordered, and laid out under glass in drawer after drawer. The tiny celadon-colored hummingbird eggs and the great ivory ostrich eggs were separated by rows of ellipsoidal globes of graduated sizes, each perfect except for the small pinprick from which the life-sustenance had been sucked. In other drawers, innumerable warblers rested on their sides, presented as if in a fashion designer's showcase like small, jeweled evening bags. Each seemed woven in a unique intricate pattern, the iridescent feathers in some shimmering. But dark wizened feet, dangling at the end of each lovely pouch and turned in on themselves, gave death away.

Living birds nest sporadically in the eaves of our house in Flint and in the trees around the cottage in the spring; all summer they continue about their own tasks in the shrubs and trees around the cottage, hovering about the docks and shore, zooming and drifting over the lake; in the winter they come in flocks to the feeders in the backyard of the house and at the cottage. The behavior of birds, along with the changes in leaves, flowers, and temperature, spells out the order of seasons. But flying in the face of expectation and order, individuals will always take you by surprise. Although it might be possible to name, identify, categorize, classify, compile them, they'll fool you into wonder. If you're out driving in the Kansas country, for example, and you stop and roll down the car window, a meadowlark, likely as not, will be right there to trill in your (h)ear(t). It may have happened countless times, but you're never prepared because each time, the song comes as a clarion call to begin the world anew. It's at Pinewoods, though, where birds began to show me wonder.

On an ordinary morning, a bald eagle crashed through the trees between our cottage and our neighbors' cottage. Branches broke; wind roared; wings rushed. It swooped and was gone, taking those things that make time—motion and sound—and leaving a visible blankness. With the eagle's departure, time started up again, and we asked ourselves if we had seen what we had seen. Another morning, a distant hammering—continuous and bold—drew me into the woods. I'm so used to my eyes doing the guiding that I felt uneasy letting my ears lead me this time. Thinking of bats and whales mapping their world by sonar and snakes and wolves mapping it by scent, I listened and followed the repeated staccato sounds, a distinct solo against the nattering forest. Thus my ears saw the pileated woodpecker, high in the oak, before my eyes.

My mind wasn't on birds the morning last summer when Howie and I headed for Lakeside in the canoe. It was mid-August, and before returning to Kansas, I needed a reassuring glimpse of fringed gentians. We paddled close to shore, with a solitary sandpiper stepping out in front along the shore like a drum majorette. I only had eyes for the shore and the bank, and if Howie hadn't told me to look up, I'd have missed the kingfisher. In my Kansas living room a Chinese woodblock print of a kingfisher hangs alongside a Japanese scroll with the poem—"My soul, like the blue-green kingfisher in the autumn moon, becomes pure"—written in bold calligraphy. But the living bird was missing, and without knowing it, I'd also missed it. Where had it been when I'd not been looking? Undoubtedly, out on the lake catching insects. But having chores to tend to on shore, it returned. It darted above us now, testing one overhanging limb and another. In every respect a snappy bird. Grateful for this glimpse, I realized on our paddle back to the cottage that I should be paying more attention, for birds—not frogs or salamanders, those critical barometers of other living bodies of water—indicate the health of Higgins.

Some birds seem to have appeared at Higgins from out of nowhere. Perhaps we, desiring control, seeking connection with the miracle of flight, seduce them. As soon as camp opens, people begin filling feeders for the ruby-throated hummingbirds, who seem to arrive from nowhere. Faster than the speed of light and just as silent, they whir in to sip. A decade ago, when the feeders were first hung in camp, everyone watched astonished, although many now take their minute and beautiful perfection as they do our neon sunsets—as a matter of course. Mother was initially concerned that when camp closed, they would starve. Realizing, however, that by the time camp ends, they're already en route to Tunis, or more likely Mexico, she now ritualistically makes her own syrup solution and fills their feeder off our pavilion daily. She nonetheless continues to protest vigorously the use of red dye in the hummers' syrup as poisonous.

Like the hummers, ducks—mallards, black ducks, mergansers—are a recent phenomenon at Higgins and a daily delight. They float by—the mother duck pulling her brood along behind her; they sit sedately on dock ends, occasionally twisting around to primp, to prune, to spread out a wing with purple epaulets; they turn upside down in the water waving bright red feet in the air, as surprising as jack-in-the-boxes. In recent summers it's been an ongoing circus, to the delight of every child, encouraging adults to give dock-end instruction: "How many ducks do you see? Which one is the mommy? Look at how silly that duck is! He must be finding some delicious seaweed to eat!" Fearing the dreaded swimmer's itch, however, we absolutely do not feed the ducks that sleep complacently every night on our dock. But more than the swimmer's itch, we fear that their proliferation will result in their accelerated harassment and eventual disappearance from the lake. In a letter to the Higgins Lake Property Owners Association on behalf of the ducks, Mother wrote in the summer of 1996: "We find waterfowl interesting, beautiful, and a part of the unfortunate waning of wildlife around and on 'our' lake. . . . We believe you should recognize that there are surely two sides as to whether mergansers and other ducks should be eliminated from Higgins Lake."[121]

At the turn of the century, the Reverend Bruske was pegging birds—their wings outspread in a stultified imitation of flight on his Pinewoods cabin walls. His son, Uncle Paul, later kept a rifle handy, according to his grandson, for "eradicating red squirrels from camp to protect the birds and 'scaring' gulls off of the raft."[122] I have stood at the end of our dock watching Uncle Paul in his motorboat out by the deep water raft. He sat low in the back of the boat, one hand on the outboard, the other bracing the rifle and aiming it skyward. Round and round the raft he drove, with the birds squalling and flying above him in broken circles. Gunshots in Pinewoods cracked the dome of heaven. Herring gulls and the occasional ring-billed gull continue to soar over the lake, to ride the waves, and to sit with distinction on our rafts as well as on boats, docks, waves, just as on the land the red squirrels still ridicule us with a flick of their tails. Other birds of the lake, like other animals of the woods, however, are fewer and fewer.

The disappearance of whippoorwills and loons has long been lamented by older members of camp. Like Shoppenagons, these birds are remembered by a few, and like him and his people, they were expelled from Higgins. Returning perhaps as shadows, slipping among the trees, diving down into black water. Who heard the last whippoorwill at Pinewoods and when? We have had glimpses of lone loons, and recently several people have reported waking at night to hear the loon's ululation rising up from the lake. One morning in the summer of 1996, for the first time since they began making their pilgrimages to the island to watch the sunrise, I joined Howie and Tammy and Ginger, the dog.

Mist mushroomed up off the lake's surface as we headed blindly through white billows toward the island. By dumb luck and instinct, we arrived in the island cove and dropped anchor. We waited, padded in fog. If the sun rose, it did so under wraps but we listened to the sounds of the island waking—stirring of insect and bird, crow caw, dove moan, thrush song, and suddenly close to us on the water, the loon's loud laugh. A cosmic voice penetrating the fog. It might have signified a Cassandra warning, a triumphant return, a desperate desire. We saw no bird at all. Still blinded by whiteness, Howie maneuvered the boat in the direction of home, trusting. To head back to Pinewoods, though, we needed those dark trees on the horizon as guides. We ended up close to the beginning of No Man's Land. By the time we were back to our dock, the mist was scrolling up from shore, and we saw the ducks. Not only were the Gang of Five and the Gang of Seven (whom we'd been seeing at Pinewoods for several weeks) gliding about, but here, out of the fog, appeared a new gang: a mother with seven ducklings, no bigger than teacups, spinning along behind her.

In 1966 Aunt Adelaide Taggart, who taught generations of campers to be sensitive bird-watchers, expressed her anxiety at the absence of birds at Pinewoods. She knew the consequences of the "widespread use of insecticides," which Rachel Carson had spelled out in 1961 in *Silent Spring*, and often felt "discouraged at the reduction of numbers of our song birds in camp, and elsewhere." She missed "the yellow-throated vireo, who sang so beautifully down in our front swale . . . ; the blue-headed vireo, whose series of phrases included a definite wolf whistle; several warblers we count upon seeing only to have them disappoint us lately, like the gorgeous Blackburnian, the cerulean, and the parula." But as I had reveled in the materialization of ducks from fog, she, too, put up a brave front. She wanted to believe that if the hermit thrush had gone, the veery had arrived. If several warblers have disappeared, the endangered Kirtland's warbler has increased its numbers. If the loon and the whippoorwill no longer call to us, the tanager does. Her account concludes, listening for, longing for, and interpreting hope in the birds she sees and the songs she hears: "Pondering on this dismal problem [of our birds' disappearance], we wandered home from the dining hall one July evening, just when the sun's rays found the tops of our tall pines. Suddenly we heard a song, a robin yet not a robin, rather a hoarse robin, as though he had a sore throat. Gazing up into the treetops we catch the flash of color, the brilliant scarlet of the tanager. He sings his song, a comforting message, which lifts our spirits. 'I'm here and I am going to stay,' he says."[123]

The tanager—its presence, color, song—took Aunt Adelaide by surprise. But in the summer of 1992 Joe Taylor, the eminent ornithologist with a life-list of all North American birds, was shocked by missing birdsong in Pinewoods. He could not rationalize. In another reference to *Silent Spring*, he called a short essay he wrote for the camp newsletter, *Pinewords*, "Silent Summer":

I wonder how many of us, other than the inveterate birdwatchers, were conscious of the almost complete absence of birdsong at Pinewoods this summer.

Particularly this summer, with its very late spring, there should have been even more than the usual number of birds singing when we arrived in mid-July, but there were almost none. It was a scarily real "silent summer." Away from the Higgins area, when we went for wildflowers or just to explore the sandy back roads, there were plenty of birds singing—four or five species of warblers, vireos, wood and hermit thrushes, downy woodpeckers drumming, blue jays screaming their warnings that "man" was on his way, flickers "bounding" down the road ahead of us, swallows after insects over the open fields and others. But at Pinewoods it was ominously quiet. One great crested flycatcher called from the highest tree tops; a pair of robins nested near our cottage and another at the dining hall; there were two or three chickadees and one palm warbler and one nuthatch, probably a white-breasted and that was all. There were no other flycatchers or warblers; no woodpeckers or vireos; no thrushes singing off in the distance; no jays to wake us up in the morning. I sadly missed the delicate little "Where's Elizabeth?" songs of the brown creepers, and there were no song sparrows working through the weeds and grasses at the lake shore and now and then popping up to sing from a taller stalk; and not a sign of the wonderful pileated woodpeckers which are such a thrill to watch.

By early August a lone peewee wandered in to call plaintively from above, and three cedar waxwings, rather than the usual dozen or more, were hawking for insects out over the lake, but except for this, it remained quiet, very, very sad and frightening.

Is it possible that BT, that "non-lethal except to gypsy moth" spray, kills the birds outright and directly as well as indirectly by starvation?[124]

The editor of *Pinewords* for 1992 provided an epilogue for Joe's essay: "Joe sent me this for *Pinewords* just a week or two before he died. It certainly shows both his concern for his beloved birds and the quality of his 'listening ear.' Several of those who have better ears than I (though not so good as Joe's) tell me that by the end of the season there was a marked increase of birdsong at Pinewoods. After reading Joe's piece, I'm going to try to listen more appreciatively next summer."[125] But Joe's essay, construed as his will and testament for Pinewoods, leaves us with a sense of urgency not just to tune our ears, not to see the kingfisher or the tanager as synecdoche for the lake. I think of my graduate school friend who, when asked what use there was in studying a dying dialect of Gaelic, replied by asking how we could understand blue in a world without yellow.

Interlude

*A*dam Gopnik queries whether we Americans, in spending June through August laboring in claustrophobic cities and in consequent obsessing about summer, have actually invented it. "Summer in America," he suggests, "is another place, to be dreamed of rather than remembered. You find it where you can, and mostly you find it by thinking you'll have it, eventually. . . . Summer is about longing for summer."[126] Contemporary writers, remembering their summers, compulsively reconstruct them as dreams. Judy Ross exclaims, "The summer cottage. The mere words evoke images of sun-dappled woods and sparkling waters, breezy screened verandas and the promise of lazy afternoons. Often our most treasured retreat, the cottage has become a metaphor for relaxation, escapism and family kinship. Above all, it's a place where we can cast off our city shoes and worries, sink into an old porch rocker and be ourselves."[127] For Christine S. Cozzens, "The house, the woods and shore [where she and her family spent their summers] have lived in my imagination, more real than when we swung in the squeaky porch swing to stir a breeze in midday heat, or played endless hands of casino by the fire in the knobby stone hearth to the steady beat of a summer rain. And they have grown to mythic dimensions, becoming the standard next to which every other place or trip or experience was doomed to fall short."[128]

Deborah Wyatt Fellows believes her memories "of life Up North" are "universal, really, . . . colors and scents so real that even now I can shut my eyes and almost touch them. In my mind, it's always the same summer, that one year before any of us could drive, before we had decided that a job was more important than having fun." Testifying that her universals are shared, she believes that other families, in addition to hers, experienced their greatest happiness Up North and are "committed to giving those experiences to their children and grandchildren."[129] Barbara Hanson Pierce, who as a child had had visions of summers such as these writers describe, married into a family who experienced them annually. She found herself captivated not only by the traditions of her husband's family's old summer home but also by a "dream—that turn-of-the-century blend of simplicity, regeneration and family." Pierce recognizes that "times have changed, but the dream remains,"[130]— alluring for her as well as for others.

The summer of 1995 has all of the characteristics of the dream summer, of the paradisal visions of my Pinewoods's ancestors and of my own conception of "A Perfect Day at Higgins Lake." That is to say, this summer of 1995 is all desire in response to labor, anxiety, anguish. The Asiatic lilies unfold their elegant petals and aroma in my Kansas backyard; here wrens chitter about and inside their box in the ash tree, and yellow swallowtails come to the orange butterfly weed. But this summer time has halted and intensified: two friends have died from cancer; my large cat languishes from an undiagnosed illness; on July 7 at 6:00 A.M. I am to appear at the University of Kansas Medical Center to prepare for a full hysterectomy. With Pinewoods only a remote possibility for this summer and a resonating memory, the yearning for its loveliness and evolving harmonies thickens.

In preparation for my surgery, I have learned a new breathing technique: a deep breath in and then an exhalation, a long sigh with the sound of a hiss or a piss. It's breathing like lake water silently approaching the shore and withdrawing with a gasp and gurgle. It's breathing which strengthens the abdomen and occupies the mind. It's breathing which corresponds to my alternate yearning for Pinewoods and my working and writing in Kansas.

After the snow melted this year, Howie and Tammy began their weekend treks to the cottage. Through Mother I'd get a word about their visits; Tammy also wrote, enclosing photos, and Howie called. They described natural sightings: four whistling swans gliding on the lake in front of the cottage, suckers spawning in the shallow waters, red fox kits tumbling outside their den just behind the camp mailboxes, a great horned owl, sedate and still, except for its blinking eyes, in a white pine in back of the garage. Repeatedly they've seen bald-headed eagles returned from the past: one, flying in low over the gulls on the island's northern spit, weighted down with a live fish in its talons; a pair screaming, rising up out of the woods in No Man's Land and soaring out over the lake, close enough for them to feel the whoosh of their wings, see the whites of their eyes. Eager to see and believe, I insisted that they tell me the exact time of day, the temperature, the sounds, the words.

Mother, at Pinewoods since June 30, called today to tell me about the Fourth of July parade through camp. Beginning at the eastern end, it wound its way down the path, collecting people ("Eighty-five in camp just now," Mother says, "a record for early July!") with their red-white-and-blue garb and banners all along the way, coming at last to our cottage at the western end of camp before heading to the dining hall. Through the spring and into the summer, these descriptions have come as messages from eternity: the lake, the woods, the life still there. I'll go into surgery naming the cottages along the path and the wildflowers on the bank above the shore in No Man's Land.

The Senses

Home, 11:30 A.M., Tuesday, July 11, 1995. One day later than anticipated. Temperature outside: 102°F.

Out of touch, taste, scent, sight, sound. Out of mind. At the hospital, I couldn't find the lake. I tried the bee trick: identifying a flower on the bank in No Man's Land and drinking deep. I tried naming the flowers, counting the flowers. I tried canoeing along No Man's Land, out to the island, around the island, along black water. I walked the trails back of camp, the path in front of camp, the road to town. I tried all my familiar wilderness stations and mandalas, and I yearned. I had lost the center.

I can move the bed up and down; I can adjust the knee position. But whatever way I move it, it becomes more uncomfortable. The plastic mattress creaks; the sheets slip over it, wrinkling and creasing. I pull myself up with my elbows; my elbows are raw from the sheets' rough texture.

Light streaming from the full moon staircases down the Venetian blinds.

TV channel surfing parallels mindsurfing.

No reading, no sustained narrative other than the one I am living.

The day nurses, the night nurses, the nurses' aides, the cleaning women come and go.

Diet of clear liquids since Tuesday, July 4: Jello (red, blue, yellow), cranberry and grape juice, tea, broth, ginger ale. Clear equals that which can be seen through; therefore, no coffee, milk, soup. Feeling so weak, I wonder if I'll survive the operation. A gas explosion. Then ice chips, liquid diet again, and at last on Monday night, July 10, food: the dried chicken breast and super sweet carrot cake come to a starving person.

Images from nowhere: a creature from an iridescent lagoon, his head squashed and turned; he, too, suffering, trying to comprehend, trying to survive.

The last morning, the nurse takes my temperature with a pistol thermometer in the ear. It registers 39°C; she tells me that translates to 105°F. How can this be? I feel no fever. She puts her hand to my forehead and proclaims that, yes, I seem hot. I *feel* no fever. "You won't be released today," she announces. I think only that I can't sleep another night in the plastic bed. Another, more conventional thermometer proves that my temperature is "normal." Dr. C releases me.

TASTE TREATS

intergreen leaves: wafers on the tongue.

Chewing pine sap.

Licking your fingers, as a kid, after devouring one of the dining hall's cinnamon sticky buns.

Sucking a wild huckleberry picked at the entrance to No Man's Land.

Sipping the first gin and tonic of the season on the pavilion.

Slurping a marshmallow, twice-baked at the fireplace in front of the cottage, before it drips off the fork tines.

Smacking on your one hotdog of the year, slathered in onions with a stripe of bright yellow mustard down the center, at lunch on the tennis court following the annual meeting.

Whoever talks too much about taste probably doesn't have any.

Thoreau gives a primary place to hearing, titling *Walden*'s fourth chapter "Sounds." He jeers at those who set time by the railroad's whistle, but praises local church bells which, by the time their melody reaches him through the Walden woods, acquire "a vibratory hum," as if from "the universal lyre."[131] He takes pleasure in the sounds of nature: of "the baying of dogs . . . the trump of bullfrogs . . . the clangor of geese . . . squirrels on the roof and under the floor, a whippoorwill on the ridge pole, a blue-jay screaming beneath the window, a hare or woodchuck under the house, a screech-owl or a cat-owl behind it, a flock of wild geese or a laughing loon on the pond, and a fox to bark in the night."[132] Sound, like smell, acknowledges no borders; throughout the day, it crossed the threshold of Thoreau's cabin, entered into his domestic space, and integrated him into nature. Like faith, it challenged belief in what wasn't seen.

Thoreau may well declare the value of sound, but his mentor, Emerson, indicates that for the transcendentalists the eyes have it, that for them sight was the dominant sense. I, too, have heard myself declare, explaining my choice of literature over philosophy, "If I can't see it, I can't understand it." Following an arduous day of visiting museums or raging about perceptual distortions caused by advertising and the media, I have also spoken of "the tyranny of the eyeball." Certainly during my days, sight governs. At night, however, sound—with touch and smell—comes into its own, connecting me in the dark and quivering air to pulsating life. I think of sperm whales, in the perpetual night of ocean depths, seeing with sonar through underwater peaks and shipwrecks. I lie in bed at the lake and listen to the day settle down and the night stir. Human voices subside on the path outside, in the rooms beneath me. Voices, unheard during the day, speak: pine needles prick the roof overhead; mice scramble in between the walls; the lake murmurs down below. I yearn for the barred owl's hoot, that metronomic call which belongs only to the night.

Although visual clues—color, size, shape, scat, track, appearance of bill or nose, design in fur or feather, shape of nest or den—are far more useful in identifying species, animals and birds are also known by specific sound. Plants, however, are known primarily by a multiplicity of visual clues. Voiceless, flowers, moss, fungi make no sound as they grow, if they suffer. Sycamore and cottonwood snap, crackle, and pop when the sap rises in spring, and wind may give trees a sound—creak and whine of branch, tick of twig, and pines and oaks can be distinguished by their very particular rustlings—but who has heard flower, moss, or fungus speak? It is we, not they, who must cry out, "Woodman, spare that tree!"[133] Yet the woods are not silent. They instruct us in listening. On a windless afternoon, you're aware of adjustments constantly being made. A branch falls; a twig twitches; a fern unfurls; dew drips; moss grows, and the delicate pine needle coverlet over it is slightly rearranged. The specific sound of crow caw, chickadee chatter, nuthatch hammer, squirrel squabble, deer snort, duck wheeze, insect buzz, and then human voice crisscrosses this intersection of clicks and creaks. Your own breathing becomes distilled with these sounds. Mother wears a hearing aid now, and as we walk through the woods, I translate sounds, conscious of her loss and of the inadequacy of my words, conscious of myself as "a sounding brass or a tinkling cymbal" (1 Corinthians, 13, 1).

Water, too, seems silent until wind gives it sound. Then we have waves pounding and crashing on the shore, up against the sailboat hull, onto each other. In lesser winds, there is a sloshing and a slurping underneath docks and around rocks. Without perceptible wind, however, Higgins generates a ceaseless motion from its hidden depths which, in turn, keeps the water in whispered conversation with the sand. All around the lake, it laps against the shore, sucking, seething. Lying on the dock in the dead of summer, you drowse off, listening to the easy rhythms of these sounds, a lullaby, beneath you. Becalmed in the center of the lake with your sails limp, you hear that "vibratory hum." Listening to it, you can be tranced. It rises up from the distant shores, throbs round and round you until you are absorbed in a condensation of pulsating spinning sound. You are lulled like Ishmael in the masthead and in his most transcendental mood by a "blending cadence of waves with thoughts."[134] You, too, run the risk of losing your identity if a cat's paw suddenly swats at your sails, gibing the Sunfish and tossing you with a splash into the mystic lake. In any event, you have to raise a clamor to get back home: you jerk the rudder rudely to get a flap and flutter in the sails, you sing lustily to rouse a wind. At last you holler out to a passing motorboat for a tow. A gull cruising by overhead screeches his ridicule.

Driving up to the lake all the summers of my girlhood, I learned to sing. Mother and Daddy in the front seat sang together, and Howie and I in the back seat sang along. We sang folk songs, rounds, spirituals, Stephen Foster, and the songs of Mother and Daddy's youth. We sang Daddy's favorite, "Beautiful Dreamer," and "Last Night the Nightingale Woke Me," Mother's favorite.

Driving up to the lake alone now, with only a cat for company and two Mars bars for nourishment, Mother still sings to keep herself company. At the lake we sang folk songs in groups at Uncle Paul's campfire, Gilbert and Sullivan in the Loomis's living room or the golden oldies, in Ted Plum's "sing-along," accompanied by ukelele, gut bucket, kazoo, moraccas, and washboard and thimble; we sang solo in BOA productions or strolling down the path. Out sailing in *Chip* or *Spindrift*, we added sea songs to the repertoire, belting them out in unison to accompany the wind.

On still evenings after supper, Mother and I canoe down to No Man's Land. Out a distance from the shore, we put our paddles across the gunwales, and Mother begins to sing from the stern, "Little Sir Echo, how do you do? Hello!" We wait for the woods to answer, "Hello!" before she goes on to the next line, "Little Sir Echo, will answer you. Hello!" and again wait for the echo to come back from the woods, mysterious and yet predictable, changed and yet the same, "Hello!" The song finishes with the line, "Won't you come over and play?" and its echoing response, "And play?" The question always hangs in the air, for we've never yet enticed Little Sir Echo out into the open. If the woods refuse their answer, I reply to Mother from the bow of the canoe, "Hello! . . . Hello! . . . And play?" When Mother finishes, I sing all the lines, pausing for her refraining echoes from the stern of the canoe. And then our paddles dipping and echoing each other are the only sounds.

Russell Baker recently commented, however, "Nowadays Whitman would not hear America singing."[135] Not on the streets, not in the shower, not at parties, not in the workplace, not in families. We no longer sing in groups at Pinewoods. Usually we talk now, even when we sail. We sail often in couples—mother and I pressed together on her Sunfish, Howie and I sprawled on his Hobie Cat, but the insularity of a boat, disturbed only by sounds of wind and water, prompts reflections and revelations rather than song. Nevertheless, reading in bed around midnight one summer recently, with the front windows of my room wide open, I heard singing coming up from the next-door deck. Teenagers, celebrating a sixteenth birthday, were harmonizing and reviving the old songs—"Blue Moon," "This Land is My Land," "Down in the Valley," "Kisses Sweeter Than Wine," and "Greensleeves," ending up with giggles and "I'm a Little Teapot." The songs of our car journeys north and our campfires are filed away in my memory, and like bicycle riding are readily retrieved.

When I sail alone, they come back one after another. And I sing and sing and sing. Not only to whistle up a wind or to talk back to the Over Soul, but also to restore a memory of simple harmony of self with other. Even if wind and water send back no echo, it's possible to sing merrily on.

The dining hall is cacophonous. Dishes clattering, coffee pots hissing, ice cubes clinking in the lemonade pitcher, hamburgers sizzling Saturday noon, the front doors creaking open, the side doors slamming shut, the kitchen doors whooshing open and shut, ice cream orders being given, people talking, people laughing, babies babbling, babies screaming, children running, somebody whistling, the bell ringing out the hours, people clapping whenever the ringer is a small child. In the background a toilet flushes, the refrigerator whirs, the generator drones. Mother's hearing aid accentuates these noises, making specific words in a conversation difficult to discern. She leaves the dining hall discussion, picking up an ice cream cone on the way out.

Howie recently confessed to me that at times the quiet he feels Mother and I impose on the cottage is intolerable. He takes comfort in sound: purring cats, yipping dogs, country music, radio ball games, chatter with Tammy. He prefers the putt-putt to the canoe, the whizzing of the Hobie Cat's rudders and the thrumming of its stays to the intermittent, humdrum slapping of the Sunfish. His manner is to move hard and fast: to thunder up and down the stairs to the lake, taking two steps at a time; to roar around the cottage in accomplishing a diversity of tasks; to crash into the lake in the early morning and thrash forward. Reading he saves for his time in the bathroom. I imagine that when he and Tammy are at the cottage with only their friends or daughters, the place jumps. Yet on those mornings when he and Tammy have taken the putt-putt over to the island, it's the sound of silence which moves him. The motor is turned off, the boat drifts, a hush prevails as they wait for the sun to rise and all the island's birds to burst into applause.

After buckling up for takeoff from Kansas City in the summer of 1996, I flipped through the pages of United Airlines' magazine. My mind was on Aunt Mary in New Jersey, and the task ahead of sorting through a lifetime of memories in preparation for her move into a retirement community. I wasn't prepared to find an essay with the irresistible title, "Love of Lakes." Its title was irresistible. The author, David Butwin, claims "an abiding kinship with lakes," especially those in the north woods which, like Higgins, are "rounded and clear and blue, small enough for one to see the opposite shore, and remote enough that [they weren't] connected by anything wider than a country road." He writes affectionately of the cottages that border these lakes, invoking the two primary sensations that greet one on arrival at a cottage: "First was The Sound: the slap of a screen door closing behind me on a summer day. Then, The Smell: a blend of must, weathered wood, and trapped air—pure perfume."[136]

I know this sound and this smell. This sound, like the sound of loons, can be recorded and played over and over on tape in the car as well as in memory, but the smell is not to be bottled up or conjured up so readily. It is not even to be named. Yet the smell of Pinewoods and our cottage seems their essence. Eric Schmitt, before leaving his family's Minnesota lake cabin, took a final walk through, breathing in its odors—"oiled pine logs, wool blankets, spices and a whiff of ash from the pot-bellied stove permeated the cabin."[137] The smells Butwin and Schmitt describe are synthesized—compiled of diverse elements—but preclude the possibility of distillation into a single word. "Pure perfume" seems a romantic generalization, a reductive cliche, and considering the ingredients, not in the least bit pure.

The catalogues of Butwin and Schmitt reflect the fact that we don't have words for smell although we form absolute moral and aesthetic judgments about it. It's either fine or foul, a stench or a fragrance. It stinks, or it just plain smells. Like taste, smell can be sweet or sour, but unlike taste, which allows other responses—salty and hot, for example—smell allows only the extremes of positive and negative, yucky and yummy. Research indicates that sight, sound, touch, and taste are registered first in the brain's cerebral cortex, its analytical apparatus, with smell alone connecting directly with the brain's limbic system. This is the area associated with the reptile brain, called primitive by neuroscientists, but this area is also the neurological center for emotions. Thus, if the smell implies the essence, evokes the memory of the place, connects to the emotional center, the search for the words becomes vital. After all, such an essence—the distilled truth—guides our lives.

When metaphor or episode seemed evasive, catalogues emboldened me in an attempt to get at the essence of Pinewoods, although I knew that the effusions from the objects on my personal list could not evoke the same response from family and friends. I'm also aware that the objects on my list do not exist autonomously; they fuse with other sights, sounds, touch, tastes of Pinewoods. George Wilson, driving as a boy with his family to Higgins from New York, always said that he knew they were almost there when he could smell the sweet fern. For me, too, the sweet fern aroma summons up the entire season of summer. Sweet fern grows dark green in a clearing with huckleberry bushes, a few wild, straggling daisies, and a profusion of butter and egg plants, along the path, just at the end of Cottage Grove and at the beginning of No Man's Land. The soil here is sandy, and if you're wearing sneakers or sandals, it's sure to get between your toes. After lunch, when the sun's hottest, sand and sweet fern bake together, drying and softening and scenting the air. A whir of unseen grasshoppers stirs this fragrant heat. Gently, gently, it seems to lift off my clothes, and I am dizzy in its presence. Through shimmering light, heat, sound, smell, I look out across the lake at ribbon after ribbon of glistening color. As I once tried to bring a sample of black water home to Flint, I gather sweet fern leaves every year in my pocket to take to Kansas where I place them in an antique box on my dresser. Black water in a vial proved to look like all water—merely transparent. Through the year the sweet fern leaves, although brown and crumpled, emit a musty odor, but without sun, sand, and huckleberry bush tangle, the essence is diminished.

I take the smell of the cottage in gradually. It begins as I lie in bed the first night, drawing in breath and smell simultaneously. In the dense darkness of my cottage bedroom, sight cannot tyrannize. I hear the tickings behind the walls of the many-footed creatures who, residing in the cottage through all seasons, claim first right of domain, and I hear pine needles scattering on the porch roof. A laugh on the path down below. And the lake murmuring against the shore. But it's the smell of the place that releases its essence. It all springs from the sheets. The sheets, pillow cases, towels, and wash cloths in our cottage are kept stacked in the upstairs linen closet along with light bulbs, broom and dustpan, comforters, dresser scarves, hand towels (cross-stitched and embroidered for a more gracious era), and extra blankets, layered with mothballs and stashed in plastic. Through fall, winter, and spring, the beds in the cottage's unused rooms wait for summer. With their blankets and pillows piled in the center and their spreads tucked in around the mattresses to keep out mice, they have the appearance of biers.

By the time I arrive at the lake, however, my bed has been made. Some of the sheets have "Stanley" written in ink still visible on an edge, indicating that they came with my grandfather and grandmother's purchase of the old Stanley cottage and that long ago they were laundered and starched in Roscommon by Swedish laundresses. Heavy linen, the sheets on my bed retain a roughness, a dampness, and the particular odor from the closet although they'd been washed and pressed the previous summer by the anonymous women at "The Wash Tub," the laundromat in Roscommon, which replaced the town's professional laundry ladies. I stretch out, seeking warmth at the end of the bed with my toes. There's none to be had, and as I move, the sheets' dank muskiness, mingled with hints of mothballs and mildew, is uncorked; it rises up and wraps me. Since I have to make my peace with this bed, however, I furiously move my arms up and down and my legs in and out as if creating a snow angel between the sheets. The bed warms; the smell dissipates into the familiar incense of initiation; I sleep, breathing deeply.

Some discrete Pinewoods smells remain only in memory, the material object which elicited them now having long gone: canvas sails folded in the chest in the corner of the living room with Mother's thick Camp Ca-Ho blankets, pineknots heaped in the old woodshed, birch logs burning in the outdoor fireplace, candles extinguished in the dining hall at the end of supper. On occasion, driving into Kansas City, I catch the whiff of skunk. Coming from the woods or a corpse by the roadside, the smell penetrates the car. It lingers after I've passed the spot, bringing back Pinewoods evenings when skunk smell used to penetrate conversations out on the pavilion, drifting ubiquitously through camp from an unseen source. It might have come from beneath a cottage, from behind the dining hall, from as far away as the Cottage Grove dump. The skunk itself never appeared, but the sharp astringency of its smell impaled the twilight, making it last a moment longer and intensifying the significance of our conversation.

Skunk smell has rivaled the loon's weird cry in popular evocations of north woods wilderness. But the loon is only now returning to Higgins, and aware of the trace of skunk in my Kansas car, I am startled to realize it's been years since I've smelled skunk at Pinewoods. Like the smell of skunk, the smells of displaced objects—canvas sails, pineknots, candles, birch logs—resemble the north woods: these smells are without boundary; they are invasive; they are organic. In losing the woods and embracing technology, we diminish our spectrum of scents. Plastic and steel, it occurs to me, are odorless, and desperate to sniff out life's possibilities, we now resort to aromatherapy.

In the pumphouse, underneath the lower pavilion and at dock and shore level, a democracy of smells—"a congress of stinks," Theodore Roethke would say[138]—prevails. When plumbing was installed in the cottage, the kerosene motor in the pumphouse, which diligently day in and day out had sent lake water up to the cottage, was removed. The pumphouse was left to accommodate tools and assorted equipment for sailing, boating, bathing. A rancid odor had already infiltrated this small space, however, for the heavy oil that had kept the pump's flywheel spinning had seeped into the workbench. In layers over this basic odor, however, is an intricate diversity of other smells—gasoline for the putt-putt, paint, paint-remover, and varnish; coils of worn and new hemp rope, feather cushions cast off from the pavilion swing for canoe seats, half-used bottles of sun-tan lotion, new tubes of sunblock, assorted shampoos, perpetually damp towels, and old rubber tennis balls; the basket of snail shells and clam shells, and the last of the canvas-covered, cork life preservers. Acrid, musty, sour, exotic, fresh, heady, it is the accumulated and compressed essence of a shoreline existence.

Access to the pumphouse is through an overhead door across the front, which allows winter entry for the canoe and summer entry for sailfish masts. All summer long, the pumphouse stands open to the lake which allows the smells of shore and lake to mingle with those inside. Depending on the day—its wind, its moisture, its temperature, one or another smells—rope, shampoo, snail—from the congress of smells within the pumphouse will be in ascendancy. Reading in the open doorway of the pumphouse, I am challenged to synthesize—not only the book in my lap with the lake before me, but also fresh breezes coming in from a far shore, carrying just a taint of fish, with the pumphouse's dense complexity of smells from its interior and from the past behind me. Sitting in the open door-way of this pumphouse, I smell myself. Summer, after all, rouses and then releases all our human odors—armpit, ass, the body entire—more profusely than any other season. (Halitosis and flatulence know no season.) I prime myself with underarm deodorant every morning, and my vulnerable areas are slathered with sun-block. To my back there is shade from the pumphouse, but before me white sun glances off dock and lake. I am steaming and sweating, and my own stink rises up comfortably around me. Who else would know it? want it? The sun shifts; in a minute Tammy will arrive with the grandchildren; Mother will be up from her nap and ready to take the Sunfish out; we'll bring sand toys and sails out from the pumphouse. But for this moment I am smug and snug and keep on reading, breathing, smelling—profound essence.

The Seasons

*T*he summer of 1995 was one of loss. At home in Kansas, just a week after I'd come home from surgery, Mother called from the lake. By doctor's orders, I was lounging about in the AC-cooled July afternoon. Not yet dressing, far from driving, and still on books and meds. Mother was not calling to inquire after my health, however. "There's been a tornado," was how she started the conversation. "The transformer's out in the dining hall. Trees are down everywhere in the back." It took a while for me to get it.

I asked her to repeat, and the implications of the phrases, one by one, began to accumulate. "Yesterday afternoon," she said, "we really had a storm. Nobody's hurt. None of the cottages. Only some boathouses and cars. The electricity's gone throughout camp, but we're all using candles. You can't believe it unless you see it. The dining hall transformer was blown out into the middle of the road. Howie's renting a generator in Flint and bringing it up on Friday. Cottage Grove can't, won't lend our hall any freezer space, and who knows how much frozen stuff we'll lose. Everybody's carrying water up from the lake in buckets to flush their toilets. But the trees are the worst of it. All the big ones. The white pines and the Norways. Not out in front, but behind the cottages it's a mess. You can't walk anywhere. They've fallen every which way, twisted off about half way up. You walk out in back now and see sky where we never could before."

Later Mother told me she had seen the storm develop, coming from a thickening darkness in the northwest. When she'd felt the wind rising and seen rain pricking the water near the dock, she went up to the cottage to take her stand at the front windows in the living room where she could watch the boats. It swept in fast and furiously, lashing the lake to whiteness. Off the end of the dock, the mooring stake for the putt-putt seemed to have come loose, and the boat was gyrating wildly on its line. She tried to keep her eye on the mast of Howie's Hobie Cat, propped above water on its hoist, but with the rain slashing across the windows, her vision of this steady vertical came and went. Thunder detonated overhead. So loud she could not hear the trees shattering and crashing in the rear. With mind and eyes focused on the lake in front, as they usually are during any shift in weather, she did not see the trees twisting and falling behind.

In about a half hour the storm had passed and the sun was out, glaring, glittering in myriad shards of light. It had left the sky an immaculate and impervious blue. Mother went down to the lake. Some young neighbors, who had gone out to perform an Anti-Storm Dance when the rain began, had ridden out the storm on the end of their dock. Now they were stranded there on an isolated dock section separated from shore, with the rest of the dock blown away. Other people, coming out of their cottages, smelled fresh pine—like Christmas potpourri, they said, like dresser-drawer sachets. Like Mother, they, too, faced the lake, not realizing what lay behind them. Only when they moved from picking up the broken branches on the path to the rear of their cottages did they see the devastation and realize, as one camper would write, that the "delicious aroma [was] rising from the heartbreaking wreck of broken trees."[139]

The damage was assessed, and the storm identified as "a second-tier tornado." It had snapped off most of the trees, not at ground level, but midway, at the waist, and not cleanly. In the woods, therefore, there were no stumps, only trunks of varying heights torqued and tortured. Later I heard that because the prevailing winds at Higgins come from the southwest, our trees had developed strength on that side, but that this storm, coming from the north, had approached on their most vulnerable side. Whole root systems of oaks and maples were exposed as a result of the great pines falling on them. But wind, like cancer, I realized, chooses erratically. Astonishingly, a few of the great trees still stood. Isolated in their splendid verticality. Some were armless, their limbs stripped off or helplessly dangling. Others leaned. But the only crutches were other vulnerable trees. The entire, lovely fabric of woods behind our cottages was rent and torn, with harsh diagonals ruining its warp and woof, and gashes opening it to harsh light. The canopy was down.

The editor of *Pinewords* felt that "Walking through the woods, the light was wrong. It was too bright up above where the trees should have been shading the road—all those trees were lying shattered in the road, the driveways and the woods."[140] But for many, a walk in the woods was no longer possible. Kids went out on scouting excursions to Cottage Grove to come back and compare notes on the damage to their woods and goods with the damage on ours, but right after the storm, no one could get through the crisscross maze of fallen trees, tangled branches, bent saplings. Even after chainsaws had restored clearance along driveways and paths, people stumbled. If our pine woods were changed forever, could Pinewoods, our community, survive unchanged?

Mother ended her phone call: "Well, I've got to start picking up." Other telephone calls came. A friend called from Phoenix in tears. A tree, she had heard, lay across their family boathouse, and her mother, so distraught by the devastation, wondered if she could return to Pinewoods. Marion rang from Boston. Her brother had told her that a tree had also fallen on their boathouse. She reported a dream. She and her mother stood on the high bank in front of their cottage looking out at the lake, noting how very agitated it was; they were joined by my mother, and together they observed that the boats down below were being smashed. My mother commented, then: "I'd better get back to our cottage to see what I can do." Realizing she'd never been in Pinewoods without her mother, who had died in April, Marion wondered how she could endure being at the lake this summer. Still grieving for her mother, she felt also bereft of trees. My Phoenix friend, weeping at the end of her call, asked me for answers: "What can I do?" I heard myself replying, "If the big trees come down, there's sunlight for the small trees to grow." But knowing that these words came from the head, I wondered if I could believe them myself. Mother's words seemed more helpful, and I repeated them, "We'll have to start picking up." If you care for something, you have to take care of it, I interpreted to myself.

Many people helped in the tornado's aftermath: Roger, assisted by numerous campers, cleared the Stage Road and the driveways; Kathy Piehl, her staff, and her family, working without lights, refrigeration, or water pumps, making breakfast in the near dark and journeying into town for fresh food daily, kept the dining hall going; Howie's generator failed, and another was acquired and trailed up from Chicago, which kept refrigerator losses to a minimum. I had to get to the lake myself to see what I could do. With the unexpected news that I needed a hysterectomy and a complex agenda of activities at the university, I had turned back my ticket to Traverse City in June and doubted that I'd get to the lake at all this summer. Yet I knew now that if I'd ever needed to be at the lake, this was the summer. Two days after burying my dear cat, whose disease had been diagnosed as cancer, behind the bench in my backyard, I left for five days at Pinewoods. Upon arrival the talk at camp, on the path, in the dining hall, on the pavilion was, inevitably, the tornado. What did I think? Everyone was judging; it was horrible, terrible, sad, bad, and I agreed. Driving in, along the familiar Stage Road, I felt that the intimacy of entering camp, always evoked by the gathering in of the pines, had been violated. In their confusion and anguish, these trees had been cruelly exposed to the sky's eye and to our eyes as we passed by.

Later, walking and stumbling through the woods behind camp and seeing the trees' abused forms close at hand, I saw for myself the storm's savage rage. I saw, too, that the natural devastation had precipitated another. The camp had signed two contracts. One contract was with our own Jean, who lived year-round in Roscommon, tending her wheelchair-bound father. She was hired to remove the tangle of storm-generated debris. Through all seasons, Jean walked the Pinewoods paths and woods, our unofficial caretaker, checking not only her family cottage, but all of our summer homes, worrying about fires, keeping an eye out, too, for owls, laying extra leaves on the paths, counting gypsy moth egg masses. We trusted Jean because of her strength as a swimmer—we had seen her stroking by camp as she began her round-the-lake swim; because of her generosity—she brought us local news and cartons of home-grown raspberries when we arrived in camp; because of her concern for Pinewoods and her tenderness for her father.

The other contract was with local lumbermen to remove fallen and "storm-damaged" trees: these were the "big boys." Strangers carrying chainsaws and measuring rods, they stalked our woods. They cut a deal with Pinewoods: their wages would be paid from the lumber in our trees. As I stumbled on behind the cottages, countless pines stretched out before me, severed into ten-foot sections, the designated length of logs for sale to lumber companies. Other trees were rigged with ropes, ready to be toppled. The sunlight streaking into the clearings was heavy with sawdust being spun into gold, and the incessant buzzing of chainsaws cancelled both birdsong and silence. The "big boys" also brought their "Timberjacks" into the woods. These forest bulldozers were equipped with jaws for lifting and twirling the ten-foot logs into piles, snouts for pushing brush and small trees out of the way and transforming them into debris, tractor pads for converting dense woods into open highways. The storm had passed in a flash, but its impact would last for years, and the "cleanup" would go on for months. The contract stipulated that the "big boys" would finish their job by November 1. "Horrible, terrible, bad, sad" repeats the sinking heart.

The mind, in its capacity to rationalize, and the soul, in its need for faith and hope, however, desperately respond, "Life. Life." The day I arrived a tripod with a telescopic lens was set up next door on the path. A loon had been spotted cruising out on the edge of black water, and a congregation of the curious—people stopping on the path, called from nearby cottages—had collected. Waiting our turns at the scope, we discussed the absence of recent bird-sightings. No pileated woodpeckers. No owls. A small thrush dead on the path in front of a picture window. But a loon's ululating awakened our neighbors at dawn several times in the past week. It seemed impossible—a small apex of desire attained—to realize that loons had returned from the other side of sleep, that one could lie in bed letting their wild cries come across the lake to pierce sleeps' mists. I squinted into the scope and gasped with pleasure when the bird's definitive shape floated into the circle of the lens. A few days later, a scarlet tanager led Mother and me on a walk through woods that had lain outside the tornado's path, but which Cottage Grove was dismembering through its forest management program. The bird flew high among the still-standing trees, a gaudy red signal flashing against green.

Martha Hansen, overwhelmed with her duties as new camp president and decisions about the woods, takes time out to fill a plastic wading pool with water, detergent, and glycerine for the delight of us all. Dipping bicycle tires, hula hoops, coat hangers shaped into rings, and Ball jar lids into the solution, we created long bubble blimps, spinning bubble beach balls, and sequences of ephemeral baubles. The kids swished quickly, spraying us with blizzards of bubbles. My bubbles seemed to stumble into existence and collapse before they could shine. The carefree play, however, was contagious, and soon we all were easing large and lovely bubbles out of our rings. We waved our wands slowly over our heads like circus impresarios, and magically, shimmering, iridescent tunnels emerged. When we brought the rings down, they wobbled off, shook themselves into proper globes, and then sailed with the dignity of galleons into the clearing, reflecting sky, trees, and us grinning on the ground in our world.

The bubbles prepared us for the last day of Paul's Store. Paul's Store, Paul Brown's gift to the children of Pinewoods, had started ten years ago behind the Big Taggart Cottage. Perhaps his wife,

Ann Taylor, had told him about The Store at the dining hall and about Uncle Paul's Bonfire Parties—that special evening every summer when Uncle Paul invited the whole camp to come to his grotto after supper. Benches, wicker loveseats, slingback canvas chairs had been set around this amphitheater for the adults, in the middle of which Uncle Paul had a roaring bonfire going. Shaking a square black popper over the fire, he called forth the children. One by one, we came forward out on the high ramp leading from the Bruske cottage down to the shore and spanning the grotto where our elders sat looking up to us. We sang, danced, recited, whistled, performed the skit we'd been rehearsing all day, or turned cartwheels down the ramp, terrified we'd go over the edge. I remember once reciting all the counties in Michigan as fast as I could, aware that if I paused, I'd never be able to start up again and grateful that this school memorization task had at last proved profitable. Our act completed, we each approached the ramp's edge and dipped forward to the grownups with a stiff curtsey or bow. Our reward was a newspaper cone brimming with salted and buttered popcorn. The triumph was not just in racing off the ramp for the popcorn and predictable praise from attendant relatives, it was also in getting through the performance without breaking out in giggles and in being able to join the party down around the bonfire, anxiety-free, to watch the antics of others.

Paul's Store, unlike Uncle Paul's bonfire, was open every day for a half hour right after lunch whenever Paul and Ann were at the lake, and children flocked to it. Since its opening, Mother had written me every summer about this new store's success. In exchange for a striped lucky stone, a dried butterfly wing, a card trick, a drawing, a riddle, a song, a somersault, a skit, Paul paid the child a nickel or a quarter. With this coin, the child could then make a purchase from among the assorted old-fashioned candies and toys displayed in a red steamer trunk on the back porch of the Big Taggart Cottage. Top prize was to have your name carved on "The Bench of Fame," which resembled the long wooden bench at the Taggart Ping-Pong table where generations had inscribed initials and mottos. Paul also set out racks of old comics and postal cards made up during the winter that depicted Pinewoods summer scenes, and one summer red T-shirts with a Paul's Store logo were available for anyone joining a kickball game. As my time at the cottage never seemed to coincide with the time Paul and Ann were in residence, however, my only opportunity to witness the joy his store brought to Pinewoods was on its closing day during this summer when the woods were destroyed. On this last day I heard Paul Brown named a "Merchant of Love."

A crowd of people waited for Paul to hang out the sign indicating that the store was Open for Business. Everyone was expectant, prepared either to be entertained or to participate, hoping to put the sorrow of the woods behind us. We had acrobatic stunts on the bar, a flute solo and a Beethoven sonata on an electric keyboard, juggling acts and dog tricks. Big kids appeared as Carmen Miranda puppets. Many privileged the letter "P." All five members of one family, appropriately appareled in pink and purple plaid patchwork pants, performed a play, titled "Paul's Pinewoods Picnic," which produced a plethora of "Ps"; four teens, naming themselves the "Polynesian Popcorn Princesses," sang skat, "Skinnery-rinky-dinky-doo. We lo-ooo-ve you." Through all the proceedings ran the mad "Prophet of Doom" proclaiming, "The Time is Near." Two young women, on the teetering brink of their teens when Paul opened his store, presented a final skit, one that thanked him for encouraging their creativity and their self-confidence. When Paul flipped the sign from "Open" to "Closed," it was a sentimental moment, with tears and tissues, and we hugged each other, gladdened by Paul Brown's generosity and believing in the goodness of one another. Before we again picked up the droning of chainsaws behind us in the woods.

In these days, I spend time with my grandniece Hillary. We make sand birthday cakes on the bit of beach by our dock, using stones for raisins and snake grass for candles, and we walk hand-in-hand down the path into Cottage Grove to check out the familiar wonders of that camp: a roof planted in grass, a bench with dragons carved into its arm rests, a great boulder which surely is a fallen star. We touch the slimy mushroom, pat the broken tree, and do not find the swing I had promised Hillary.

I also turn toward the lake. Before dinner the day I arrive, we sit in the pavilion with drinks, our chairs, as usual, facing the water. It's been a somber, gray day, and out across the lake the water looks like foil. Hard to tell what it signifies. I stare hard. The island, a dark and solid shape against the water's dull gleaming, seems, by comparison, so simple to grasp. One afternoon Howie takes Mother and me in the motorboat to swim at Stony Point. To the north, the sand is as soft as ever and the drop-off as astonishing. Getting out of the boat, I'm only ankle-deep in water, but in two steps, just as I anticipated, I'm in over my head and treading water like mad. I borrow Howie's snorkel and fins and swim off to the south. Here are strange wonders! An abyss looms. From its murky interior spring gigantic soft plumes, Brobdingnagian seaweed. They sway silently, and fish I have never seen—some with flashing speckles, others with long silver stripes—swim languidly, contrasting with the fronds' drab green. Is this Mike Taggart's enchanted underwater forest or is it a transplanted tropical reef, with the dreaded Eurasian water milfoil substituting for coral? I shiver and kick back to the boat, eager to divest myself of mask, fins, and this vision of Higgins transformed.

On another afternoon I tack out across the lake on Mother's Sunfish. It's a dead on-shore breeze, and it takes a while to clear the boats and swimmers in close to shore. After that, it's a nice run to the east and another to the west, with the sail pulled taut and the hull steeply pitched all the way. I plan a long downwind run home. The boat planes well, but three jet skis and a power cruiser cut before me, each time causing tidal waves to swamp the bow, snap the sheet, and jostle the certainty of the small boat's steady progress. One evening, Mother and I take the canoe out, tacking this time not against the wind, but the glare of the setting sun. When it goes down, we turn back, paddling into our own deepening shadows which stretch out elongated before us.

Two friends and I walk after lunch on the path through No Man's Land to Lakeside. It is an azure and emerald Higgins day of precise outline and sparkle. Along the path sunlight polishes separate pine needles to a glitter, while through the trees, we can see the whole gleaming lake. I am aware that Martha carries anxieties from the camp's divided responses over the cleanup of the devastated woods, and that Marion bears the ongoing sorrow of her mother's death. I tell my friends that in coming to the lake for these few days, I had hoped for clarity—for light. The truth is that since my arrival on the Stage Road and my perception of an excess of light that day, I've felt a weight of darkness within.

The sound of trees crashing intersects the chainsaw's persistent clamor. Escapable only in No Man's Land or out on the lake or at the end of the day. Howie, however, has walked into the hornet's nest. Although on this brilliant day he'd rather be sailing his Hobie, he's drawn into the tangled and tormented woods. He takes axe and saw and goes alone, to Tammy's distress. She fears the flying wood splinter, the arbitrarily falling tree. I remember Daddy on the summer's loveliest days going into the woods to chop dead trees or to dig out pineknots. Howie clears the Pinewoods trails of trunks and branches which fall across them at every angle, making them impassable for dogs or people. He is careful to lift fallen limbs over to the side, to straighten young trees bowed over the paths, and to cut through only when he's confronted with an entire tree trunk or an impenetrable tangle across a trail. Howie's method is to lay by, lay off, and let lie. His work is a labor of love, for he knows that no one else will tend to the trails if he doesn't. He arrives down on the shore in late afternoon in time for a sail. From this endeavor to rearrange the forest and restore the trails, his face is nicked and scratched, and his hair, matted with sawdust, a wig. Wind and water are cleansers.

Two days before I leave, he brings a beer down on the dock at midafternoon. As he was working in his solitary way this afternoon in the woods, Curt, the boss lumberman, had appeared and accused Howie in vehement terms of violating the contract Pinewoods had signed with him. By sawing out the two-foot sections of trees where they crossed the trails, he was interfering with the possibility of transforming these trunks into profitably correct ten-foot sections. Down on the dock, Howie was struck by the growing realization that the "big boys" were "cleaning-up" in more ways than one by cashing in on our devastation and grief. For some days, we had been aware that they were moving through the woods, behind the cottages as well as around the dining hall and the tennis court, designating with red ribbons many trees as "storm-damaged," which we perceived to be sturdily standing. Claiming that these trees were doomed to fall with the pressure of wind and time, the lumbermen staked their claim to take them down. Collectively, we at Pinewoods were subdued by their apparent expertise, by the legalities of the contract, by our grief, and silently we watched them lower, one after another, in a few minutes' time, the great pines that had been growing for centuries behind our cottages, the great pines that Uncle Paul had designated as our legacy, but which we also knew to belong only to themselves and to the ages. Who could say if a tree was "storm-damaged" or if it would be strong enough to resist subsequent storms? Because the trees could not, Howie, usually shy with words, had to speak. On September 11 he addressed a desperate letter to Martha:

A couple of years ago we Pinewoods people so valued natural forests that in consideration of Cottage Grove's activities of "improving" their forests we pledged $70,000 so we could buy some of their land and save them—and they could continue without man's intrusions or interference. Cottage Grove turned down our offer and we were left with only our ten acres of woods. How sad—only ten acres. But we are Pinewoods—and we are proud, even though we don't have a high profile. . . . We have fun with each other and we tilt towards harmony with ourselves and with nature. Our name says who we are—Pinewoods. We like the woods.

We have a problem in our woods now. Jean is cleaning up brush from downed trees as fast as she can and [Curt] is pursuing his mission by cutting down more trees. Some trees are storm damaged and some are not. We say it's okay because the trees will bring money to Pinewoods and that money will pay for Jean's work. And [Curt] cuts down another tree and Jean has more brush to pick up, and Pinewoods will make more money. Is this a "Catch 22" with our woods paying the price?

A forestry committee was appointed, but it spent its time discussing the fate of 3 pines behind the dining hall. These are great trees. They survived the storm. The result of the committee's deliberations—one tree stays, one tree can be negotiated (it's [Curt's] tree but we can have it for $400–$600) and one tree goes. So much for the committee.

The wolf is guarding the henhouse, and Pinewoods is a pawn for [Curt's] greed. What we should be about is saving our woods, but we are willingly ruining them. For the promise of money we are allowing [Curt] into our woods with his machinery to take our trees and to trample everything in the way. Some folks say we are bound by the contract and that we should honor it. Truly there's no honor in this contract. We should save the woods. That is where there is honor.

Under normal circumstances for [Curt], things would be okay. He has a contract which will provide him with income by harvesting trees and the landowner mutually benefits. Our Pinewoods trees are hardly a commodity, and we are not in the business of making money.

I am afraid [Curt] is on a path of destruction. Please do something so [Curt] will cut down no more of our trees and he will leave our small woods to take care of themselves.[141]

By October, countless trees had been reduced to logs. Their stumps, as big as card tables, remained. Their limbs were litter. Trees and shrubs too small to be profitable had been bulldozed into indiscriminate brush heaps. On a weekend early in October, Mother, Howie, and Tammy went to the cottage. Mother called me Sunday morning as she always does: all three were agreed; they felt it would be impossible to come back to Pinewoods. Howie decided he would resign from the position he had held for twenty years of serving as the camp treasurer and of keeping the camp's books. In a call a month later, however, Mother told me that they all realized, "This is what we have. This is what is left. This, after all, is Pinewoods," and "We [after all] are Pinewoods." So they would return. So we do shore up our remnants, I thought. But through the fall, Mother's distress, like Howie's, persisted. She prepared her own statement to be delivered to everyone at Pinewoods:

Our common holding of ancient forest land is so small. I suspect it is not the size of a pinprick on a map of Roscommon County. Yet we did not revere this treasure. The storm of July 13, 1995, put our trees at the mercy of a rapacious outsider. We did not understand well enough that the way a tree dies adds to the diversity, beauty, and health of a forest. Except for freeing wires and clearing our paths and roads, we could have let our forest be.

When a tree snaps off, keep it for bird food, nests, and look-outs. When the root system comes up creating soil perturbation, save it for animal homes. If the trunk is twisted by wild gale winds, keep the dying tree for eventual enrichment of the forest soil. Our trees suffered every variety of snapping, falling, and twisting. Sadly they and their neighbors were felled for logs and wood chips. An article in *Audubon* states, "Nobody listens to the importance of dead trees." That was certainly us.[142]

Martha's letter in the fall issue of *Pinewords* cited recent ecological investigations representing an alternative environmental perspective: "Studies of forest regeneration after catastrophic blowdowns indicate that we can expect a dramatic increase in plant species diversity, tree seedling density and shade intolerant herbs and shrubs in the next six years, with the greatest burst occurring in years 1–3. Keep your eyes open this spring."[143] Elizabeth Burrows Huntington, in her early *Memories of Lakeside Camp,* gives a detailed account of storms in both 1880 and 1908 when "great pines that had withstood the storms of a century were uprooted like toothpicks"[144] in a ten-minute blast. Included in her *Memories* is a photograph of well-dressed ladies posing on the fallen trees as if they were theatrical props. It helped me see our choices: to believe that our lives are tragic dramas with conclusive final scenes and strewn bodies or cyclical epics, following rhythms and seasons in a continuing narrative.

December 26–29, 1991. *(Written after returning to Pinewoods with Mother for the first time out of season since 1954; written as a memo to myself, with no thought then of writing more.)*

I am a marginal person. Long before the adjective "marginal" and the verb "marginalize" came into fashion, I've been aware that I stand on the marge, the edge, the strand. Looking two ways, in and out, back and forward. Separated from the mainstream, yet not quite adrift.

The first day I walk down to the lake morning and evening. I stand on the shore. Conscious always of the bank behind me. Of the pumphouse, the cascade of stairs moving up to the tall dark cottage and the woods. Yet drawn to the lake. It's frozen. An expanse of ice. But there's an edge where water meets ice beyond which are the colors of summer—turquoise and cobalt. The whole western end of the lake seems open. Everywhere is such a glistening. Light glancing off the small sea waves, spinning in sheets off the ice, and all around the pine needles flash like blue blades.

On the next day, fog, and the open water is invisible. The ice seems to move on endlessly, shrouded over. No distinct line between its solidity and the gray mist which has erased the island and the shoreline opposite. At my feet, between the slabs of ice pressed up against each other like geological plates, are pools of water, holding each stone in a clear outline. The ice speaks. Not yet the whooping which Thoreau associates with the spring thaw, but creaks and sputters. Where is its mouth? On the eastern side of the lake, some tempt the ice. Snowmobiles roar; skaters appear; dogs frolic around them. It could be a Dutch Renaissance painting.

And the woods. Mother and I boot up. Tammy's boots are a perfect fit, and instinctively I remember what to do with these skis and poles, surprised by and grateful for kinetic memory. I last skied in Japan in the winter of 1958, yet the muscles recall how the foot lifts up on the ball and pushes forward. We move out behind the cottage, taking the old path to the mailbox first, and then moving onto the trails and roads that intersect throughout the woods. Others have preceded us on these trails as they do unseen in summer. Inscribed in the snow, a maze of animal tracks is visible now. Deer prints, clear ditto marks, crisscross fonts less easy to decipher. Raccoon, fox, squirrel? Mother identifies the passages made by porcupines dragging their tails behind them as they go to and fro from the pile of castoff boats, furniture, docks, and stumps that is the Cottage Grove dump. On the snow's parchment, a multitude of signs are evident: circlings, nuzzlings below the surface, middens, scat, and spores. The summer's skeletons—dried heads of Indian pipes, spidery twigs of huckleberry bushes, brown fern fronds—protrude from this parchment. The question has been, always will be: how to read it? Emily Dickinson had it right:

> Nature is what we know—
> Yet have no art to say—
> So impotent Our Wisdom is
> To her Simplicity.[145]

Watching our skis' linear tracks cross these notations, watching our progress through the woods, I'm too busy to translate sounds. This is possible only when we stop. When the shushing, shushing of the skis stops. Time stops in this silence. Such hush. Can I hear a pin drop? A pine needle? Somewhere the narrative is resumed: a pileated woodpecker taps. We move on, searching the trees above for a red crest. But there's no other sign. Only the elusive tapping. Looking up at the trees, I invoke bird: an ancestor who has heard and seen it all.

We ski into the wooded area Cottage Grove had designated for clear-cutting. Through thinning trees appears the apparition of heavy machinery for lifting and hauling logs. All twisted trees, all double trees, all fallen trees, all trees signifying diversity have been taken. Only those deemed straight and tall remain, piles and piles of logs stacked alongside them. Is this the end that the designers of Cottage Grove's forest management plan seek? In their desire for a park's purity, their red ties around these gnarled trees might seem six-pointed yellow stars. Here in this devastated woods, quite suddenly the tidy black type of deer prints have vanished from the snow. The heavy marks of bulldozers, jeeps, cleated boots instead spell out confusion.

At the kitchen window inside the cottage, I watch birds and squirrels come to the feeder. Black squirrels, gray squirrels, a red squirrel; the birds only chickadees, nuthatches, a brown creeper. Mother's list of birds, started two decades ago, updated regularly, and posted above the can-opener by the kitchen sink, indicates decrease in kinds and numbers. The once-common cardinals, titmice, juncos, red-breasted and evening grosbeaks, blue jays, woodpeckers are elsewhere this winter. To watch these few that are here flit and frisk must be to believe in continuity and connections. The planet is not yet Winter, sterile science-fiction world, devoid of wings and the dream of flying.

SPRING

Booming ice, honking geese, thawing earth. The signs of spring were all the testimony necessary to Thoreau for belief in immanence. Proof of life's perpetual re-creation and renewal. Basis for hope and faith. With the simple observation, "Walden was dead and is alive again,"[146] he embodies his gospel. Although historically he concluded his stay at the pond in early fall, he arranged the book to bring us around through summer, fall, and winter to spring in his next-to-the-last chapter of *Walden*. So as the readers of this sacred text, we also wait for spring and experience the conclusion, not as ending, but as beginning. As a child growing up in Michigan, however, spring seemed an abstraction, a remote poetic possibility: in Flint, we trudged through endless winter straight into summer vacation.

If there was a spring in Michigan, it occurred only on those rare occasions when we went north over Memorial Day. Behind the cottage Daddy pointed out the woods' secret signs. He pushed aside dark, damp leaves to uncover the trailing arbutus's sweet flowers. He also had us all on the lookout for pink and yellow lady slipper orchids. Few and far between, they poised among the greening underbrush, teetering delicately on their slender stalks. Entirely vanished by summer, these lady slippers seemed more magical than Cinderella's. But such revelations are isolated memories, and unlike Dickinson who could make a prairie from one clover,[147] I couldn't make a spring at Higgins from them. My Michigan spring remains a memory of soot-spotted snow heaped alongside driveways and sidewalks like piles of dirty linen that didn't go away. In college I spent spring breaks writing term papers, shocked to realize sometime during the summer that the season of tender leaves could come and go without my noticing.

In Japan following college, where spring is a cultural ritual, celebrated with ceremony, I began to understand how bereft of spring I'd been all along. Here the first plum blossoms to dot winter's blank boughs are featured in newspaper headlines, TV programs, greeting cards, shopping arcades, sweet bean-paste cakes. In traditional homes, they flower on scrolls, kimono prints, embroidery, teacups, lacquerware brought out of storerooms and chests to announce the season. Their round pink petals and the assurance they evoke of spring's pregnancy have made them the flower of Girls Day, March 3. The plum blossom is followed by the cherry with cherry-blossom-viewing parties, reverential and drunken, at well-known sites. The cherry blossom is, in turn, followed by the iris, with its spear-shaped leaves the floral representative for Boys Day, May 5.

Kansas taught me spring, however. Disappointed by the autumn my first fall in Kansas, I had no reason to look for spring. There was no warning. It burst upon me. Redbuds, unknown to me in previous lives, suddenly appeared from nowhere. Nothing subtle about this Kansas spring. These redbuds were shocking. In the singular, a tiny knotted bloom, but in the plural, a haze of magenta on hillsides, along roads, up against a building. A parade followed closely after them—crab apple, cherry, apricot, quince—and all bloomed simultaneously in red, pink, orange revelry. The colors of that first Kansas spring, 1968, were intensified by an unrequited romance, by my students drafted for Vietnam, by the deaths of King, Kennedy, and the big cat, who had seen me through graduate school. The redbuds were bred out of the dead land, with these other flowering trees following gaiety in excess. In subsequent years, I wait for the heraldic redbuds. I pay annual visits to favorite trees—an ancient one at a friend's where the buds cluster on the gnarled trunk like fuschia-colored honey bees and another in a grove on campus whose branches twist and intersect to shape a perfect clover. I anticipate the appearance of the redbuds' tiny, tentative green leaves which, in time, darken and unfold into hearts, and then for a few days, while the blossoms are falling, I watch the spreading magenta shadow beneath the trees.

The first tree I planted after I bought my own house in Kansas had to be a redbud. It's in the southeast corner of the backyard, and it's proliferating. I pull up infant redbud trees along with dandelions, plantain, nettle, hen bane, poke weed, bind weed, shepherd's purse from the garden every spring and learn again the tenacity of weeds. My spring garden in Kansas has provided diverse lessons. A garden instructs in all seasons. But perhaps lessons in the spring come most easily because their context is the marvel of growth itself. There's a predictability about some events in this springtime garden, an assurance about the orderly transformation of the redbud, of tender green protrudings into multiple colors, of the perennials' tumescent gropings above ground into peony's gawky stems, iris's elegant blades, bleeding hearts's leafy extravagances.

It's the unpredictable, however, which teaches. Scientists still can't say what prompts a plant to bloom in the spring. When those small blue flowers—the grape hyacinths and sporellas—emerge from the dark earth in my backyard, I wonder how I could have forgotten them. Impetuous miracles! Each exquisitely colored and distinctly shaped, they appear when I'm not looking to remind me of sky-blue perfection. The big bulbs I put down in the fall also fool me. From these hard fists the intricacies of the daffodil bloom emerge. Some bulbs migrate underground during the winter to emerge in unexpected locations. From one spring to another some perennials—cone flowers, columbine, lythrum—multiply wildly; some appear from out of nowhere—black-eyed susan and mint; others, ordered by catalogue or transplanted from local nurseries—the delicate blue flax and the brilliant delphinium—disappear. Some mutate, changing colors—a deep red tulip becomes striped, a purple larkspur, a little later in the season, becomes pink. I may plot and plan my garden, but springtime shows me the quirky power of plants to chart their own courses. An ice storm, however, can break your blooms and break your heart. In the spring of 1996, a late deep freeze stunted the daffodils, obliterated the aconites, and hardened the forsythia buds, depriving us of yellow for a season. Red and blue survived, but we yearned for lost yellow.

I see now that as a teenager in Michigan I didn't know how to look for spring. It was there all the time. At home in Kansas in the spring, I am grateful for phone calls from Howie and Tammy who always call during their early visits to Pinewoods to help me see what I'm missing. In the spring of

1996, Howie reports on feral cats and raccoons beneath the cottage, tearing up the insulation. Talk proceeds to Mother's concern about the need for a new, creature-tight foundation for the cottage. He does not report on arbutus and lady slipper. This spring he and Tammy keep to the lake—the suckers swirl over the sand and eagles soar near the island; they try not to see the wracked woods behind the cottage. It's not my brother's way to use violent language, but his call from Pinewoods this spring is vehement as he refers to the logger responsible for "cleaning up" and clearing out our woods in the wake of the tornado: "If [Curt] didn't clear-cut, he did the next damn thing. It's not a woods any more; it's the creation of an enemy." With the loss of the woods and the loss of faith resulting from communal misjudgment, Howie grieves this spring for more than the loss of yellow. Will anyone notice if beneath the dark, damp leaves the arbutus and lady slipper will appear this year in the slashed land?

SUMMER

Everything here is about summer: the time of ripening.

O n my first evening at the lake during my brief, five-day visit following the storm of 1995, I talked with Marion in her back cottage. Musing over our realization that our culture neither allows for nor helps one with extended grief, we discussed the loss of the woods and her loss of her mother. She told me she is glad her mother did not have to suffer from seeing the destruction of Pinewoods's great trees. She told me she believes that one way she can accept her mother's death is by trying to assume her nurturing qualities. I reminded her then of a dream she once had shared with me in which her mother appeared as a marvelous fish-shaped fountain ceaselessly spouting and spurting cascades of water, and I shared with her the words I'd received the day before my hysterectomy from a wise woman in Kansas: "The healing begins as soon as the first cut is made. Think of that."

In June 1996, a bulletin reaches Kansas, summarizing the history of events in the past year and the camp's reactions to these changes; it suggests a healing process:

This special letter is being sent out because there are issues we all need to think about and reflect upon before this year's annual meeting. Having a natural disaster (tornado) in our woods has been catastrophic, catalytic, and very painful for many. In addition, Howard Schultz's well deserved transition out of the position of financial officer is another very big change. These events alter a relatively peaceful stability that Pinewoods has had for the last twenty years and have forced us to reexamine the structure of the Association. It has been difficult because these types of changes carry with them a sense of loss, anger, confusion, even grief. Those involved in the forest clean-up realize that if it were to happen again (and hopefully it won't in our lifetime) the organization and orchestration of it would be better. However, all of us did the best we were able to do with the information we had at the time. Which brings us to some questions we need to be asking ourselves as an association. How do we learn from this experience, take that knowledge and use it to create what we want in the future? . . .

Love, caring, family and history are the glue that keep Pinewoods together. This has not changed. While the events of the last year have drained our financial and emotional resources, they have also provided us with an opportunity to make adjustments that will fortify the bonds of the Association as we move into the 21st century.[148]

The bulletin, signed by Martha, proposes a set of critical areas to be discussed at informal sessions in camp prior to the seventy-seventh annual meeting, to be held in the Pinewoods dining hall on 27 July 1996. These areas, all pointing to the difficult need for changes in our communal traditions, are identified as "Communication," "Finances," "Organization of Governing Bodies," and "Catastrophes and Emergencies."

For the meeting the dining hall is rearranged, tables pushed back and chairs set in concentric half circles facing a single board of directors table. About eighty of us gather; Martha presides. There is a welcome; a moment of silence for a member who had died in the spring; an acknowledgement of marriages, engagements, and births—six baby girls in the past year. The roll of members is read, proxies of absent members accounted for, a quorum established. The president, the treasurer, and the chairs of standing committees—Dining Hall, Property and Grounds, Fire Safety, Higgins Lake Foundation, Higgins Lake Property Owners, Memorial Fund, Trails—deliver their reports. This is business as usual with intermittent laughter. The chair of the Dining Hall Committee asserts, "If you complain more than two times about the food, you're on the committee." A few people leave their seats to go to the coffee urn for a breakfast follow-up. Some stragglers arrive during the reports. We listen to Jack Wade deliver an informed and detailed account of the concerns of the Higgins Lake Property Owners organization:

- Zebra mussels, which now infest nearby Lake St. Helen, haven't hit Higgins yet;
- Eurasian water milfoil continues despite the DNR's use of 2-4-D;
- Swimmer's itch cases are up;
- The lake level continues to be a critical issue with heavy rain and snow causing washouts of banks and at roadends;
- Realtors are promoting "funneling"—the purchase of large tracts of land with a narrow access to the lake—and their subsequent subdividing into multiple lots, making new zoning laws a pressing necessity;

- The need to protect Higgins's entire watershed, not just the riparian environment, is increasingly imperative.[149]

Reports from standing committees reflect on the upheavals caused by the previous summer. The Trail Committee report acknowledges the storm's destruction of the camp's trails as well as the good work done in restoring paths to the tennis court, Mr. Wiseman's Road, and the mailboxes. The Property and Grounds Committee report makes note of the proliferation of poison ivy due to increased sunlight in the woods and urges caution in spraying. For her special work in cleaning the storm debris, Jean receives a yellow rain poncho, inscribed with "Thanks" from many Pinewoods people; it replaces the black trash bag she'd worn through the fall during her labors in the woods.

The camp also expresses its gratitude to Howie for his years of service as Pinewoods's bookkeeper. Howie is stunned to receive two large gifts, one wrapped in paper printed with dollar bills, the other in newspaper. The first is a framed aerial photograph of the lake in its full array of colors with a small brass plaque of appreciation. The second gift is wheeled to the front of the dining hall. It is a child's wagon, but nailed to its bed is the wooden seat from our outhouse, torn down to make way for the new toolshed and washer and dryer; the toilet seat and the lime box next to it are intact, saved from demolition by the camp caretaker and brought to light for this occasion. Laughter erupts through the dining hall with the recognition and exposure of this intimate and familiar relic. After the meeting, we will place it on the pavilion for all to admire.

Martha begins the president's report with a statement of collective gratitude to the many who participated and cooperated in leading Pinewoods beyond the experience of disaster. She is concerned that everyone in camp have an opportunity to speak and to be heard. We talk through multiple necessities and possibilities: a dining hall budget, a contact person from each cottage, a list of camp members' skills, the availability of First Aid kits, an emergency phone or e-mail tree, a hired tax consultant, an extended presidential term, a "Dining Hall Scramble" which would mix up families at the tables. I have heard the grief of my mother and my brother; I have seen the ravaged forest; I have written about these sorrows. A marginal person, holding no office and sitting on no committee, arriving at Pinewoods on a late-night flight and leaving after a brief interlude, coming from Kansas and academia—*terrae incognitae* for almost everyone present, I have not spoken. From the shoreline of past and present, of sorrow and hope, it occurs to me what I need to say at the end of the meeting: "As we have a moment of silence to remember the beloved friends and family lost in the preceding year to death, I ask for a moment of silence to remember the great trees lost in the preceding year to storm and greed. I ask, too, that we pray for the growth of the seedlings from these great trees and the restoration of the forest."

Walking back to the cottage with Mother after the meeting, she points to a small white pine along the path. It appears in a barren area where before last year there was a stand of tall pines. Mother found the small tree smashed into the ground after the removal of the fallen giants around it. Its branches hung battered and broken. An orphan tree. But a survivor. With stakes and cords, she has plucked it up and propped it up. She brings water to it daily. Back in Kansas later, she calls to tell me that she's contracted with a local nursery to have young red and white pines planted in the open spaces along the path to the mailboxes.

This summer I take to the lake and the woods daily. Although as a kid, returning home late from the Loomises and refusing a flashlight, I could take a wrong turn off the path and end up down the bank, I was never lost for long. Setting out alone into the woods at dusk and without a compass might have more serious consequences. I start out after supper, planning to try Julia trails. I want to see how they have fared in her long absence and during the months of abuse in the woods. Access to Julia's trails are off the firebreak. It's dry out here; few mushrooms and fungi punctuate this sandy stretch with color. But even in this diminishing light, you see the scurrying of ants. You keep walking west and enter the woods where Julia laid a log perpendicular to the firebreak, just at the point where you spot the singleton red pine. Her trails dip and circle through the woods, running through groves of poplar and oak and out across mossy meadows. This year they are overgrown with fern and huckleberry bush, but I find Julia's decaying markers, following one after the other, and I move along. Light and shadow flicker soundlessly as I pass through these groves of straight, slender trees.

Except for a distant woodpecker tapping, the woods are quiet. The first deer appears between the slats of light. Stands and gazes, its eyes still, its ears held out like large leaves. I cluck and step forward. I am allowed. Approach closer. The deer swivels its head on its lovely, stalk-like neck, and it's off, giving me the high sign—its startlingly white tail. I continue tracing out Julia's path. It's harder now to see the branches she has placed end to end to outline it. I find myself with ferns as high as my knees. Three deer emerge up ahead. They stare for a quick second, and with a snort from one, they turn as triplets and disappear like shining knives plunged into darkness. They do not slip back into the woods noiselessly, however. There is a thrashing of underbrush from out of which leaps the sound of the woodpecker's tapping. I look for the trail and do not find it. I backtrack through broken ferns.

I look more closely at the signs I've left in this wilderness—my disruption of plants, my imprint on moss. There, once again, is Julia's trail. I follow her markers carefully, coming out of the woods unexpectedly onto an unknown road. I check the sun and put its burning orb behind me, knowing the way home is east. Walking awhile, with my shadow extended out before me to lead the way, I come to realize I've left Julia's trail for a road made by Timberjack devastation. The woodpecker tapping seems closer. Up ahead in an open, cutover space are five deer this time, heads down grazing among stumps. No longer occasional visitors, the deer are occupying these woods in herds. The sun's liquid light pours over them, setting them aglow. Lifting their heads casually, languidly, they look about with wide-eyed innocence. They are etched in light. The scene of desecration becomes radiant, a sense of the original pastoral restored. I clasp my hands and greet these holy beings. The woodpecker's tapping rouses me from my transfixion. I see the bird now; persisting with its tapping, it twists about the trunk of an oak, out of sight for one instant, but back in view the next. It flies on ahead of me, its blood-red head my sure flashlight and guide the rest of the way home.

1. Gertrude Stein, *The Autobiography of Alice B. Toklas* (New York: Random House, 1933), 18.

2. Henry David Thoreau, *Walden and Civil Disobedience* (1854; reprint, New York: Viking Penguin, Inc., 1983), 125.

3. *Ibid.*, 135.

4. *Ibid.*, 240.

5. Lucy Schultz, letter to author, 18 September 1995.

6. Mrs. A. F. Bruske, "Fifty Summers of Higgins Lake," *A History of Pinewoods Camp* (Higgins Lake, Mich.: n.p., 1929), n. pag.

7. Thoreau, 45.

8. Quoted in Arthur W. Rosenau, *Lakeside: A History of Lakeside Association on Higgins Lake in Roscommon County, Michigan* (N.p.: Lakeside Association, 1979), 23.

9. Quoted from "U. S. Field Notes of William Burt," *Gerrish Township, 1880–1980* (Roscommon, Mich.: Graphic Arts Press, 1980), 3.

10. Quoted in Rosenau, 20.

11. Quoted from *Roscommon Herald News* (July 1949) in *Gerrish Township, 1880–1980*, 11.

12. Mrs. A. F. Bruske, "From the Forest Primeval," *A History of Pinewoods Camp*, n. pag.

13. Charles E. Cleland, *A Brief History of Michigan Indians* ([Lansing]: Michigan Department of State, 1975), 25–26.

14. James M. McClurken, "The Ottawa," *People of the Three Fires* (Grand Rapids, Mich.: West Michigan

Printing, Inc., 1992), 38.

15. Elizabeth Burrows Huntington, *Memories of Lakeside Camp* (N. p.: n. p., 1984), n. pag.

16. "David Shoppenagons," *The First Hundred Years: An Introduction to the History of the Grayling Area* (Grayling, Mich.: Northern Litho Printing, 1972), 106–9.

17. Quoted in Rosenau, 40.

18. Quoted in Rosenau, 37.

19. See Chapter 8, titled "Backwoods Production Line" in Bruce Catton's *Michigan: A History* (New York and London: W. W. Norton & Company, 1976), 128–47.

20. Terry E. Jones, *Higgins Lake: Past, Present, Future*, ed. Robert King and Bess Behnke ([Mt. Pleasant, Mich.]: n.p., n.d.), 84–85.

21. Dan Fishel, comp., *Roscommon—1885* ([Roscommon, Mich.]: n.p., 1981), 1

22. Chief Mack-e-te-be-nessy (A. J. Blackbird), *History of the Ottawa and Chippewa Indians of Michigan* (Ypsilanti, Mich.: Ypsilanti Job Printing House, 1887), 101–2.

23. *A History of Pinewoods Camp*, n. pag.

24. Rosenau, 14.

25. *Gerrish Township*, 39.

26. *Ibid.*

27. Rosenau, 3.

28. *Gerrish Township*, 41.

29. Cindy S. Aron, *Working at Play: A History of Vacations in the United States* (New York and Oxford: Oxford University Press, 1999), 8–9.

30. Quoted from *The Independent* (2 July 1903) in Harvey H. Kaiser's *Great Camps of the Adirondacks* (Boston: David R. Godine, 1982), 63.

31. *Ibid.*, 58.

32. *Ibid.*, 66.

33. Paul Hale Bruske, "Early Days at Higgins," *A History of Pinewoods Camp*, n. pag.

34. Lucy Schultz, *Loon Echoes* (May 1992), 3.

35. Herman Melville, *Moby-Dick*, ed. Harrison Heyford, Hershel Parker, and G. Thomas Tanselle (1851; reprint, Evanston and Chicago: Northwestern University Press and the Newberry Library, 1988), 55.

36. Mrs. A. F. Bruske, "Fifty Summers of Higgins Lake," n. pag.

37. Lucy Schultz, "Shaw-Schultz Cottage," *Pinewoods, 1920–1987*, ed. Florie Foster and Ted Lawrence (N.p.: n.p., 1987), 16.

38. Minutes of the Pinewoods Camp Association Annual Meeting, (29 July 1995), 2.

39. Thoreau, 136.

40. *Ibid.*, 371.

41. *Ibid.*, 45.

42. Barbara Hanson Pierce, "To Grandmother's House We (All) Go," *Town & Country* (August 1992), 124.

43. "The Pinewoods Camp Association," *A History of Pinewoods Camp*, n. pag.

44. Fischel, *Roscommon—1885*, 5.

45. Lucy Schultz, "The Beginnings of the Pinewoods Dining Hall," *The Pinewoods Scrapbook, 1992* ([Roscommon, Mich.]: n. p., 1992), 64.

46. "Our Pinewoods Camp War Record," *A History of Pinewoods Camp*, n. pag.

47. Anna Ring Conroy, *Memoirs of Early Days at Higgins Lake* ([N.p.: n.p.,] 1923), 11.

48. Mrs. A. F. Bruske, "Fifty Summers of Higgins Lake," n. pag.

49. *Funk & Wagnells Standard College Dictionary* (New York: Harcourt, Brace & World, 1963), 990.

50. Mrs. A. F. Bruske, "Fifty Summers of Higgins Lake," n. pag.

51. Paul Hale Bruske, "Early Days at Higgins," n. pag.

52. Quoted from Kendrick Fritz by William Least-Heat Moon in *Blue Highways* (1983; reprint, New York: Ballantine Books, 1984), 193.

53. Jens Peter Jacobsen, *Niels Lyhne*, trans. Tiina Nunnally (1880; reprint, Seattle: Fjord Press, 1990), 143.

54. Christina Rossetti, "Who Has Seen the Wind?" in *Poems and Prose*, ed. Jan Marsh (1869; reprint, London: J. M. Dent, 1994), 136.

55. Melville, 543.

56. Toni Morrison, *Song of Solomon* (New York: Alfred A. Knopf, 1977), 337.

57. Patty Taggart McKibbin, "The E. B. Taggart Cottage," *Pinewoods, 1920–1987*, 55–56.

58. Ted Lawrence, "Lawrence Cottage—Aloha," *Pinewoods, 1920–1987*, 67.

59. Thoreau, 59.

60. *Ibid.*, 57.

61. Quoted in Rosenau, 30.

62. *Ibid.*, 30–31.

63. Edwin G. Plum, "Recollections of Pinewoods Camp," *Pinewoods Camp, 1920–1987*, 7.

64. *Ibid.*, 6.

65. Philip Will, Jr., "The Siscos and the Dining Hall," *Pinewoods, 1948–1966* ([Evanston]: The Willage Press, 1967), 25.

66. Quoted by Patty Taggart McKibbin, 59.

67. *The Compact Edition of the Oxford English Dictionary*, I (Oxford: Oxford University Press, 1971), 1112.

68. Sally Loomis, "The 'H C's,'" *A History of Pinewoods Camp*, n. pag.

69. *Ibid.*

70. Emily Dickinson, #333, *The Complete Poems of Emily Dickinson*, ed. Thomas H. Johnson (Boston and Toronto: Little, Brown and Co., 1960), 158.

71. Melville, 5.

72. Eugene Field, *Cradle Lullabies* (Chicago: The Canterbury Company, 1909), 9.

73. Kenneth Grahame, *The Wind in the Willows* (1908; reprint, New York: Dell Publishing Co., Inc., 1974), 5.

74. Plato, *The Collected Dialogues of Plato*, ed. Edith Hamilton and Huntington Cairns (New York: Pantheon Books, 1961), 1208.

75. Nick Dewey, "Bruske-Dewey Cottage," *Pinewoods, 1920–1987*, 40.

76. Paul Hale Bruske, "Early Days at Higgins," n. pag.

77. Edwin G. Plum, "Recollections of Pinewoods Camp," 8.

78. George L. Harman, Jr., "The George L. Harman Cottage," *Pinewoods, 1920–1987*, 34–35.

79. Lucy Schultz, "Shaw-Schultz Cottage," 15.

80. Thoreau, 148. The third chapter of *Walden* is titled "Reading."

81. *Ibid.*, 46.

82. *Ibid.*, 95–96.

83. Louise G. Humphrey, "Betty Wright's Wedding—Aug. 24, 1921," *A History of Pinewoods Camp*, n. pag.

84. Henry James, *The Portrait of a Lady* (1881; reprint, New York: The Modern Library, 1951), 1.

85. Melville, 167.

86. Rosenau, 42.

87. Melville, 164.

88. Michael Taggart, as told to Marion Foster, "Forest Lodge," *Pinewoods, 1920–1987*, 42.

89. *Ibid.*, 43.

90. G. Lloyd Harman, "The Hermit," *A History of Pinewoods Camp*, n. pag.

91. *Ibid.*

92. *Ibid.*

93. Edwin G. Plum, "Recollections of Pinewoods Camp," 11.

94. *Ibid.*, 8–9.

95. Walt Whitman, "Out of the Cradle Endlessly Rocking," *Leaves of Grass and Selected Poems* (New York: The Modern Library, 1950), 198.

96. Mrs. A. F. Bruske, "Fifty Summers of Higgins Lake," n. pag.

97. Thoreau, 366.

98. Robert Pogue Harrison, *Forests: The Shadow of Civilization* (Chicago and London: University of Chicago Press, 1992), 6.

99. Patty Taggart McKibbin, "The E.B. Taggart Cottage," 62.

100. Paul Hale Bruske, "Our Pinewoods Pines," *A History of Pinewoods Camp*, n. pag.

101. Quoted in John H. Bland's *Forests of Lilliput: The Realm of Mosses and Lichens* (Englewood Cliffs, N.J.: Prentice-Hall, Inc., 1971), 1.

102. Henry T. Darlington, *The Mosses of Michigan* (Bloomfield Hills, Mich.: Cranbrook Institute of Science, 1964), 31.

103. Kent H. McKnight and Vera B. McKnight, *A Field Guide to Mushrooms* in the Peterson Field Guide Series (Boston and New York: Houghton Mifflin Company, 1987), 127.

104. Darlington, viii.

105. McKnight and McKnight, 11.

106. Caroline Kirkland, *A New Home, Who'll Follow?* ed. Sandra A. Zagarell (1839; reprint, New Brunswick, N.J.: Rutgers University Press, 1996), 5.

107. Gary Snyder, "For the Children," *Turtle Island* (New York: New Directions, 1974), 86.

108. Clinton S. Owensby, *Kansas Prairie Wildflowers* (Ames: Iowa State University Press, 1980), 58.

109. Kathryn Loomis, "Pinewoods Nature Notes," *Pinewoods, 1948–1966*, 16.

110. Philippa Nicolson, ed., *Vita Sackville-West's Garden Book* (New York: Atheneum, 1969), 119.

111. William Butler Yeats, "Lapis Lazuli," *The Collected Poems of W. B. Yeats* (New York: The Macmillan Company, 1940), 292.

112. Whitman, "A Noiseless Patient Spider," *Leaves of Grass*, 351.

113. Henry James's term for his penchant for seeing life as "ferocious and sinister." *Letters to A. C. Benson and Auguste Monod*, ed. E. F. Benson (London: Elkin Mathews & Marrot, 1930), 35.

114. *Higgins Lake Foundation News*, 6, no. 3 (Fall 1995): 8.

115. Lucy Schultz, letter to Higgins Lake Property Owners Association, 25 June 1996.

116. Quoted by Rosenau, 3.

117. Paul Hale Bruske, "Early Days at Higgins," n. pag.

118. Mrs. A. F. Bruske, "The 'Scientific Purpose' Deer," *A History of Pinewoods Camp*, n. pag.

119. Peter J. Schmitt, "Birds in the Bush," *Back to Nature: The Arcadian Myth in Urban America* (New York: Oxford University Press, 1969), 33–44.

120. Neltje Blanchan, *Bird Neighbors* (New York: Doubleday and McClure Co., 1901), n. pag.

121. Lucy Schultz, letter to Higgins Lake Property Owners Association, 25 June 1996.

122. Nick Dewey, "Bruske-Dewey Cottage," 40

123. Adelaide Taggart, "Birds of Pinewoods," *Pinewoods, 1948–1966*, 1–2.

124. Joe Taylor, *Pinewords* (November 1992), n. pag.

125. Laura Gauss, *Pinewords* (November 1992), n. pag.

126. Adam Gopnik, "The Myth of Summer," *New Yorker* (22 and 29 June 1998): 11–12.

127. Judy Ross, *Summer Cottages* (Toronto: Stoddart Publishing Co. Limited, 1991), 7.

128. Christine S. Cozzens, "A Cabin, a Lake, a Memory," *New York Times*, 8 September 1996, 33.

129. Deborah Wyatt Fellows, "Editor's Notes," *Traverse: Northern Michigan's Magazine* (August 1997): 1.

130. Pierce, 124.

131. Thoreau, 168.

132. *Ibid.*, 171.

133. George P. Morris, "Woodman, Spare That Tree!" quoted in John Bartlett's *Familiar Quotations* (Boston: Little, Brown, and Company, 1899), 595.

134. Melville, 159.

135. Russell Baker, *New York Times*, 2 November 1991, sec. 1: 23.

136. David Butwin, "Love of Lakes: In Praise of Clear Cool Waters," *Hemispheres* (June 1996): 84.

137. Eric Schmitt, *New York Times*, 14 December 1986, sec. 10: 37.

138. Theodore Roethke, "Root Cellar," *Words for the Wind: The Collected Verse of Theodore Roethke* (Bloomington: Indiana University Press, 1963), 39.

139. Paul Bennett, *Pinewords* (Summer 1995), n. pag.

140. *Ibid.*

141. Howard Schultz, letter to Martha Hansen, 11 September 1995.

142. Lucy Schultz, statement presented to Pinewoods Camp Association Annual Meeting, 27 July 1996.

143. Martha Hansen, *Pinewords* (Fall 1995), n. pag.

144. Elizabeth Burrows Huntington, n. pag.

145. Dickinson, #668, 332.

146. Thoreau, 360.

147. Dickinson, #1755, 710.

148. Martha Hansen, letter to Pinewoods Camp Association, 19 June 1996.

149. Minutes of the Pinewoods Camp Association Annual Meeting (27 July 1996), 3–4.